'In my view, autobiographies by well-known people – especially those in the show business world – should be entertaining. This was my aim in my previous books, *For Adults Only* and *Behind Closed Dors*, but there were many who asked why I had not related my true life story in full.

'The answer was that I considered that everyone had read and re-read stories about my personal life over the years and had also observed most of my personal tragedies and troubles, so why would they wish to be depressed again?

'But now the public may, if it wishes, take a long, hard look at my personal life. What I write is the truth and, like many other women, I have made more than my fair share of mistakes as I fumbled through the incredible entanglement of what I still firmly believe to be "a man's world".'

DORS BY DIANA

Futura
Macdonald & Co
London & Sydney

A Futura Book

First published in Great Britain by
Macdonald Futura Publishers Ltd in 1981
Reprinted 1981

ISBN 0 7088 20205 5

Photoset by
Rowland Phototypesetting Ltd,
Bury St Edmunds, Suffolk.
Printed in Great Britain by
Hunt Barnard Printing, Aylesbury.

Futura Publications
A Division of
Macdonald & Co (Publishers) Ltd
Holywell House
Worship Street
London EC2A 2 EN

Man that is born of woman
hath but a short time to live,
and is full of misery.
He cometh up,
and is cut down, like a flower;
he fleeth as it were a shadow,
and never continueth in one stay.

FOREWORD

In my view, autobiographies by well-known people – especially those in the show-business world – should be entertaining. This was my aim in both previous books, *For Adults Only* and *Behind Closed Dors*, but there were many who asked why I had not related my true life story in full.

The answer was that I considered everyone had read and re-read stories about my professional life over the years, and also observed most of the personal tragedies and troubles that have pursued me throughout life. Why, therefore, would they wish to be depressed again? There is too much misery in the world today, and my strong belief is that people want to laugh. But now the public may, if it wishes, take a long, hard look at my own personal story, that hitherto has never been written, and judge for itself. I hope it does not make me sound too much of an idiot!

Let me state strongly, before we begin, that I am not an advocate of Women's Lib, nor am I the sort of woman who has a deep-rooted fear or dislike of men. On the contrary I adore them, but it is because I have always done so that I feel compelled to write this seemingly 'anti-male' book, describing not only my own experiences but those of others – together with my thoughts and opinions on men.

I hope, too, that readers will not think I am presenting myself in the role of a martyr who has been persecuted by the male sex! For if my words suggest I have behaved like some sort of 'shrinking violet' throughout life, totally used and abused, I must deny it emphatically. What I write is the truth and, like many other women, I have made more than my fair share of mistakes as I fumbled through the

incredible entanglement of what I still firmly believe to be
'a man's world'.

However, there are always two sides to every story;
where there is laughter, tears will also flow. Perhaps my life
has been filled with too many of the latter where men are
concerned but, regardless of this, I would not change one
part of it. With the exception of the loss of two sons, and of a
vast fortune along the way, I have enjoyed the whole
absurd mess to the highest possible degree.

And so I will endeavour to write about myself and men,
even though they have hampered my journey through life
and caused me much unhappiness in what would, and
should, have been a wonderful experience. I choose to think
it is more than just coincidence that the illness which struck
me down, nearly causing my death some years ago,
was . . . *men*ingitis!

CHAPTER ONE

HONOUR THY FATHER

Cry baby bunting,
Daddy's gone a-hunting.

It is a wise child that knows his own father, or so the saying goes. Did I really know mine? Perhaps now I am older I can understand a little of what he was trying to do for me and the wisdom of his philosophy of life. But then much has happened since I was a child.

From the beginning I did not like my father. Indeed, looking back to those far-off days, there were occasions when I detested him and everything he stood for. He, for his part, probably disliked me at times, for I was certainly not the daughter he would have wanted. Perhaps he might have been luckier if he could have had another roll of the dice; but I was an only child.

No-one remembers his or her first encounter with either parent but, as my mother later recalled, I was still very young when she came to realise that the war between him and me was on. Within me was an inborn resentment and opposition to this man whose name I bore, and with whom I was forced to live. I do not know why, yet it was as if the mould of my attitude towards men set itself then. I was never a 'Daddy's girl' – my love and affection went completely to my mother – but I adored every other male in sight and grew up with a desire to captivate the opposite sex. My adoration of boys was such that I yearned for brothers all through childhood – not younger, but older ones – and the bane of my life was that my best school-friend, Christine, not only had two brothers but also

sported natural platinum-blonde hair, whereas mine was
merely mousey.

Somewhere, in the recesses of the mind, all this must
have had an enormous effect on me. Sitting in class
plodding over sums, which *she* did brilliantly, and troubled
by an eye which turned inwards, necessitating the wearing
of a black disc on one side of my glasses; then was born the
dream of becoming a blonde, alluring film star, a woman
who enchanted men and lived a life of glamour and fame.
Happiness did not enter into it. To a child, life holds neither
sadness nor pain until the moment it occurs.

My parents had been married for thirteen years before I
was born, during which time their lives had been a combination of work and pleasure, as any childless couple in the
upper middle-class might know. They had long given up
any idea of a family, but at the age of forty-two my mother
discovered she was pregnant, and the shock was unimagin-
able.

For some years prior to this, during the twenties, she and
my father had been great friends with a young bachelor
named Gerry Lack. All three had gone around in a sort of
'ménage-à-trois', taking holidays together at seaside resorts
or my grandmother's cottage in Wales, buying a car jointly,
and generally having fun, attending parties in London or
giving them themselves at home. My father loved playing
cards; he also loved his club, together with the drinks and
camaraderie it provided. So while he spent most of his
evenings there, it was left to Gerry to escort my mother to
the theatre or keep her company at home. Such an association could lead to only one outcome as far as I'm concerned,
but it seemed to present no problem to my father, who
regarded it as a great relief from his own responsibilities as
a husband. To this day I cannot imagine how he could have
been so naïve. Unless that enormous male ego most men
possess prevented him from suspecting that someone else
might attract his wife's attentions.

Whatever occurred between her and 'Uncle' Gerry –
subsequently my godfather – I will never know. But as I see
it, my destiny was woven by two men: one of whom grew

tired of my mother when I arrived on the scene and went in search of another; and one who, although legally my father yet completely unsuspecting as to the reality of his fatherhood, was extremely jealous of my presence and never really came to terms with the fact that his wife's affections were now centred on her child. Maybe this was the cause of my own feelings for and my rejection of him, or maybe it was a deep-rooted, subconscious knowledge that perhaps he was not my real father. Whatever the truth it is lost in time, for only my dear mother knew what came to pass before I was born.

This, then, is how it all began for me. During my formative years the first man in my life was to be my mother's husband. When they met he was a handsome Army captain who loved to dance, played the piano beautifully, and in those uncertain days of the 1914–18 war was never seen with fewer than two girls on his arm. But after a bout of malaria in India, which left him with a weak heart, and being shelled in France, which nearly cost him the sight of an eye, he was invalided out of the Army and told he had not ten years to live. The dancing days were truly over, and from my earliest days I lived with the ever-constant reminder that Daddy might die at any time. There was even an important letter in the desk drawer so that my mother and I would know what to do when it happened. As events turned out, however, my mother looked after him so well and was such a wonderful wife – disregarding Uncle Gerry – that my father lived to be sixty-eight and died nine years after she did. So the desk-drawer letter was never opened.

My ancestors and relatives were, as far as I could tell, ordinary country folk; farmers from Somerset and Gloucestershire. This no doubt explains my love of the country, and the attraction of earthy men! But then I am a strange mixture really, thoroughly enjoying the company of intelligent, courteous, well-bred men but *not* wanting them as lovers. I have a high regard for the aristocracy, but I also respect the working-classes. Their ignorance may frighten me, but I have always admired the genuine, rough, down-to-earth way they live and think. The middle-classes I detest, probably because, by the time I was born, my parents had made the climb from working-class to *upper* middle-class (a notch even worse than *lower* middle-class). My early life, therefore, was one of continual torment and upheaval over a 'what will the neighbours think?' attitude – the result of a snobbish, respectable, bourgeois lifestyle; of being the only daughter of an ex-Army captain living in a hypocritical, narrow-minded community.

These ancestors and relatives were vast and uncountable. Catherine Carter, my paternal grandmother, had been the youngest but one of twenty-five children of a Gloucestershire farmer – who, I hasten to say, had mercifully married twice! Even so, I never dared enquire how many relations I had on her side of the family, or that of her late husband, my grandfather, whom I never knew. Just to complicate matters further she had married – when my father was in his teens – a widower with five children, so taking on even more relatives and responsibilities. This may well have been why I always thought of her as a hard woman who loved her 'drop of drink' – either a tot of gin, if she could get down to the local with her friends, or the bottle of stout she kept hidden in the cupboard by her armchair. I say 'hidden' as she genuinely did not think my mother and I knew it was there and would wait until we left before retrieving it and swigging it down, no doubt with great relief at our departure. Never did she realise we were peeping at her through the window. I used to call her 'Grandma with the Teapots', but why I can't remember? It should have been 'Grandma with the Stout Bottles'.

Not that I'm trying to imply she was an alcoholic. Far from it. Looking back now, I suppose the poor old girl had had enough in her life to make her welcome a drink whenever she could get it. Again because of the complete absence of any feeling for my father, my interest in her, or anyone on *his* side of the family, was non-existent. I used to dread the compulsory Sunday teatime visits at which she droned on about her life as a young model – with an eighteen-inch waist – in a dressmaker's shop in Gloucester. The effects of my grandfather's Victorian dominance over her were evident in her daughter, my Aunty Gwen, nearly being named 'Spite' when she was born. Apparently she was conceived after a row, and he spoke not one word to her during the entire nine months' pregnancy! Certainly my Aunty Gwen looked like a product of misery. She abhorred cosmetics, seemed permanently vinegary, and joined the Salvation Army where she met and married a cornet player. Together, childless themselves, they would 'spread the word' on Sunday evenings at the corner of various streets in Swindon, which is where we all lived.

Perhaps this was why Grandma kept her booze hidden. But whatever the reason, I do know that those boring, dreary Sunday evening teas gave birth to my loathing of Sunday, with its closed shops and everyone sitting around, doing nothing interesting within the sound of church bells. To this day I cannot hear church bells on a Sunday without being reminded of that time in my life.

Georgina Dors, my maternal grandmother from whom I took my stage name, was completely different from 'Grandma with the Teapots'. She was not hard, in fact quite the opposite, though she too had every reason to be so. I called her 'Grandma with the Chick-Chicks', because she kept chickens at the remote little pink-washed cottage in Wales where she lived all alone. When we went there for holidays I had to climb over the stile and go into that exciting feathered world with a basket to collect eggs. It was all very adventurous until one day, as I crept into the straw-smelling wonder of the stone hen-house, a large black hen flew at me in a rage for disturbing her. I ran out petrified. It might have made me wary of hens, as indeed some people are frightened of birds, but happily it did not. Grandma also had a rather savage cat named Deedles, though to me it always sounded like Needles, which would have been appropriate considering the sharpness of its claws. The poor thing was never fed and had to hunt rabbits when it was hungry, so perhaps it was entitled to be vicious. Anyway, Deedles didn't make me frightened of cats either, despite the fact that it scratched me often!

I loved going to Grandma Dors': the fun in hayfields during summer, and the sight of a slightly sinister tree in the distance which I called the 'umbrella tree'. It resembled some evil-looking ogre waiting to catch me if I dared go anywhere near it. Moreover, the only relations I cared about were to be found there. My mother had seven brothers and one sister, and with the exception of her brother Gerald, killed in the First World War, all the family, uncles, aunts and cousins, lived nearby. As an only child I delighted in finding myself among a big family. Two of my uncles I especially worshipped, for I thought them very handsome.

In many ways I think I am more like Grandma Dors than my own mother. For one thing, Grandma let her heart rule her head where men were concerned and was, like me, a perfect target for Cupid's arrows when a dark-eyed man appeared. As with me, too, this was to prove to be her downfall, but that is anticipating both our stories. The second daughter of a happy, respectable farming family in Somerset, Georgina Dors married at sixteen a young farmer and bore him three children, one of whom was my mother. There was another, a little girl named Melinda, but she died of pneumonia when only two, and all this had happened by the time Grandma had reached her early twenties.

One can but surmise how hard life was in those days at the latter end of the nineteenth century, but in my estimation she was then in an extremely vulnerable position. Certainly it is not difficult for me to understand how she came to fall in love with the dark-eyed, sullenly handsome brother of her husband, who toiled in the fields unaware of his wife's emotions. In short, she and James Payne ran away from their little village in the Mendips, Georgina dragging her three children along too – admirably, I think, for James did not want them. Her husband, another grandfather I never knew, gave chase on his horse but failed to find the lovers, for they had fled to Wales, more than likely crossing the Bristol Channel which separates it from the coast of Somerset.

This act ostracised Georgina from her father's family and friends for the rest of her life. For apart from the disgrace of her deed, actually to live with a man as his wife without being married was an unforgivable sin. Nor was life idyllic for her and James in Wales. They had no money; he had no permanent work. And as further children inevitably came along, the family was forced to move from one village to the next, all the while existing in abject poverty. Little wonder, then, that romance flew quickly out the window, although the runaway lovers did stay together, raising six children.

On reaching her teens, my mother, who hated her 'uncle' James, had been placed as a lady's maid at the local manor house, from where my grandmother took in washing to make ends meet. There my mother met and fell in love with a young groom named William Padget, a ne'er-do-well whose chief passion was gambling. In spite of this, though, she married him, mainly to get away from her step-father and the grim circumstances in which she lived. Her elder brother, meanwhile, had become engaged to a young village girl before going to fight in France, asking his mother to look after her during his absence. This she did willingly, but apparently James still had a keen eye for a pretty face, as once my Grandmother's had been. It was not long before he disappeared with his new flame, leaving alone the now-lined face and work-torn body of his old love after all the years of struggle, childbirth and strife.

For all that, Grandma still loved him, and who knows how many lonely hours she experienced after his departure, her children now grown up and making their own lives? When he died she demanded that each of their sons went to his funeral to pay their last respects. 'Whatever he did, he was your father', she told them.

My mother, by this time, was living far away in Swindon, Wiltshire, where she had gone to live with her husband's family for the duration of the war. William Padget, it seems, had been given a shilling by Grandma to 'join the army' instead of idling away his time gambling. Not that my mother was idle. She was rather proud of the distinction of being one of the first postwomen in the country, but this would soon be overshadowed by the news that William Padget had been killed in action.

There she was then, a lovely young widow in a strange town. Eventually she met my father, a young, local fellow who had recently acquired his commission and, when on leave, was usually to be seen at dances surrounded by girls. Fate certainly played a hand in that meeting, for it occurred at a place where both had arranged to meet someone else. But on seeing each other they went off in a dream, completely forgetting their respective 'dates'. I sometimes wonder what happened to those other two.

After a fairly difficult courtship, for no love blossoms easily during a war, they married on 9 March, 1918, and then informed my father's mother, who was not at all pleased. My mother was again obliged to live with her mother-in-law until the war ended, a state of affairs with which I sympathise after experiencing those Sunday teas.

Her ordeal finally came to an end when my father was invalided out of the Army and sent to convalesce at Osborne House on the Isle of Wight. Once the home of Queen Victoria, it was at that time reserved for officers and their wives, and there, at least, life was pleasant. As both my parents were musical – my mother having trained as a singer and my father as a pianist – they were in constant demand at social evenings and functions. Quite how my father was such a good pianist was something of a mystery for, after his father's death, 'Grandma with the Teapots' had sold his piano to get it out of the house. Subsequently, I assume, my father had to struggle along without one, and yet he played so well. It was one of his great disappointments that I never followed in his footsteps. Twice he tried to teach me – a disaster – and once he placed me with a tutor, but that didn't work either for I never practised. I'd cheat by putting down the hours of practice I'd supposedly done, and in the end he gave up and 'washed his hands of me'. Not for the first or last time.

Indeed, during my childhood I lost count of the times my father said that. But just as I did not get along with him, he must have been wretchedly sorry to have me for a daughter.

As far as I can make out, I had not one single point of which
he approved. For my part I was intolerant of his criticisms,
his principles, his honesty, and so on. Yet, looking back
now, I do feel guilty about those early days and realise he
wanted only what was best for a girl child. I came to
understand, when it was all too late, that whereas one can
rebel against a father, mother, or husband, one cannot do
so against one's own children. Though I have never had
daughters, who must be much more difficult in many ways,
I see now how hard it must have been for him.

It was also hard for me to honour my father, as the Bible
says, when I did not even understand his motives and
ideals, let alone *him*; if indeed he was my father. But however confused I felt about everything, *he* was the first man
with whom I had to cope and, as in each emotional
relationship involving men throughout my life, I made a
hopeless mess of it.

Is it all so surprising? Not really. Scientists, doctors,
and psychiatrists might be able to explain the problem with
words like 'distribution of genes', 'hereditary factors', and
so on. From where I am at this moment, looking back
through the swirling emptiness of time, I was born into a
world in which one grandfather had, in anger, forced his
wife into conjugal submission and pregnancy, then cruelly
refused to speak a word until the child was born . . . my
great-uncle, having seduced and run away with my other
grandmother, had left her after years of child-bearing and
misery for a younger woman who was already engaged to
her eldest son . . . my father resented my presence after
thirteen magical years with the woman who had catered to
his every wish and whim.

And, finally, a world in which one more man, the
mysterious 'Uncle' Gerry, played his part by disappearing
into the arms of another woman soon after I was born. In
search of the love and pleasure he had received from my
mother before she found herself burdened with me? And
was it 'Uncle' Gerry, whom my mother would never admit
to the house again, despite their having been such close
friends, who should really take the blame for placing that

burden on her? I do see much more resemblance to him than to my legal father when I peer at faded snapshots of their carefree days together. And if this is so, why, I wonder, did my father not see what was staring him in the face? Did he never wonder why their friendship had turned sour? Perhaps he suspected and then dismissed it from his mind.

Therein, surely, lies the answer to all the discord between us. But whichever way I study the situation, I cannot help feeling that fate and my forebears had not properly prepared me to tackle the one stumbling-block that would upset and affect my life over and over again – a complex animal known as man . . . born of woman.

CHAPTER TWO

RIDE A COCK HORSE

To Banbury Cross,
See a fine lady on a white horse.

'Born 23 October, 1931, at "The Haven" Nursing Home, Kent Road, Swindon, Wilts. to Mary, wife of Peter Fluck, a daughter (Diana Mary).'

So ran the announcement in the *Evening Advertiser*, but it did not say that Mary had taken nearly a week to give birth and had almost died as a result. Nor that Diana Mary was born black in the face, thrown aside for dead as doctors battled to save her mother, and was revived by a nurse in another room. The result of this near-suffocation as I fought for survival has been lifelong claustrophobia.

Banbury and its famous Cross were not far from my birthplace, though they are of little significance really. But my mother, when she recovered from the ordeal of giving birth so late in life, realised that she at last had her own little girl and that child was going to have everything, and do everything, she herself had never dared dream of. 'Rings on her fingers, bells on her toes, she shall have music wherever she goes' were only some of the beautiful things she wanted for me.

It is small wonder that my father became jealous of this screaming bundle of humanity when I was brought home, even though Aunty Kit – my mother's sister who knew more about babies than my mother, cared for me while my mother regained her strength. I now took up all his wife's time and affection, destroyed his hours of sleep, and generally upset his former perfectly organised existence.

Even 'Uncle' Gerry had an excuse, although I hate to admit it, for deserting his post as escort, companion or whatever he was labelled in their social circle and going off with another woman. For the parties at my parents' home had to stop. There was a baby asleep upstairs. Later in life, in moments of anger, my mother would complain how I had completely changed her life, reminding me of the sacrifices she'd had to make as a result of having me. 'It hasn't altered your father's life at all', she often grumbled. For it was true that he still went his own way and was hardly ever at home, going to the office or to his various clubs, concerts and Masonic meetings.

Once I had been christened, on 13 December, 1931, with 'Uncle' Gerry as godfather and Aunties Gwen and Kit as godmothers, everyone seemed to go his or her own way. 'Uncle' Gerry, as far as I can make out, must have begun his philanderings soon after, for Aunty Kit, whom I adored, told me years later of an occasion when my mother had left me asleep in my cot while she followed him as he went to keep a romantic tryst.

'What would Peter have said if he'd known you left Diana alone?' Aunty Kit had enquired incredulously.

'Well, he never knew', my mother replied, with just a hint of bitterness. It was obvious she was hurt, her suspicions confirmed regarding the loyalty of her once 'best friend'.

By the time I was two, 'Uncle' Gerry's name must have been blackened to the extent that I regarded him as a two-headed monster. Aunty Kit recalled another occasion when, seeing him in the street while we were travelling on a bus, I said vehemently, *'Nasty "Uncle" Gerry'*. However, having presumably got over this man, and with my father out most of the time, my mother allowed her obsession for me to become stronger than ever, especially as all her fun-loving friends had gone off too.

I was always the best-dressed tot in the neighbourhood, and nothing I wanted was too much. Birthdays were always celebrated with large parties, often at a hired hall, dancing-class was a must, and, as she was a great cinema fan, my mother took me to see my first film when I was three. Here began my own love of films. Sitting there in the dark with my mother, we were transported to a world far away from Swindon; to glamorous Hollywood homes and nightclubs where people wore beautiful clothes, swam in luxurious pools, and sang, danced or acted their way across lavish sets.

When it was time for me to go to school, at great expense and against my father's wishes I was sent to a small private one, Selwood House, run by two prim spinster sisters, Miss Daisy and Miss Ruth. Considering where my interests lay, it was not surprising that, instead of concentrating on sums – my weak point – I would sit writing film stars' names down the margin where I should have been adding up figures. My father raged over my school reports, but I was always strongly defended by my mother, who said something one day that was to become the understatement of the decade: 'What does it matter, just so long as she knows how to count up the few pounds she'll earn at the end of the week?'

My father, at this point, doubted if I would even be able to do *that*, much less make millions as would eventuate. So he washed his hands of me, as usual, and after yet another argument, which they now had endlessly, went off to his club.

On one occasion at school during English – my best subject – I wrote, in an essay entitled 'what you would like to be when grown-up', that 'I was *going* to be a film star, with a cream telephone and a swimming-pool'. I cannot remember how the two headmistresses reacted when they read that, but as their opinion of me was similar to my father's, I was probably written off as a thoroughly 'bad lot'. If they had their favourites, I was certainly not one of them. Indeed, they often branded me a ringleader of all the misbehaviour that occurred in class.

Even my first day at school had been traumatic – and, as if setting the pattern of things to come, all because of a boy! I adored members of the opposite sex and, being an only child cosseted by her mother, had been looking forward to

going to school. I thought it would be all fun and games
with other children. Not long after my arrival, I was getting
along fine with a boy named Eric Barrett when, for no
apparent reason, he placed his cap over my face and
punched me in the eye, causing me to return home, much to
my mother's horror, sporting a big black shiner! Perhaps
this should have been a warning of how boys behaved,
whether they were angry or playful. But I took no heed and
transferred my affections to David Colbourne, the only boy
in our class. We were sweethearts, and announced our
intention to marry when the time came. Naturally the affair
floundered, and David disappeared from my life after his
last appearance at one of my birthday parties – when he
gave me a toy tea-set which, he announced proudly, was
made of *real* china.

Eric Barrett's punch may or may not have been the cause
of my first set of troubles, but suddenly my right eye began
to turn inwards. After lengthy sessions with the oculist, I
was prescribed spectacles and, much worse, a black disc
over the offending eye for an hour a day to encourage the
'lazy' one to work. Both my mother and I were mortified by
this, and the disc treatment was singularly frightening. I
couldn't, and still cannot, see very well out of that eye, so
my world was very dark during that hour-a-day treatment.
As for the spectacles, they were the bane of my life.
Although I wore them only for reading and at the cinema,
my vanity, encouraged by my mother, was prevalent even
then and I was terrified of anyone, particularly a boy,
seeing me wearing the wretched things.

One day, in an effort to make me look and feel pretty, my
mother took me to the hairdressers to have my straight hair
permed. We both thought it was rather nice, and it saved
the ghastly hot curling-tongs' routine we had to go through
each day so that I could have fashionably curly hair. In
those days little girls were supposed to have curls, perhaps
because of Shirley Temple. But when my father found out
he was furious! I couldn't understand his reasoning. What
did it matter to him if my hair was curly? Where was the
crime in that?

In the ensuing explosion over this latest 'act of irres-
ponsibility' on my mother's part, I discovered that when
they met she possessed the most beautiful long hair.
Apparently she could sit on it when the tresses fell down.
But during the twenties, when the short bob became
fashionable, she had committed the unforgivable sin of
having it all lopped off (an early Women's Lib fashion, no
doubt). It upset my father so much that he didn't speak to
her for three weeks. 'You ruined your own hair, now you're
going to do the same with hers', he stormed, waving his
'commanding officer' finger in my direction. Still, what was
done was done, and I suppose he washed his hands of the
pair of us that day.

As time went on, it seemed that my mother and I had
become united against him. She could never resist giving in
to me, and, as I hated school so much, there were days
when I would plead with her not to be sent back in the
afternoon, insisting nothing important was happening
there and coaxing her to take me to the cinema. Not that she
needed much coaxing. The cinema was her only escape to
the sort of life she had dreamed of when she trained as a
singer. So off we'd romp, hand in hand, and for a couple of
magical hours watch our film star idols before rushing
home to have my father's tea ready on the table when he
returned from the office. The poor man never knew, as he
deftly spread fish paste on his bread and butter, that I had
skipped school. Sometimes I nearly let it slip, but we always
managed to cover up by pretending I was talking of a film
we'd seen some nights before. Officially, I was permitted to
go to the cinema only *once* a week.

My mother, to prevent me from speaking with a broad
Swindon accent, persuaded my father to let me have elocution lessons. Unlike my school studies, I enjoyed and
became rather good at these, and my elocution mistress,
who came from Cheltenham, entered me in various poetry
festivals and competitions. Whatever I entered – even
exams – I won, and before long my collection of prizes and
medals was becoming quite large. In a small way I was also
gaining some local recognition, my picture often appearing

in the local newspaper with a caption like 'Swindon Child Prodigy Does it Again'. Not that my successes in any way impressed my headmistresses. 'Your conduct in class is what we are more interested in' was all I received when I proudly displayed my newest silver medal. I loathed them, and their stuffy little school, vowing that when I grew up I really would become that famous film star I'd written about. Then I'd show them! Indeed, the eternity of waiting to grow up and achieve all that was beginning to frustrate me a great deal. But by reading as many books as I could, when I wasn't in the cinema, I tried to escape from the dreary world in which I felt myself living.

It was while snooping around with nothing better to do one day that I discovered my mother had been married before. For deep in a drawer of my father's desk I found their marriage certificate which, I noted as I casually perused it, described her as a 'widow'. Naturally I rushed to ask her what it all meant, but she pushed me away with a quick excuse about it being some sort of mistake.

Later that day I heard both parents talking. 'What did you tell her?' my father asked gravely, as if I'd discovered some dreadful crime they'd committed before I was born. 'I said it was all a mistake', my mother whispered.

Suddenly I found myself in the middle of a domestic drama. It was all quite exciting really, but I couldn't understand why they both looked so grim when they called me into the drawing-room. They wore the expression of two deserters about to give themselves up! My father explained, in his usual sensible way and as carefully as he could, the secret and serious truth that my mother had once been married to somebody other than him.

'But why didn't you tell *me*?' I enquired when he finished his speech.

'It is a chapter in my life that I wish to forget', my mother announced somewhat dramatically.

And that was the end of the matter. Later I often asked her what her husband, William Padget, had been like, for my vivid imagination was building up quite a fantasy about him. Whoever he was, to my mind he *must* have been more interesting than the husband she had now! But she would never say much about him, and it was from Aunty Kit that I learnt more of the facts after my mother's death.

It was soon after this incident that my father said something which will remain with me for the rest of my life. Whether it was due to the discovery of my mother's previous marriage, or yet another abysmal school report – my mother was again berated for ruining me, and told that I'd be good for nothing when I grew up, except possibly going into domestic service – I don't know. But on this particular day he turned to me and calmly said: 'You know, my dear, when you leave school I would like to see you get a good job, possibly that of a secretary.'

This was not what I had in mind at all; a very far cry from Hollywood with my swimming-pool and cream telephone. But it was his next statement that really made my heart sink, though quite why I have never discovered. 'Eventually, I'd like to see you settle down and marry some decent sort of chap. . . .' His words trailed off there as far as I was concerned. For even at the tender age of seven, the prospect of marrying 'a decent sort of chap' filled me with absolute horror. Yet I could not and still cannot understand why.

If I thought a few storm clouds would darken my horizon after all this, they were nothing compared to those clouds that were coming for real. The year was 1939, and the threat of war had been looming for some time. Finally it happened and, although I could not possibly understand why they looked so unhappy, my parents and I heard the announcement over the radio on that fateful September day that England was at war with Germany.

Like discovering my mother's previous marriage, it was all quite exciting to me. Anything was preferable to the dull, uneventful time I was experiencing in Swindon, and a war might liven things up a bit. How could I realise the full, terrible meaning of it? What did I know about life other than my comfortable, sheltered home in a quiet suburban town? The sad part of life for many of us is that we never know how good something is until it's no longer there. In the years to come there would be many times when I would have welcomed the peace of my secure, simple existence in Swindon.

The first major problem at our house was where to go for our annual summer holiday. Where would now be safe from Hitler's bombs? Grandma Dors had died in 1937, so the lovely country vacations at her cottage had come to an end, and the pleasant little seaside resort of Weston-super-Mare – my father said the air there did *him* good and refused to go anywhere else – might now be dangerous with a war on. We tried it for a weekend, but there was an air-raid and the beach was covered in sandbags. It was not the old comfortable Weston to which we had grown accustomed.

It was decided we'd go to my mother's Uncle Joe Dors' farm, tucked away in the Mendip Hills of Somerset. She probably had some misgivings, though she never spoke of them, as it would be the first time she'd returned there since her mother dragged her off to Wales. I, of course, was oblivious to all this as I happily looked forward to a real country holiday on a farm, and my father savoured the fact that Great-Uncle Joe's also boasted a little pub named Hunters' Lodge. His beer supply would be all right despite the change in holiday plans. What none of us knew, and my parents *never* knew, was that it would be the first time in my life that I was nearly raped!

Dear Grandma Dors had another brother besides Joseph, and Arthur Dors was one of the worst old rogues that tiny little village of Priddy had ever seen. As the youngest of the family of John and Anne Dors he may have been spoilt, and now he was the black sheep – except for Grandma, of course, for no-one could have behaved worse than she had. A rough, cider-swilling ne'er-do-well, he hung around Great-Uncle Joe's pub at all hours of the day and night, doing farm work if he was made to and getting drunk whenever possible. He spoke with a broad Somerset accent, liberally laced with swear words, which I think not even he could understand, and in a battered old hat and with trousers tied up with string, he presented an odd picture to my parents when they first encountered him. But he fascinated me.

As we revelled in the glorious life at Great-Uncle Joe's, eating now-rationed food like eggs and sides of ham, drinking milk fresh from his cows and hob-nobbing with the local squire, who called regularly with his hounds for a stirrup-cup, no-one gave much thought to Great-Uncle Arthur. He would totter back and forth to his cottage and second wife – he had managed to bury the first one, a poor, long-suffering soul named Annie who, I am sure, died of exhaustion from being married to him.

One evening I was loitering in the stable watching the horses contentedly chew their hay when a shadow appeared in the doorway. I looked up quickly, and there staggered Great-Uncle Arthur. Presumably he was drunk, but he held himself fairly steadily – let's face it, he'd had enough practice over the years. Exactly what followed his entry I can't remember; that is, I don't know if we spoke. But if we did, our conversation could only have been the sort which might take place between an eight-year-old girl and an incorrigible old drunkard. Then, before I knew what was happening, he seized me in a rough embrace and gripped me against his body so hard that I thought all my breath was being squeezed away. Moreover the cider fumes were nearly making me sick.

I couldn't understand why this elderly relation was suddenly displaying such affection. Until then he'd never seemed to notice me, or so I had thought! Things were getting hot in that barn, and even as a child of eight I sensed something was not as it should be. His passions now aroused to fever-pitch, he kept pressing his mouth on mine with kisses decidedly dissimilar from those I'd received from my other uncles. Beginning to panic, I realised I must get away. But how? Using all my strength I pushed him as hard as I could, and luckily he lost balance and tottered backwards. That was my chance, and I ran from the stable as fast as I could.

For several days I remained confused about the whole affair. Knowing nothing about sex, I couldn't work out why he'd kissed me like that, or the meaning of it. And I daren't tell my mother; I felt too embarrassed. As for my father! God knows what he'd have done had he ever learnt that the colourful old character he regarded with tolerant amusement had tried to take advantage of his little girl. In years to come he would probably have blamed me for leading the fellow on, but this was one occasion when my behaviour, even in my father's critical eyes, would have been completely blameless.

As the war continued, and with everyone trying to do his or her bit, my theatrical career got off to a start. Concerts were frequently staged at Army camps, usually under canvas, to entertain the troops, and as my father had continued with his music at local functions – even professionally accompanying artistes performing at Swindon's variety theatre – he was the obvious man to arrange these shows. Furthermore, apart from being the senior ARP warden of our area, it was his way of contributing to a war in which he could not possibly fight.

Often, when one of the artistes couldn't make it, I would be roped in at the last minute, which suited me admirably. Hardly looking like Shirley Temple, but with a pair of red tap-shoes, my heart beating with excitement and butterflies performing acrobatics in my stomach, I would eagerly await the moment when I stepped on to the stage and gave the poor soldiers the benefit of my somewhat limited talents. My act consisted of topical tunes like 'Ma, I Miss Your Apple Pie' (always a wartime favourite), followed by a carefully contrived little tap-dance which I had learnt at my dancing-school, where now I took private lessons. If the show was really short on acts, I would throw in a recitation or two for good measure and always received a thunderous ovation. Naturally I thought this was because the troops immediately recognised my Hollywood potential, and believed it was merely a matter of waiting for the war to finish before I would be whisked over there to become a star. I never dreamt for one moment that their generous applause was due to two things: a child usually gets sympathetic approval from adults, whoever they are; and I had a captive audience. What else could they do?

By now I was obsessed with becoming a film star. I read silly stories in magazines and papers saying that some of my idols had been discovered in most unlikely places – Lana Turner while sipping an ice-cream soda in a Hollywood drug-store – and I went to great lengths to see if something similar could happen to me. How could I know then about the workings of studio publicity machines, and of all the rubbish that was printed to titillate the public?

And speaking of rubbish, my first idea was a classic. I would leave a note in the dustbin, stating that I was a talented young girl living at 210 Marlborough Road (well, the rubbish collectors would know that as they came for the dustbin, so I need not bother with the address), that I could sing, dance, act and recite, and would somebody please inform someone of my whereabouts so that I could get into films. It never occurred to me, in the optimistic fantasy world of childhood, that the dustbin men did not actually have a private line to Louis B. Mayer at Metro-Goldwyn Studios – where Lana Turner was – otherwise they wouldn't be emptying my mother's rubbish; or that if indeed Lana really *was* discovered in a drug-store in Hollywood, the same thing would not happen to me if I sat in the Kardomah coffee bar in Swindon's High Street! And so, having carefully placed the precious note at the top of the bin, I sat back and waited for the summons, probably by telegram from Louis B. Mayer himself, or from Twentieth Century Fox.

Disappointment number one!

My other big disappointment was a frequent event. Because I read countless books, especially fairy stories, my imagination and belief in the possibility of acquiring anything if you wished long enough – shades of the song in a Walt Disney film I'd seen, not to mention the *Wizard of Oz* with Judy Garland – knew no bounds. And the one thing I wanted so much was my very own swimming-pool.

I could not swim well, owing to the claustrophobia which had plagued me from birth. And every time I went to the local pool, some nasty little boy would push me in, I'd disappear under the water and then emerge choking and too terrified to go near the water's edge again until the place was empty of people. If only I had my own private pool where no-one could interfere with my swimming!

The nearest I ever got to privacy or Hollywood-style luxury was to stand in the rainwater butt at home and pretend it was a beautiful blue swimming-pool – like the ones in the movies. For in my world anything was possible. I contrived all kinds of wishes and dreams with my eyes closed, fully believing that when I opened them there, at the end of the garden, would be the pool of my dreams. Time and time again I enacted this fantasy, only to be disappointed bitterly when the fairies did not come through as they did in story books and Disney films. All that was there was the plot of land which once boasted a lawn, but which had now been dug up to grow vegetables in the 'Dig for Victory' campaign.

Even with a good memory like mine I cannot remember exactly the year when I fell seriously in love for the first time. To the best of my recollection, it was the summer of 1943 when my father announced that, as there was a war on and as I was getting too old for them anyway, my birthday parties had to stop. His name was Michael Wheeler, and we shared an idyllic summer, sitting around in the field between our homes, gradually getting to know each other, talking of our hopes and aspirations, and doing all the things that very young lovers do in the gradual process of becoming interested in the opposite sex. Our names are still carved on the tree which stands there, concealed in a tiny copse which we considered to be our own 'private place'.

Although I'd known Michael most of my life, it was not until that magic summer that I really became interested in him. He sang in the choir at the church where I was christened, but had hardly ever set foot in since, and so, typical of a female in love, I started attending church regularly every Sunday, always placing myself in the front pew so that Michael could gaze at me, and I at him. My father, unsuspecting, must have thought I had seen the light at last and that there was some hope for me after all!

Perhaps, when we grew up, Michael would have been the 'decent sort of chap' he had wished upon me. But the course of true love never runs smoothly, and my last birthday party was also the end of our romance.

Poor Michael! It was not his fault that, at twelve years old, he did not have any long trousers. There was, after all, a war on, and clothing was rationed. But as the other boys trooped in I realised he was the only one in short trousers, which brought some sniggers from the other, more fortunate fellows *and* from a handful of girls, who knew he was my sweetheart and wondered what I saw in him anyway. I felt humiliated, and suddenly the whole idea of that 'decent chap' seemed to be coming true. Spoilt little shrew that I was, *his* embarrassment never occurred to me; for in his short trousers he looked as awkward as he no doubt was feeling. All I could think of were my father's words, and how sophisticated the other boys looked beside him.

Our secret meetings in the field and the private copse ceased from that day on, and he never could truly understand why. My churchgoing, of course, ended abruptly, and every time Michael tried to contact me I would turn an icy shoulder. When I think now of that poor bewildered boy, it makes me feel guilty even after all these years. I still remember the last time we met, accidentally in the street, and he stared at me with those big dark eyes for which I had first fallen. 'Don't throw away that book I gave you', he said quietly. 'It's a good book, really it is.' Oh Michael; I don't even remember its title.

As the war dragged on, a new and exciting time, such as I had never dreamed, was approaching. I was going to meet *real* Americans! It was 1944, and with the approach of D-Day, the allied invasion of Europe, thousands upon thousands of them were entering Britain. There was not enough space to billet them at camps and barracks in and around the town, and anyone who had a spare room had to accommodate one, or even two, GIs.

I was ecstatic! We had a bedroom free, and I truly thought my luck was in when our soldier turned out to be from California. I bombarded him with questions about

Hollywood, which he tried hard to answer, but as his family had an orange farm some hundred miles north of the film capital he was hardly in a position to tell me what Lana Turner ate for breakfast, or who Tyrone Power was dating.

Eventually Joe was moved on, and then we acquired an officer nurse named Elizabeth Maguire, who was charming but from Massachusetts, a state I'd never heard of before, let alone tried to spell. Being three thousand miles across the other side of the United States, it was not really the sort of place in which I was interested. None the less, it was all wonderful, and the more Americans I met the better, for I truly believed that anyone who was an American had to be a film star. After all, they spoke like the stars I saw on the screen, chewed gum, smoked cigarettes the way Humphrey Bogart did, and had lots of money, sweets, plus so much else that we starved British had never seen.

I was now twelve and a half, but I looked older and had taken to wearing make-up when my father wasn't around. (He had forbidden me to do so after catching me wearing lipstick one evening.) My hair was now long and fairly honey coloured – with a little help from some lightener – and as I walked about the town, cries of 'It's Veronica Lake!' rang out from passing GI trucks. Veronica Lake was then in her prime, appearing in films with Alan Ladd. And she had also gained some unwanted notoriety by upsetting the war effort. Girls in factories had tried to emulate her hairstyle and got their own hair caught in the machines – with dreadful results. Flattered at first, I became tired of hearing her name everywhere I went, almost as tired as I became of being compared with Marilyn Monroe many years later; and yet such are life's ironies that there would come a day when my surname would actually be Lake.

The night I was invited to my first dance, at an American party, was just about the most thrilling thing that had ever happened to me. My mother and I were returning home from the cinema, of course, when we were met by droves of GIs who begged us to go to a hotel where some big celebration was going on. My mother hesitated, but as my father was playing the piano somewhere, and likely to be late back, she finally gave in, much to my delight. We rushed home and I put on my most grown-up dress – a red one handed down by a young friend of my mother – did my hair in as glamorous a style as I could manage, donned a pair of real nylons which the American nurse had sent me, plus a pair of semi-high-heeled shoes, and off I went, accompanied by my doting mother.

Cinderella's evening at the ball could never have been as wonderful as mine that night. I danced every dance and lost count of the GIs I danced with and met. My head was a-whirl with sweet nothings and compliments whispered in my ear, and although I drank only Coca Cola, it might as well have been champagne. I also had fun pretending to be older than I really was, casually giving my age as seventeen when asked, and revelling in the fact that they believed me! I had grown up at last. All those years of waiting and yearning to be an adult and do adult things, this now was *it*. But suppose I had been a few years older. Would I have married an American and become a GI bride? And if so, what would have been my fate then?

Having experienced the enchantment of that first evening, I pleaded with my mother to let me go every Saturday night to the local dance hall. I don't recall my father's reaction to this idea; perhaps he was too busy with other matters. For we did start going regularly, and also to parties at American camps. My mother's main purpose, in addition to chaperoning me, was to get to know the camp cook, and we'd return home from our evenings out with a large bag filled with sugar, butter, and anything else she could obtain. I used to think this was a terrible act; I could never understand why she was so obsessed with getting food at dances when there were much better things to do. But then, for all my grown-up ways, I was too young to appreciate the struggle she and millions like her endured to make ends meet.

My wonderful new life wasn't without its hazards, however.

Because some of the GIs I danced with were stationed at an American headquarters in the same road as my school, I had to sneak along that road on school days, full of fear that my dancing partners would see Saturday's seventeen-year-old swinger reduced to a thirteen-year-old schoolgirl! Only as I entered the school precincts would I place the wretched regulation beret on my head so it looked as though I'd obeyed the rules and worn my uniform proudly in the street. While at home there was still the problem of my father's unsympathetic attitude to my wearing make-up.

There was, too, the night when the worst almost happened. How I escaped being seduced I do not know. I'd been invited to a party at this headquarters, by an American MP whom my mother trusted, and I even had my father's permission. It wasn't much of an affair really; plenty of food and drink and some music.

Usually, when asked what I'd have to drink, I said Coke, but this night I saw there was pineapple juice, something we'd not had since the war, and at once opted for this. What I didn't realise was that my drink, and the ones that followed, were laced with gin, and halfway through the evening I began to feel giddy. However, despite this sly attempt to get me stoned, I managed to remain upright and intact, though the room was really spinning by the time I left the party and was taken home in the MP's jeep.

'What on earth's the matter with her?' demanded my father as I made a somewhat unsteady entrance.

'Oh, she's just tired and nervous', answered my ever-defensive mother as I climbed the stairs to bed. 'There's a big exam at school tomorrow.'

There was an exam all right, but not of the kind my mother had intimated. One of the younger teachers asked me to stay behind at the end of her class that day. I couldn't imagine what I'd done wrong, but it turned out that her steady boyfriend was one of the Americans who had more than likely laced my drink. We'd spoken for a few minutes, mostly about the fact he knew my teacher, and as usual I was busy pretending that I was older than thirteen. Now, it seemed, my teacher was jealous that I'd been at the party whereas she had not been invited, and I received a few terse words about keeping my nose out of her affairs.

So life went on in a happy, carefree whirl of dances, dates and parties. There was nothing to worry about, except what would happen when the war ended and all these exciting Americans went home. By late 1945, the war in Europe was over and coming to a halt in the Pacific. There were VE celebrations, more parties, more dances, and less and less time for school work. But my burning ambition was still there. To go to this enchanted land called America, and of course to become a famous film star.

Compared to the Americans, the local boys at the high school across the road from my school all seemed very tame; even the ones who'd worn long trousers to my birthday party. Usually they were forced to take a back seat, but I did try to keep some interest going with Swindon boys – more as insurance than anything else – by organising small parties at my mother's friend's dancing studio. I'd seen films of American teenagers 'jiving', as it was called then, in drug stores, and I tried desperately to introduce this to the Swindon teenagers. One night I even wore what would now be described as a mini-skirt, just as I'd seen on the screen, so that I could 'jitterbug' and be thrown around and over my partner's shoulder easily. Usually, though, they were rather boring evenings. We played Postman's Knock and did quite a bit of smooching, but they somehow lacked the thrill of the American parties. Even the wind-up gramophone in the corner, blaring out music which I normally danced to on a Saturday night, was a reminder of what I'd become accustomed to.

Among the boys was Eric Barrett, villain of my first day at school but now more interested in kissing than punching, and another Swindonian who later attained fame and fortune. Desmond Morris, whose mother had a tobacconist shop in Victoria Road, lived in a house with its own small private lake where, some lazy summer afternoons, we would float in a little canoe. Desmond was a bit older than the rest of us, by which I mean he was about seventeen, and, of great importance, he had a car. Some evenings four of us would go out into the country, perhaps to a village fair

like the Marlborough Mop, or we'd park the car in a field
and have a 'necking session'.

Towards the end of their stay near Swindon, the
Americans opened a large college for servicemen whose
studies had been interrupted by the war and who wished to
resume them. And it was about this same time that my
parents and I returned to Weston for our annual summer
holiday. One day, as my father quietly sat by the sea
reading his copy of *The Daily Telegraph*, I entered, with my
mother's help, a beauty contest to find a pin-up girl for
Soldier magazine. Having given my age as seventeen, I
strutted around the Lido pool in a scarlet and white swimsuit, trying to look as much like Betty Grable as possible,
and to my delight and amazement I came third. Now my
father *had* to be told, for my picture would be in the
Swindon newspaper once again, reporting the latest exploit
of the town's 'bad girl', as I was rapidly becoming known.
It was with the publication of my photo that an art professor at the American college called and asked if I would
pose for his art classes . . . in a swimsuit, of course.

Very flattered, I accepted a fee of one guinea an hour,
and as I posed on the platform I felt that at last things were
getting somewhere. Especially as the professor was comparing me with the Powers and Conover models whom I'd
seen in the American film magazines my GI friends gave
me.

Before long I was asked to take part in theatre produc-
tions there, too, for I lost no time in making it known that I
wished to be a film actress. I appeared first in *A Weekend In
Paris* and then *Death Takes a Holiday*, in which I played the
lead for one week and received rave reviews in the campus
paper. I also sang a few songs on the college radio station,
which my parents managed to pick up on their own radio
dial. It was all very exciting, and with so much going on I
decided to leave school altogether, wheedling my way
round my father to let me attend an acting academy in
London once a week instead. He wasn't happy about me
'going on the stage' as he put it. 'I've seen too much of what
happens, and too often the way to success is through a

bedroom door', he announced. But realising he was wasting his money sending me to an ordinary school, he permitted me to go there, on the understanding that I study for a teacher's diploma and return to Swindon to teach elocution. Thrilled with yet another victory, I left my hated school and journeyed to London each week for a private acting class with Miss Kathleen Cunningham at the London Academy of Dramatic Art. My mother, as usual, accompanied me.

There was also another treat in store. An American photographer at the college, knowing I longed to get into films, gave me a letter of introduction to a film director he knew in London, and so, on one of our day trips to LAMDA, my mother and I made our way to a film studio in Islington. They were shooting *This Man Is Mine*, starring Glynis Johns, and the director's name was Keating. I remember standing in what I considered to be *paradise*, watching him rushing about, giving orders and generally sounding most important. As I waited in the darkness of the studio, staring in awe at the incredible set with artificial snow, a large house with real trees around it, and the dozens of arc lights, I felt an indescribable thrill. Perhaps someone like Margaret Lockwood had actually stood on the same spot as me.

Mr Keating finally came over, was very polite, and read the letter. But no bells rang that day, and it wasn't until much later that I discovered he was only an assistant director, the person employed to do all the dirty work for the real director. Still it was a start, and I'd had my first look inside a real film studio.

Finally it happened; the Americans went home. Never before had I felt so disconsolate or miserable. The bottom had dropped out of my world and nothing could make me feel better. Swindon seemed duller and greyer than ever, and not even the odd night out with one of the local boys could compensate me for what I had lost. I had to get out of there; it was my new driving force. If I was to see any of my American friends again, go to their country, or attain my ambition of becoming a Hollywood star, then there wasn't a moment to lose. Time was slipping by. I was fourteen years old and I'd done nothing with my life except physically grow up.

CHAPTER THREE

FAREWELL TO FANTASY

Mary, Mary quite contrary,
How does your garden grow?

Believing that I would return one day to teach elocution,
and not continue with my plan to become an actress, my
father finally agreed that I might attend the London
Academy full-time, instead of once a week. He had been
assured by Miss Cunningham, and by my elocution
teacher, Mrs Barraclough, that this was the one area in
which I shone. He had been promised by the head of the
Academy, Wilfred Foulis, whose eyes turned outwards
above his pince-nez, that I would come to no harm under
his guidance. And my welfare had been solemnly and
sensibly confirmed by Miss Whipp, who ran the YWCA
hostel around the corner from LAMDA.

I left Swindon one cold January afternoon in 1946,
sporting a green suitcase and a return ticket, promising that
I would return home every weekend. My father had
lectured me all the way to the station, letting me know he
was giving me my big chance in life. 'Failure is unthinkable', he said, and would occur if I did not work hard and
concentrate on my studies. What his private thoughts were
that winter day I'll never know; nor those of my mother
who, although happy that I was setting out to do things
she'd never had the opportunity to do, must have felt
broken-hearted. Her life was ending, for the void I left
would never be filled again.

Whatever either of them was feeling did not enter my
mind, however. The failure my father spoke of so gravely

could not possibly happen to me. I was young, the world was mine for the taking, and I was on my way to everything I had ever wanted. As for the hard work, how could he describe being a glamorous film star as hard work?

No-one cried as the train pulled out. Not that there was anything to cry about as far as I was concerned; it was a day for celebration. But how many tears and misgivings did my mother know that night? Doubtless my father went to his club as usual, leaving her alone without me for the first time in fourteen years. But as I sped further and further away from the town of my birth, I experienced no misgivings. There I sat, puffing away dramatically at a cigarette taken from an old cigarette case belonging to my mother, trying to look like Bette Davis and remembering the short life now left behind. Everything was in the past, rather like a dream: calling myself 'Dander' because I was unable to pronounce 'Diana', and having it as a nickname all through childhood; my early fears of the dark and being afraid to go upstairs on my own, always sleeping with a nightlight because of my terror of waking and feeling buried alive if I was in blackness; the wolf which had pursued me for years in dreams or imagination, scaring me out of my wits and always waiting with claws and teeth to kill me.

Good times, too, were past. Summer holidays at the seaside, harvest festivals with the fresh-picked fruit, flowers and vegetables on display, picnics in the bluebell woods, village fairs, Grandma Dors' cottage in Wales, Great-Uncle Joe's farm in Somerset and the haymaking on long summer evenings, play-hours with childhood friends, Christmas pantomimes, concerts organised by my father, the local boys, parties, dances, even the war. The war had brought me the Americans, and now they, too, were part of the past. So was school, and all those sneering people in Swindon who'd shaken their heads, saying I was doomed to failure and would soon be running home to my mother. 'Whatever was she thinking of, allowing so young a girl to go to London alone anyway?'

That brought me back to reality with a start. I'd show them. I *was* going to be a success, and I *was* capable of living

alone in London, even if I was only fourteen. No way would
I give anyone back there the chance of saying they were
right.

From Paddington station I took the underground to
Earls Court, where my mother and I had journeyed on
those weekly trips to LAMDA, and saw a large poster of
Margaret Lockwood, the number one British film star at
the time, advertising Drene shampoo. 'The Shampoo of the
Stars', it said boldly, displaying a beautiful colour picture
of her with tiny stars superimposed in her hair, to make it
look as though Drene had put them there. 'It never did that
to my hair', I thought ruefully as I envied Margaret
Lockwood her fame and wondered how long it would be
before my picture was up there advertising Drene.

On arrival at the YWCA I gave Miss Whipp my blue
ration book, for being under eighteen I was entitled to extra
food, which was still rationed even though the war was
over. And then I settled down to my first night away from
home; in a room with three other girls, two of whom were
also studying at LAMDA.

At seven the following morning I was awakened from my
sleep, not by my mother's gentle call, but by a loud,
clanging bell. Thinking the place had caught fire, I leapt
out of bed in alarm, only to find that – rather like a prison –
it was the waking-up bell. There was now half an hour to
get washed, dressed and downstairs to the dining-room in
time for the next deafening command, which was sounded
for breakfast. We sat at tables of four, to hot porridge, toast
and a small pat of butter and marmalade each – our ration
for the day. The YWCA did not provide lunch, only an
evening meal. I had been given £2 by my father, £1.50
(thirty shillings as it was then) for room and board and the
remaining 50p (ten shillings) for my lunches throughout
the week. He apparently intended that I venture no further
than Earls Court and the acting academy each day, and
have enough to pay for the underground back to Paddington on Friday, plus my bus fare from Swindon station to
home.

At ten, classes commenced at LAMDA, and I presented

myself there, feeling that I had begun my first steps towards stardom – and maybe that Drene shampoo advertisement, too. At fourteen I was the youngest full-time student the academy had had, but there was another nearly as young; a boy from Grimsby, George Raestrick, with whom I promptly fell in love. Like me, he was much older than his fourteen years and looked, as I recall now, rather like a forties' version of Elvis Presley . . . the same black hair and incredible green eyes.

No time was lost in making a date for that evening to go to the cinema in Kensington. But for some reason we took along another boy, Arthur Bentley; for laughs, I suppose, as he was LAMDA's comedian. The film we saw was *Captain Kidd*, starring Charles Laughton, but George and I were not too interested in the plot or, for that matter, Laughton's fine acting. On the way home we all went to a pub in the Earls Court Road, and such was our adult appearance that no-one asked us our age or refused us a drink. I can't remember what particular tipple we ordered, but as I never liked drinking it couldn't have been too strong. Besides, I only had eyes for George, so drink came a far second. Moreover, for the three of us, the biggest thrill was going into a pub at all as it was a freezing cold January night, and where else could we go?

The rule I detested most at the YWCA was the one which stated that each young woman must be indoors safely by eleven each night. Everyone was issued with a key and put on her honour to do so, but as I was only fourteen I was not allowed my own key, and was instructed that *I* must be in by ten. It was my first real taste of what I felt to be injustice! Many were the nights, in months to come, when I would borrow someone's key and sneak in later than my allotted time, creeping past Miss Whipp's door, without shoes, for fear she would catch me. My room was on the fifth floor, up seventy-eight stairs which all creaked at the slightest provocation.

As those first months went by, my life took a rather uniform path. Days began with the wretched bell at seven, and then there were classes where we aspiring artistes studied the art of stage make-up, improvisation, film technique, Shakespeare, the other classics, miming and fencing. There were also lessons in how to fall down dead on the floor, in various ways depending on the cause of death, and other more unusual exercises.

Lunch each day was at a small café in the Earls Court Road where one could buy beans on toast for sixpence and a jam roll and custard for fivepence. So my ten shillings' allowance stood me in fairly good stead! Evenings, unless I had a date with George, were spent listening to the radio at the YWCA – no television in those days – and on Fridays, after class, I caught the train home for the weekend where my eager mother awaited me with open arms. Somehow even then, in spite of my ambitions, Sunday afternoons always seemed to disappoint, marking the end of what had now become a pleasant period at home. The return journey to London always seemed to take hours, and those dark Sunday nights on the underground, and walking back to the YWCA, were particularly cheerless. Not at all the sort of life I had envisaged as that of a glamorous film star. But I kept telling myself it was all part of the price I must pay to attain my goal; and *that* I was determined to do, no matter what happened on the way.

My romance with George had cooled considerably by now, though I still used to give him all my sweet ration in an attempt to rekindle some of his earlier interest in me. But George had other things on his mind, and becoming serious with just one girl was not for him.

During these days I also acquired an agent. He wrote to me as a result of my meeting the year before with Mr Keating, the assistant film director, who had after all kept his word about trying to help me, informing the Gordon Harbord Agency that I was a likely young girl for films. Mr Harbord asked me to call to discuss a film which was being cast, *Black Narcissus*, and I hurried to his office in St Martin's Lane, my heart pounding with excitement at the thought that my chance to become a film star had arrived. Imagine my disappointment when Mr Harbord announced that the role was that of a black girl! Was this to be the fate of Swindon's answer to Betty Grable? What would all those people back there think if they saw me stained with boot polish, or whatever they used? And yet it never dawned on me that I might not even get the role, which incidentally I didn't. It went to Jean Simmons, whose career at the time was soaring high and who played the part beautifully.

Having experienced what I considered to be the first major setback to my ambitions, I attempted, with the wonderful optimism of youth, to rebuild my career. One of my efforts, through the help of a newspaper photographer from the *Swindon Advertiser*, resulted in an evening job, for the princely sum of one guinea an hour, posing as a photographic model with London's Camera Club. It was a rule among these amateur photographers never to touch the models, and, as some of them posed in the nude, it must have been quite an achievement for the men who rushed along there, armed with their cameras, for an evening away from their wives. Eventually I, too, was asked if, with the strictest propriety, I'd be prepared to remove my swimsuit and allow the photographers to snap me in my birthday suit. A serious discussion with my mother followed, and as my guinea was such a help with the expense of keeping me in London, it was decided I should do it. On this occasion, perhaps because she felt somewhat frightened by the idea, my mother actually consulted my father, and to my astonishment his reaction was that, if I was prepared to pose nude for art classes, it was entirely up to me. With hindsight, I now wonder if his reasoning was simply that of a weary father who knew in his heart that I would go my own way, no matter what he said.

All went well at the Camera Club, and the extra money from posing nude came in most handy. A photographer there showed me a picture of a girl named Susan Shaw, and told me she was going to be a big star in British films one day. He seemed pleased to have in his collection what were probably to be the only photographs of her in the nude, and when I expressed my own hopes of achieving the same success, he gave me the name of a modelling agency Susan used, together with a letter of introduction.

Once again I felt something might happen, and so I presented myself at the Pearl Beresford Agency with great excitement. Pearl, a rather fat, heavily made-up lady, appeared to like me and agreed to put me on her books. I explained that I was studying at LAMDA, could work only in the evenings, and also told her that my ambition was to attain stardom in films, rather than be a model, slyly hoping that she might see in me the same potential as Susan Shaw. But she merely wished me luck in that area and said she would contact me when the first modelling job came along. I was to receive *more* than a guinea an hour if I posed for independent photographers, and she would receive ten per cent commission for placing me.

Weeks went by, and I continued with my studies. I was due to take my acting exam at the end of the summer term, and this involved doing several pieces from Shakespeare and other well-known plays before an adjudicator. Peter Ustinov had already awarded me with a bronze medal the previous term, and now I was attempting a silver. At LAMDA, students aimed for a gold medal and finally a diploma, all of which were most important within that world of the drama school. As I was to discover later on, none of it meant anything out in the big cruel world.

My first call from Pearl Beresford proved quite easy and uneventful. The photographer was interested only in his work, taking great care over photographing me rather like a bronze statue! Frankly, I found the whole thing boring, with nothing to think about during the endless time he took to arrange his lights. And it made me all the more determined, if that was possible, to get into films and start acting for real.

The second call came on what was a monumental day for me: the beginning of my screen career. The adjudicator for my silver medal exam was a casting director named Eric L'Epine Smith, and having watched me go through my paces, with scenes from *As You Like It*, *While Parents Sleep* and *Wuthering Heights*, he called me out into the dark auditorium and told me I had won the medal with Honours. But the best news had nothing to do with LAMDA.

'I'm casting a film called *The Shop At Sly Corner*, which was a big success in the London theatre', he said. 'I think you'd be perfect for a small part in it.'

My head swam, I was breathless with excitement. What did it matter that it was a small part? Anything would suit me, even a 'walk on', just as long as I could get in front of that camera in a film studio. 'There is one thing though', he continued. 'I've seen you act today, and I know you can play the part easily. But it is the villain's girlfriend, and she should be older than you. I gather you are, incredibly, only fourteen years old.'

'Nearly fifteen', I added eagerly, for I couldn't bear the thought of losing this golden opportunity merely because of my age.

'Yes, yes I understand', he smiled. 'But for the moment I'm going to keep your age quiet. The producer will think I've gone mad if I suggest such a young girl for this kind of role. You'll be able to prove your worth when we give you a screen test, so until then pretend you're seventeen.'

My joy was indescribable. To say I was seventeen was something I'd been doing since the GIs invaded Swindon. And now a screen test! At long last they would see what I could do, and in no time I'd be on my way to Hollywood! LAMDA was buzzing with the news, and my mother was ecstatic. As for my father? His plan for me to become an elocution teacher had finally been terminated, and good riddance as far as I was concerned. It was typical of the sort of life he wanted for me and the last thing I ever considered.

As I excitedly waited to hear when my screen test would be, I received a call from Pearl Beresford, saying she had a client who wished to take some nude photos the next morning at eleven-thirty. This was child's play for me now as I sat back at the YWCA preparing to make my great début in films. But I agreed to do it for the few pounds it would bring in, and took down the address, the private home, somewhere near Bond Street, of a retired naval officer.

Upon arrival I was greeted by an elderly, white-haired

man whose nervous state I put down to his age and politely accepted the large drink he quickly poured for me. It didn't taste particularly nice, but I got through it and wondered when we'd begin the photo session. Meanwhile he rushed around like a cat on hot bricks, insisting I have another drink, and by the time I went into an adjoining room to undress I was feeling distinctly giddy.

No sooner had I walked back to the drawing-room, clad only in the bath towel he provided, than there was a sharp ring at the door. The naval officer went white and shoved me through the door into a cloakroom, from where I heard sounds of much rearranging of the cameras and lights he'd earlier set up to photograph me. I also heard a woman's voice in the hall, and I remember thinking with some amusement that, if he'd reacted as nervously to situations during the war, his ship would surely have been sunk by the enemy. In a frenzy he threw in my clothes from where I'd left them and ordered me, in best naval terms, to dress again; adding that he'd show me out a different way and that the photo session was off. I could only assume that his wife had returned unexpectedly, for the old devil was terrified. Apart from which his plans for me had been thwarted, and the drinks so liberally poured down my throat, for whatever reasons, wasted.

However, they were certainly working well, for I staggered out of there with 'The Admiral' in spluttering attendance, shoving a five-pound note in my hand to keep me quiet about the whole affair. How I made my way back to the YWCA I cannot recall, but once there I was called to the phone to be told my screen test was that very afternoon. Would I rush down to Isleworth studios as soon as possible?

My journey on various trains is barely remembered, yet get there I did, my head still fuzzy from the wretched man's drinks. Certainly, the way I felt prevented me from relishing all the preliminaries, going through make-up and so on, but perhaps the alcohol gave me the relaxation needed for being in front of the cameras. I sailed through my scene in a kind of haze and, as the role was that of a sexy tart, the effect was exactly as required. Mr L'Epine Smith emerged triumphant with his 'discovery', and whispered that he'd tell the director my real age at a later date. A salary was fixed at eight pounds a day, and the contract for my first film was drawn up by Gordon Harbord, who was also delighted. There was only one problem, and that was my name.

Earlier on Gordon Harbord had suggested I call myself Diana Scarlett, after the heroine in *Gone With The Wind*, and although I went along with this, I had also used the name Diana Carroll when modelling. I envisaged it in lights above the cinema marquees and thought it would look rather glamorous. Neither name suited Eric L'Epine Smith, however. And he tactfully suggested that I lose my original surname 'in case some people put vulgar connotations on it'. This led to a somewhat heated scene in Harbord's office when my father went to London to sign my contract, as I was still very much a minor. Fluck, he told my bewildered agent, was a perfectly suitable name, and 'If it was all right for my father and myself, it should be good enough for her!'

I was not present when this conversation took place, and can only imagine the problem it presented to Harbord. But as usual my mother came up with a solution by announcing that Dors had been my grandmother's maiden name and that, in her opinion, two names beginning with the same letter had a strong sound for a film star. Diana Dors it should most decidedly be!

I was not enamoured of the idea really, for it didn't seem as glamorous to me as Lana Turner or Hedy Lamarr, two of my favourites then. However, a name had to be found quickly if I wasn't going to be left, through my father's insistence, with *Diana Fluck* flickering dangerously in lights. So Dors it was, with the excuse that it was a family name. *Diana Dors* was duly born, signed for, and launched on her way to the stars.

*   *   *

My role in the film took exactly three days to complete, and afterwards I returned triumphantly to LAMDA, where

everyone seemed to treat me with a certain amount of awe.
I had appeared professionally in a film. Even Wilfred
Foulis viewed my chances in a different light, for he had
begun to assume the same opinion of me as my father; that I
was a silly young girl who didn't want to accept responsibilities and who would probably come to a 'no-good end'.
His forecast seemed even less likely when, some weeks later,
I received a call from my agent to enquire if I could dance
the 'jitterbug'. There was a sequence in a film called *Holiday
Camps*, being shot at Gainsborough Studios, and they'd pay
the princely sum of ten pounds for the day. Could I jitterbug indeed? I was the best in the country, for hadn't I
performed this crazy dance every Saturday night with
countless Americans at the Bradford Hall, Swindon?

Off to the studios I went, once again revelling in the
atmosphere of the place, the arc lights, the actors and even
the extras, of whom there were dozens on the day I was
called. A large crowd-call had been assembled for the
dance-hall scenes in which I was appearing. I was introduced to my partner, a young actor named John Blythe,
with whom I was later to appear in several films for the J.
Arthur Rank Organisation. But on that winter day in 1946
the future was some distance away, although my ambitions
were still set high and my hopes of Hollywood stardom
seemed fast becoming more than dreams.

Back at LAMDA, where I was now preparing to take my
gold medal for acting, life was made more exciting by
two arrivals from Nottingham on scholarships. Kenneth
Wilkins and Geoffrey Loach were an interesting pair,
particularly Geoffrey, who was dark and strikingly handsome with an irrepressible sense of humour and a strong
personality, both of which appealed to me tremendously.
Kenneth was much quieter, and Geoffrey used him as his
foil, but they made a fascinating combination for me and
my closest girlfriend, Daphne Alford, who now shared my
room at the YWCA. Needless to say, we promptly fell in
love, she with Kenneth and I with Geoffrey, who was to be
the first man who touched my emotions seriously, even
though he was only nineteen.

Our days passed happily, exhilarating and full of fun
with Geoffrey always in the lead. His language was pep-
pered with swear words I'd never heard before; his attitude
to life and acting ambitions were as strong and vital as
mine, but much wilder! Above all, he continually made me
laugh. Even at the age of fifteen, my Achilles' heel was a
weakness for laughing and being amused, and Geoffrey
played on it from the start.

We acted together in every well-known play that had
been written, and Geoffrey inspired me to new heights,
insisting I attempt roles I never thought possible for my
limited range such as the poor, down-trodden Bella in
Gaslight while he ranted and raged as the sadistic husband.
Lunchtimes in our little restaurant in the Earls Court Road
were a riot as many of the students, led by the inimitable
Geoffrey, enacted scenes and ran amok among the staff.
And then there were the nights when, for want of somewhere better to go after the cinema, he and I, Kenneth
and Daphne, would wander round in Hyde Park under the
lamplights or try to make frustrated love on the park
benches.

I worshipped him. He had all the panache and mascu-
linity I found attractive and, although I was very young, he
seemed to me such a man of the world in every way,
particularly in the mysterious world of sex, still a
frighteningly strange place where I had never dared tread.
For despite all my outward sophistication and the times
spent cavorting with Americans at dances, my mother's
warnings of the disgrace an illegitimate baby could bring to
any girl's – not to mention her family's – reputation were
prevalent in my mind. She never really discussed sex with
me, waving the subject away as an awful experience which
women had to undergo in marriage and which culminated
in the ordeal of childbirth.

Sex, to my mother, was a rather disgusting fact of life,
and the thought of her beloved daughter, married or not,
having to go through the agony of bearing a child was
something she preferred not to think about. My father, too,
occasionally referred to men's opinions of women who

made themselves 'easy meat', reminding me how every man expected his bride to be a virgin on her wedding night.

Such thoughts, and countless other taboos, confused me and curtailed my emotions on those park-bench nights with Geoffrey. It wasn't that I didn't desire him; indeed, I wanted to do anything to please and show him how much I cared. But my parents' warnings and threats always ruled my mind. The sheer terror of 'giving in' to a man and becoming pregnant! For, in the less enlightened days of my youth, there was no safe pill, only a great deal of ignorance and the danger of finding oneself destitute and disgraced. Through my mind ran a stupid little rhyme one of the boys at LAMDA had once recited to me.

> Here we come gathering nuts 'n' may,
> I put a girl in the family way,
> Now I've got sixteen and six to pay,
> Every Saturday morning!

Was this to be the only result of my love affair with Geoffrey? After all our dreams and aspirations, was I to be left in the position of facing my parents with the ghastly news that I was pregnant? Imagine hiding that from people in Swindon, most of whom were waiting to see my downfall anyway, and being obliged to give up everything I'd ever wanted in life. Shuffling off to some welfare centre every Saturday to collect my 16/6 – presumably the allowance given to an unmarried girl – and rearing a child born 'on the wrong side of the blanket', as my mother put it. No; it was out of the question.

As I tried to explain my fears to Geoffrey, the selfishness of men and their total disregard of a woman's feelings in matters of sex gradually dawned. In no way was he prepared to understand what a dreadful and shaming situation I might be placed in if I allowed myself to succumb to both our emotions by throwing caution to the winds for a sexually stimulating adventure in Hyde Park. Or at one of the various student parties where cooking sherry and beer were liberally drunk so that everybody had a good time, in

and out of bed. Yet there were also times when I almost
made up my mind to have sex with him and to hell with
the consequences. For my situation was becoming very
difficult. Geoffrey always made me feel unsophisticated and
stupid over my attitude towards sex, as if I was uniquely
boring by being a virgin. Other girls in his life had
obviously indulged in sex, and as a result were 'sophisticated and worldly'. Why then, with two films behind me
and all my adult-style behaviour, did *I* not go the whole
route and prove that I was everything I pretended to be?

There was one memorable evening, at a party, when I
swallowed countless glasses of cheap sherry in an effort to
abandon my principles and my virginity to Geoffrey once
and for all. Sadly, instead of plunging into the exciting
mysteries of sex, I succeeded in doing nothing more than
plunging into the bathroom violently ill, with Geoffrey
looking on helplessly. I prayed he would go away and leave
me to die, for now all ideas of sex and romance had gone for
ever. How could he ever desire me again, having witnessed
such a dreadful scene?

Strangely enough he did, and so our affair continued in
the same rather futile manner. But that incident did prove
one thing which would be invaluable through the coming
years. I could not drink much without feeling very ill, and
so, despite everything that was to happen to my life, I was
never in danger of becoming an alcoholic.

During the Christmas holidays that year, Geoffrey wrote
many letters declaring passionate affection for me. And in a
flamboyant style, typical of his volatile moods and temperament, he would sign off with phrases like 'Love you like
hell'. I also wore the ring he gave me, a black onyx which
was again typical of his character, and Grandma with the
Teapots asked smilingly if he was going to be the one I
would marry. With all the confidence and romanticism of
youth I truly felt he would be. And in the fantasy of infatuation I envisaged us living and working together, acting
brilliantly in the theatre, going from success to success,
hailed as the new Oliviers, and all the while thrilling to the
joy of physical togetherness.

Before LAMDA was due to commence its spring term of 1947, I was summoned back to London to begin another film, in which I played a dance-hall hostess. *Dancing With Crime*, starring a young actor who was showing great promise, Richard Attenborough, began shooting at Twickenham Studios in what proved to be the coldest winter for nearly fifty years. So cold was it that I wore slacks under my evening-dress! To make matters worse there was an electricity strike, and when everyone arrived in the mornings at 6.30, frozen and weary, the make-up men were often obliged to apply their cosmetics by candlelight! Yet, despite the lack of arc lamps and the general misery, filming went on. My salary had been fixed at ten pounds a day, and so by the time I completed two full weeks, I had in my possession about £150, having been paid in cash at the end of each day's filming.

Working for it was not as easy as it once seemed, however, and any ideas ever cherished about the glamorous life of film-stars were swept away during that time. My day started at four-thirty when the alarm clock my mother gave me pierced my dreams with its shrill ring. Shivering, I would dress, brush my teeth and then creep down the seventy-eight stairs to the dining-room for a bowl of corn-flakes which had been left out for breakfast. My imagination, for all that I was fifteen, still did leaps and bounds as it had done throughout my childhood, and that walk downstairs in the tomb-like silence of the sleeping building filled me with terror. Not only the childhood wolf pursued me then. I'd also seen films like *The Spiral Staircase*, in which George Brent (with whom I would one day work) set his grisly trap for Dorothy Maguire and tried to murder her. How was I to know *he* was not waiting at the bottom of the YWCA staircase to spring out on *me*. It seemed irrelevant that he was only an actor like myself who had had to get up early and report to a film studio. The difference, though, was that he worked in Hollywood, where the sun shone most of the time, and I was *en route* to the ice-blocked building in Twickenham.

Nor did my ordeal end once I made it to the dining-room.

For having swallowed down my breakfast, all the while nervously looking over my shoulder for monster-actor Todd Slaughter (another film which had terrified me in childhood was *The Face at the Window*) I put on my thick winter coat, a hand-down from a friend of my mother, and prepared to go into the outside world. This meant walking up Lexham Gardens and into the Earls Court Road, where I kept strictly to the middle – there was no traffic about at that hour – for fear that someone might jump from an alley and stab me. I was convinced that every murderer in London knew where I was and was waiting for me somewhere along that five-minute walk. But finally the sickly warmth of Earls Court underground station assured me I was safe for at least another day, and I proceeded on assorted trains and buses to the film studio. Once there, of course, everything changed and I could resume my original fantasies about films and film stars.

The last morning of filming saw me creeping in total terror down the Earls Court Road, clutching my green suitcase containing all the money I had earned and in a frenzy wondering whether I'd make it to the tube before thieves grabbed the suitcase first. In the event I arrived home in Swindon that night with my money safely intact. I will never forget the sight of my mother's face when she nervously counted it all on the drawing-room sofa. Nor for that matter my father's. 'Ridiculous', he mumbled. 'A fifteen-year-old girl earning more money than I do at my time of life!'

And so, with yet another film under my belt, it was back to LAMDA and Geoffrey. The term had already started and, although I enjoyed the acclaim that came my way as a result of being employed professionally in a film, there was something rotten in the state of Denmark. Geoffrey's welcome lacked its usual effervescence, and the reason was soon apparent in the shape of a blonde named Pat, a new student.

Pat was everything Geoffrey liked. She smoked, swore, dressed sophisticatedly, and presumably knew a great deal more about sex than I. In the weeks that followed I grew to like her myself, but I couldn't help feeling jealous because of so many things. I'd made three films by then and felt I should have been the one on top in all the situations, apart from Geoffrey! I had also returned his ring, on his request, and now I noted with dismay that Pat was wearing it.

However, there was also work to do, and my acting diploma to be won, and so I tried to ignore Geoffrey's affair with Pat, consoling myself with the thought that at least *I* was getting somewhere with my career. Which is more than could be said for either of them, giggling and winking at every opportunity. The climax to that term came when Wilfred Foulis, having decided that his previous doubts about me were unfounded, announced that he was awarding me the London Films Cup, which had been presented to LAMDA by film-maker Sir Alexander Korda. The presentation was made at the academy's theatre, in front of an audience, and to make the occasion worthwhile, for publicity purposes, a leading film star, Greta Gynt, was invited to present the cup to 'the girl most likely to succeed in British films'. As I watched her perform the ceremony, gazing in awe at her clothes and jewellery, little did I know what my connections with her would be just a year from then. However, I recited the speech of thanks my father had written for me, finishing by saying that 'I would try to keep the banner of LAMDA flying high in the world of films', which it seemed I had now entered officially.

I do not know what became of Geoffrey or Pat, except that I remember them, on that particular day, fooling around in their usual manner behind the wings. Perhaps she married him and they starred in rep. somewhere? He and I had intended doing so during our early days of play-acting and romance; before I came to experience my first broken love affair.

My life was moving along quickly now. *The Shop At Sly Corner* had been released, and for the first time I watched myself on the screen. An incredible experience! It was duly distributed in Swindon, and there was much fuss over the fact that their 'own Diana Dors' was appearing in it. My name featured in all the posters around the town, and I was asked to make a personal appearance at the opening. Come the night, dressed in a white evening-dress trimmed with silver sequins and wearing a beaver-lamb coat that my mother had bought for me at vast expense, I was driven to the cinema, with my father, suavely dressed in evening-suit and black bow-tie, acting as escort. The manager greeted us and took me on to the stage, where once again, as my parents watched proudly from the stalls, I recited a speech written by my father.

After all this excitement, the idea of returning to LAMDA was beginning to wane, but as I didn't know what else to do for the summer I enrolled anyway. It was to prove a fruitless venture, for the next big step in my career was just around the corner.

'Get down to Pinewood Studios', said my agent on the telephone. 'David Lean is making a film of *Oliver Twist* and they want to test you for the part of Charlotte.' She, I recalled, was the sluttish maid in the coffin-maker's shop.

Thrilled at the prospect, for Lean's previous success had been *Great Expectations*, I made my way to Pinewood and was prepared for the part by wardrobe and make-up. In Dickensian clothes and with dirt smeared on my face, I looked a far cry from Swindon's answer to Betty Grable. Still, I can't have looked too horrendous, for a young assistant-runner, known around the studios as 'Kipp', showed keen interest in me. A dark-haired, good-looking boy, he had a personality not unlike Geoffrey's, except that he had no ambitions to be an actor and was, therefore, not as egotistical. Nevertheless, for all his seventeen summers, he possessed great confidence where girls were concerned, which was one of the things that attracted me.

We arranged to meet the following evening, which necessitated my taking the train to Ruislip, where he lived with his parents. There, Kipp lost no time in guiding me, not to a restaurant or cinema, but straight to the Ruislip woods! I'm sure they were very beautiful but I was not much interested in the scenery on that date. I only had eyes for him, while it was apparent he had only one thing in mind for both of us. Once more in my life sex reared its ugly head, and there we lay in the long grass, fighting a desperate battle over my virginity. But the only things to triumph were the gnats, for as a result of this frustrating amorous encounter, my legs and arms were covered in bites for several days.

Kipp was obviously disappointed that the sexy-looking girl he had carefully wooed at the studios was something of a fraud when it came to love-making. But his ardour had not been completely quelled, and he made a date to meet me again the following week, perhaps seeing me as the first real challenge of his short love life. For my part, I felt like a failure where the opposite sex was concerned; and worse than that, a very dull one, too. But I was boosted by the fact that he wanted to see me again, and in my own sweet way I truly believed that we were in love, and that love would prove sex was not of the greatest importance anyway. How wrong I was. Our second date was even more abysmal than the previous one. Once again we lay in the woods at Ruislip, grappling with each other and the gnats, and after several agonising hours Kipp gave up the fight.

His disappointment, combined with my misery, resulted in his walking me back to the train and muttering something about 'calling me sometime'. Those awful words, 'I'll see you around', were to echo with hollowness in my head many times in life, but at fifteen they were like the pronouncement of a death sentence. Something that was beautiful and wonderful had been lost and possibly would never be found again.

The thought that the object of my adoration had not even had the courtesy to take me anywhere other than his local undergrowth, or to pay me the compliment of escorting me home, never entered my mind. All I knew was that another boy I had fallen for was passing me up in favour of somebody else who would no doubt be happy to make love, regardless of the consequences. Why couldn't I behave like that, too? Why was I so uptight, so rigidly disciplined by the rules set down by my parents? Other girls took a chance. What was so special about *my* virginity?

Years and years later I saw Kipp again. He had become

the successful film producer he always wanted to be, and, after one broken marriage, had wed the beautiful and talented Hollywood actress, Lee Remick. Then, however, I could laugh with him over our frustrated summer-evening trysts. But at the time the hurt lingered on after our last date as I waited for him to call me.

Professionally, something good has always happened in my life, no matter how bad life seems personally. And so I arrived home one weekend to be greeted by my excited mother with the news that not only had I got the part in *Oliver Twist*, but that J. Arthur Rank had offered me a ten-year contract, beginning at ten pounds a week, then fifteen, twenty and so on until my salary reached the astronomical sum of three hundred pounds a week – if I was still with them at the end of ten years. Of course, they had an annual option to decide my fate. Our joy and elation were unparalleled. Even my father showed a certain pleasure at my early success, though as always he never displayed his feelings very much, preferring if possible to bring me down from my pink cloud by issuing warnings of what would happen if I did not work hard. As usual, all the old lectures I'd heard before.

The Rank contract was duly signed and I received my first pay cheque, which my father placed in a bank account for me, my first. He would handle all my money, he said, and see that I used it wisely. But money was the last thing I cared about. My real concern was acting and making films.

Working on *Oliver Twist* was a marvellous experience, and as Kipp had been assigned to another production, I was not hampered by any left-over feelings for him. Though my heart did skip a beat one day when I saw him on the back lot at Pinewood. What I did not realise, however, was how quickly word went round the studios that we'd dated and, as I looked and behaved older than my fifteen years, I was continually fighting off advances by almost every man there. Far from finding it a boost to my ego, I was learning that an abundance of sex appeal, plus being as friendly as I was with everyone, was not too advantageous. Kipp had obviously not let on that I was a virgin, possibly letting it be thought we'd gone all the way for fear of appearing a failure himself – that male ego working overtime again! I was constantly embarrassed by all the passes being made, and indeed have never really learned how to deal with the conceit and behaviour of the male animal.

Having undergone a great deal of this, which was the only blot on my otherwise good working life at the studios, I found myself in another highly embarrassing situation one day when the director, David Lean, told me that he would be coming to my dressing-room to go over my lines. Up till then I'd regarded him as someone well above the sordid world of sexual activities, and so I happily opened the door to him, script in hand, only to find that this 'god' was merely a man like all the others. Instead of listening to my well-rehearsed lines, he seized me in an embrace and covered me with kisses. As he was very much a man of the world, I suppose he quickly realised that I was, for all my behaviour and sex appeal, just an innocent little girl. For he soon removed himself politely from my virginal presence with the excuse that he had to get back to the set!

To his credit, at no time during the rest of the filming did he make me feel embarrassed about that silly dressing-room fiasco. I like to think he was considering *my* feelings, but somehow, knowing men as I do now, it was probably a scene he wished he'd never attempted to direct.

Having completed my role in *Oliver Twist*, I was commanded by the Rank Organisation to attend their school for young actors at Highbury, in north London. Located in a disused church hall, it bore little resemblance to the somewhat glamorous title bestowed on it by the press – namely the Charm School. Originally the idea, to teach boys and girls under contract to J. Arthur Rank to act, had been a good one, for it was most beneficial to those starry-eyed youngsters who had had little or no experience in the field of acting. But to someone like myself, the Company of Youth was a dreadful waste of time. Had I not completed a year and a half at LAMDA, with a gold medal and diploma to my credit? Admittedly David Henley, head of the contract artistes department, had merely sniffed when told of these attributes, making me realise that all the hard work and glittering prizes at LAMDA were not worth much in the outside world.

But for certain young starlets, like Constance Smith, the school was a wonderful place. Connie, a beautiful Irish girl, had won a local contest to find 'The girl who looked most like Hedy Lamarr', the prize being a screen test and contract with J. Arthur Rank. Yet, Connie, through no fault of her own, could neither read nor write, so her days were spent learning to do so, as well as walking around in circles with a book on her head to give her proper deportment. Others, too, needed all the help that the former actors and actresses employed there could give them, although some of the boys – among them Christopher Lee, Anthony Steel, Pete Murray and Bill Travers – could hardly be expected to benefit from book-balancing exercises.

Few of the girls there ever amounted to anything, in my recollection. But two who did were Susan Shaw, who had inadvertently inspired me to become a photographic model, and Barbara Murray, whom I had met one morning on the five o'clock train to Twickenham. Barbara was only seventeen then and working as an extra on *Dancing With Crime*, but she finally won a film contract and arrived at the Charm School full of hope and ambition.

Connie Smith made it, too, finding stardom in Hollywood, but her success was brief. For the discipline so essential to survive in a place like that is not learnt in the wilds of Ireland, and there were – and still are – many temptations. Ultimately, after a seedy phase in Rome, she was charged with the attempted murder of her lover, a film producer with whom she lived after the break-up of her marriage to actor-director Bryan Forbes. Nor did success provide a happy story for Susan Shaw, who died of alcoholism, alone in a sleazy flat above a Soho sex shop. Only Barbara Murray and I survived, though not without disastrous results in our personal lives.

All this, however, is racing far ahead of that hot summer of 1947 when, as Mr Rank's starlets, we climbed aboard the number 19 bus that took us each day to Highbury and the dreary church hall. 'Being paid to learn' was how one rather embittered actress-teacher often put it.

From time to time we would appear in small parts in films, being released from the school until we'd completed them. In *Good-Time Girl* I was a delinquent with Flora Robson explaining the facts of life to me; In *It's Not Cricket*, the comedy team of Basil Radford and Naunton Wayne ogled me in a fairly amusing scene in which I applied for a job in their office. *The Calendar* saw me as a primly uniformed maid serving tea to Greta Gynt – once more – and in *My Sister and I*, I was a young girl in pigtails delivering a script to that film's star, Sally Ann Howes, daughter of twenties idol Bobby Howes. Only seventeen herself, *she* wasn't made to attend the wretched Charm School like the rest of us, as I often reflected ruefully. *Penny and the Pownall Case*, a modest low-budget film made at the studios in Highbury next to the school, saw me as a secretary who, the director insisted, should take down shorthand without looking at her notepad. He even rebuked me on the set for not acting the part as a secretary would. But when the film was reviewed, a critic promptly criticised me for being the only secretary he'd seen who took dictation without once glancing at her notepad!

I hated this film, for apart from having to be at the studios at six – a return to my old *Dancing With Crime* mornings in the dark, empty streets of London – I had to catch the charwomen's bus to Highbury. It was hardly the kind of life I'd envisaged leading in my childhood fantasies in Swindon. Furthermore, the producers made me cut my lovely thick long hair. I protested violently about this, and was severely reprimanded by the Charm School's dreaded matriarch, Molly Terraine, whose main interest anyway was coaching Jean Simmons.

'What kind of an actress do you call yourself?' she demanded. 'Do you think Laurence Olivier enjoys walking around Denham with dyed blonde hair while he's playing Hamlet?'

This point was presumably made because Jean Simmons was also at Denham, playing Ophelia, and she spent every moment she could with her. But I refrained from pointing out that Olivier's portrayal in a Shakespearian classic was somewhat more important than mine in a low-budget B picture; especially when it came to my locks being shorn. Not that I'd have minded had it been a case of 'art for art's sake'. But the real reason was that the hairdresser could not be bothered styling my hair so early in the morning. And as I was not the star, a quick answer was to lop it off! I made a mental note to remember her name when I finally did become one.

It was about this time that I met the man who was to have the most serious effect on my emotions I had yet experienced. I was at Denham, doing a screen test for a film called *Precious Bane* which was being set up by American director Robert Siodmak. As the part was similar to that I'd played in *Oliver Twist*, I assumed it was why I'd been considered. The test went well, too, with Siodmak running around like a small-time Cecil B. de Mille, shouting that he wanted *realism* at all times and for my hair to look as though I'd been 'scratching'. Afterwards, as I sat in make-up trying to remove all traces of the animal-type girl I'd tried to create, I heard the most beautiful masculine voice in the corridor outside. 'Where is this little girl?' boomed loud for everyone to hear and, as I swivelled round to see who it was, in strode a tall, dark man whose gaunt good looks came second in attractiveness only to his powerful voice.

'So *you* are Diana Dors', he exclaimed, dropping to his knee beside me and exploring me with the eye of an antique dealer about to make a purchase. 'Everyone's talking about you, so I thought I'd come and have a look for myself.' A deliberate pause, and then, 'Not bad!'

His manner, if ironic, was seductive, and I did not know how to react.

'Have you finished your test?' he enquired abruptly. 'How did it go?'

I replied that I thought it had gone as well as could be expected, to which he commented sneeringly: 'Well, what the hell would that mad Hungarian Siodmak know any-way?'

After some more whirlwind banter, during which I learnt that he, too, had been tested – for the starring role of Gideon, a part he coveted and one which he considered 'No-one else was capable of playing' – he told me he was Guy Rolfe and that he was also under contract to the Rank Organisation. They'd never try to make him go to the Charm School, I thought. But then he was a man in his thirties and no doubt already a star with much acting experience.

'Come on then, Agatha,' he said, rising to his full height of six feet four inches, 'if you want a ride back to London, I'll take you in my car.'

The fact that he had his own car was marvellous, and the relief of not having to travel on buses and trains filled me with delight. The only other time I'd been driven back in style from a film studio was when David Lean had offered me a ride in his chauffeur-driven limousine as it glided out of Pinewood and he saw me waiting at the bus stop. That was *before* our disastrous dressing-room encounter.

'Where do you live, Agatha?' Guy enquired as I struggled to keep up with his long strides down the Denham corridors.

'At the YWCA in Earls Court', I replied. 'I hope it doesn't take you out of your way.'

'The what!', he shouted, throwing back his head and laughing loudly. I repeated my answer, which this time sounded extremely silly. Indeed, every time I spoke there was something about his attitude that made me feel awkward.

'My God!' he announced to an electrician as we passed by. 'Trust me to find a girl who lives in an institution.'

I hastily tried to set straight his opinion of the YWCA, but he waved my explanations away. 'At fifteen, it's probably the safest place for you', he said gravely, as if being fifteen was some sort of affliction. And when we arrived at the wretched place, my embarrassment grew worse.

'I am allowed to live my own life', I remonstrated in defence.

'How late do they let you stay out?' he asked, this time with a smile.

'Eleven o'clock', I lied, not daring to tell him ten was my real curfew.

'Then I'll pick you up tomorrow evening at seven', he said. 'We'll have dinner, and I'll have you back in the institution on time.' There were no ifs and buts; he did not even bother to ask if I was busy. That supreme male ego presumed I couldn't possibly resist such an offer, and of course it was right.

'I've just met the most wonderful man', I dreamily informed Daphne, who at that time was completely disenchanted with men, having discovered that the love of her life was married. And the following night, ignoring Daphne's warnings and her questions whether this new phenomenon was also married – the thought had never entered my mind – I prepared myself for our date. Guy arrived punctually, and away we drove to a little Soho restaurant where, from the way the head waiter bowed us in, he was obviously well known.

Food rationing was still severe, but no-one would have known it in this establishment. Steaks were served as though they were commonplace, though I'd never seen such a large one in my life. Which did not stop me pretending steaks were something I was quite used to. After dinner we went to Guy's flat, which was nearby, and he introduced me to his adorable dog, Henrietta. Somehow this small but luxurious residence revealed a woman's presence and, as it was nine in the evening, I wondered where she was. If she existed. But I asked no questions. Guy, talking endlessly, was impressing me greatly with his conversation and *savoir-faire*, never making a move towards me all evening. And just as I was wondering what time I'd have to creep into the hostel unnoticed, he looked at his watch and announced he'd have me back at the institution by the early hour of ten o'clock.

As each evening went by, this became our pattern; going to dinner and then back to his flat. Except, of course, at weekends when I returned home to my parents as usual.

The knowledge that I was a virgin and 'not doing that sort of thing' he found fascinating; he may even have seen it as a challenge. I'm sure most thirty-seven-year-old men would in the company of a young girl of limited experience.

But gradually the fun gave way to something more serious, and frustration found me becoming more and more the target of Guy's cynicism and sarcasm. Remarks about my make-up, my clothes, the way I spoke and behaved, soon gave me an enormous complex about myself, for each one was delivered with complete accuracy. It was almost as if he was trying to possess my mind and emotions because he could not have me physically.

Not that I was his only target, for in Guy's book no-one was right about anything but him. I put this down to the fact that, for all his sophistication, he had come from a very poor family and, as he once told me, had not been able to speak English properly until he joined a repertory company early in his youth. Determined to better himself, he worked on his speech endlessly until he had no trace of accent, and had perfected the kind of beautiful voice everyone dreams of having.

His ancestors, he informed me, were not mere ordinary folk like his parents. On his mother's side was a Red Indian princess, hence his striking, dark good looks. His extremely slim build he attributed to contracting consumption as a child, and apparently it still plagued him even then. All this I found intensely romantic, and yet, infatuated and bewitched by him as I was, fear always prevented me from casting off the loathed virginal mantle I'd so carefully woven round myself.

He was married, too, as Daphne had warned, and this was another important factor. Although he never discussed the matter, I did have my suspicions and discovered that his wife was appearing in a play, just around the corner from their flat at the Phoenix theatre. Which was why he always whisked me home so punctually every evening! It had nothing to do with my curfew, or his concern for my tender years. He had to pick his wife up at the stage-door and possibly take *her* to dinner, too.

Sometimes we would drive out to the country where Guy was converting a lovely old house, and, armed with antiques he had bought, he would stride around displaying great flair for interior design and educating me about furniture, paintings and so on. Other days we would visit actor friends of his, at their homes or in pubs near theatres where they were appearing, and always I saw the looks in their eyes. What was this incorrigible rogue doing with such a young girl? How wrong they all were!

On one occasion we had dinner at The Caprice, a very fashionable restaurant, having been to see *Born Yesterday* in which the American actress, Yolande Donlan, was starring. Yolande was being courted by a friend of his, Val Guest, the writer-director, though this would not have deterred Guy. As he said to me before the show, if he preferred Donlan to Dors, that would be the end of me. I sat through the play terrified. What would happen if he really meant it and took me out no more? My life revolved so much around him that I dared not venture a step without his instruction or advice. Later, at The Caprice, my fears intensified as the three of them conversed about subjects of which I knew nothing. I felt gauche and insignificant, especially when they sent a cryptic note across to the well-known musical-comedy star, Frances Day, telling me to add 'Dors' to the signatures of 'Rolfe, Donlan and Guest'.

Whether Rolfe really did not fancy Donlan, or Guest saw to it that he never got too close to her, I do not know. But to my relief our meetings continued along the usual lines. However, little changes did occur. Where once Guy had telephoned at a given time each night before coming to collect me, there were now nights when he never phoned at all. I think this is how I developed my phobia about waiting for anyone to ring me. Those dreadful hours sitting by the telephone, jumping up excitedly as it rang, only to find it was for some other girl. The endless torture of waiting for her to finish, sick with worry that he might stop trying if he couldn't get through. And then the rest of the night and the following day at the Charm School, wondering if he would call again. Ironically, my bus to Highbury passed his flat, and my misery would only deepen as I gazed up at his window and wondered what he and his wife were doing in there.

I realise now just how much he had me in his power, for I was always available when he wanted to indulge his whims. I didn't even mind when he rang and told me to take a taxi to his flat. At least he gave me the fare when I arrived, and, depending on his mood, some more to catch another taxi home.

Guy cared not one ounce for anyone's opinion of him. 'Let them all think I'm a conceited bastard', he once said, grinning with pleasure at the thought.

As my sixteenth birthday approached, I waited breathlessly, in between our on-and-off dates, to see what he would plan for me. The day came, and that evening I sat in my usual position by the phone, dressed and ready for his summons. Nerve-racking hours passed, but there was no call. I couldn't understand why, for everything had been fine the night before – or as fine as things could be between a thirty-seven-year-old film star, two-timing his wife, and a love-struck teenage virgin!

A Canadian actor I'd known at LAMDA called instead, inviting me to go to see him in a play at the King's Theatre, Hammersmith, and so miserably, for the want of anything better to do on my birthday, I went. I must have been a very poor companion. But the next night Guy called.

'I thought it was all over', I stammered. 'You didn't ring yesterday and it was my birthday.'

He sounded mortified, and told me to grab a taxi immediately. We would go out to dinner. *We*, however, did not both have dinner, for Guy sat back and watched me eat. (He was probably dining with his wife after the theatre.) As usual we went back to his flat, where an abortive love session was held, and before dismissing me he pressed ten pounds into my hand. 'That's for your birthday. I know how you must have felt when I didn't call. It's a terrible thing for a child to have its birthday forgotten.' He spoke of me as if I was an object he intended to place in his house in the country. (Years later I heard of another blonde starlet, also infatuated by him, whom he actually invited to spend the weekend there with him and his wife. It wasn't hard to imagine her misery at being made to sleep in the guestroom while they occupied the main bedroom.)

I was now beginning to realise that our relationship had little future, though I could not decide whether his callous treatment of me was because his life had made him that way, or because I'd proved myself inadequate in our ridiculous little affair. His calls grew fewer, and our frequent dates diminished into the odd one or two nights a week; sometimes not even that.

One weekend, as I journeyed home to Swindon, I met a young soldier who seemed pleasant; quite different in fact from other soldiers. He had a car waiting for him at the station, but before he drove off we made a date for coffee the next morning. I thought it would ease some of the unhappiness I was experiencing over Guy, but I was due for another lesson about men. He turned up with a married woman well known in the town, and all I got was a rather sheepish look in my direction. Quite by chance, two years later I learnt that my simple soldier was actually heir to part of a huge chain-store fortune and that his mother had a penthouse in Grosvenor Square, where I attended several incredible parties he gave: thousands of bottles of champagne and bands playing on the terrace. I was also invited once – with some others – to his home on the Sussex coast, but there I saw another side of him. He became quite crazed when I refused to go to bed with him, though little did I realise at the time how lucky I was to escape with a tantrum. Twenty years on, he was sent to prison for severely assaulting some other unfortunate girl who incurred his wrath by refusing him.

But that was later. In early 1948 I was still getting over what was then the biggest emotional upheaval of my young life. I tried going out with different boys, but compared with Guy they were so unsophisticated and uninteresting. My old friend Desmond Morris, who was now doing his National Service in the RAF, took me to an overnight party at the home of a millionaire who lived near Swindon, and that was a marvellous evening for there were some extra-ordinary people there. The host, being slightly eccentric, adored colourful characters, one of whom was an Indian poet named Tambi who sat reciting his poetry in a nearby cornfield as the dawn come up.

It was after this dawn reading that we all made our way to bed where, not entirely to my surprise, I was joined by one of the host's sons. He'd taken an immediate fancy to me and I hadn't exactly discouraged him. But my old inhibitions about sex, plus the lateness – or earliness – of the hour, prevailed and we both fell asleep.

When I returned home, my mother, who was preparing the Sunday lunch, enquired whether or not I'd had a good time. My having a 'good time' was one of her obsessions, along with not getting serious about anyone or marrying until I was much older.

'Yes, I did', was my stock answer, but this time I couldn't resist a little tease. 'Tell me', I asked innocently, 'is it possible to spend the night in bed with a man and not have sex with him?'

'Of course it isn't', she replied.

I smiled inwardly, but not without certain misgivings. Perhaps I really was on my own over this business of sex before marriage. Or was I just a freak, and a failure where men were concerned?

The end of the Guy Rolfe affair came the day I went to our Soho restaurant with some friends and saw him lunching with his wife. Although it was natural that he should ignore me, I choked on my food and had to rush out alone with never a glance behind. My life was finished, or so I felt then.

I saw him again many years later, when I was reaching my zenith in films. He was his usual self, but as we lunched together at the studios he did admit that I'd done *quite* well; though he added a rider that he preferred the old Dors he once knew to the glossy image I'd become. I didn't mention the stories I'd heard about him from time to time, but on another occasion in Hollywood, when *he* actually phoned *me*, I couldn't resist reminding him of the passing of time.

'Isn't life fleeting, Guy?' I reminisced. 'Do you realise I've known you since I was fifteen, and now I'm twenty-nine.'

'Christ!' he answered dryly. 'Have you stopped to consider just how old that makes me!' Not old enough to stop chasing young actresses around Hollywood, I thought.

During those emotionally racked months of what I came to regard as the Guy Rolfe era, I was still having to report to the Charm School, as well as struggling along in small film roles. I also had to attend, along with all Rank contract artistes, the weekly cocktail party given by David Henley. For many of the starlets this provided an opportunity to mingle with directors and producers in the hope of being cast in their films – often, though unofficially, for services rendered. Here, for once in my life, my age saved me, for Sydney Box, the top producer at Gainsborough Studios who claimed to have discovered me and who cast me in some of my early films, had sent out a memo that I was under sixteen, and therefore 'jailbait'. No matter how much the men lusted over my sexy image, they were to 'keep off'.

For a while I got away with it, and even after I was sixteen everyone behaved with propriety. But one day I received a message, via the Charm School secretary, that a senior Rank executive wanted to see me on Saturday evening 'on an important matter'. At last, I thought, they're going to take me away from that wretched school and cast me in a starring role. David Henley and the powers that be had finally realised my star potential and were ready to launch me on my way to Hollywood, just as they had done for Jean Simmons.

My weekend visit home had to be cancelled, but when I informed my parents of the importance of this meeting, they were as excited as I. I spent all day Saturday on tenterhooks, foreliving the moment when he told me that possibly a Twentieth Century Fox producer had made an offer for my services, and it would necessitate the Rank Organisation releasing my contract, the way they sold Jean Simmons to Howard Hughes. At seven-thirty, I rang his doorbell and he ushered me in, looking serious.

We were obviously alone, and as trivial conversation droned on, I wondered where his secretary was. Apart from the fact that she should have been there helping to discuss my new contract, she was, I knew, having an affair with him. Only half-listening as I waited nervously for him to get to the point of our meeting, I suddenly became aware that he was talking about my weight.

'We all know the camera magnifies, and as you're still at the puppy-fat stage this might present a problem in your next films. Whatever they are.'

Was I hearing right? Surely this wasn't why I'd been summoned to his presence?

'I'd like to see for myself just how much you've put on in the last few months. Take all your clothes off so that I can have a look', he said without a trace of a smile! 'I'll go into the other room while you undress. Call me when you're ready.'

I sat stunned. My heart had begun beating faster, and my face was flushed with embarrassment. What would I tell my parents? I could hardly explain that the old lecher had begun by berating me about my appearance, and for allowing my appetite and zest for living to overshadow my responsibilities as one of Mr Rank's young ladies. 'We cannot put old heads on young shoulders', was how he'd phrased that part of his sly speech. But there was more than my disappointment to worry about. What did he intend doing once I'd taken my clothes off? And if I refused to disrobe, he might possibly have the Organisation cancel my contract when it was time to renew the option. There seemed no way out.

Miserably I began to unbutton the jacket and skirt of my ballerina suit, then the latest fashion, when I heard a key in the lock of the front door. Never have I been so happy to see someone's secretary. Her pretext was that she was looking for some papers, but I had no doubt why she was really there. Her fears were probably confirmed when she noticed my jacket lying across a chair and my half-undone skirt.

Amidst the general fluster – not to mention embarrassment – I was ordered to put my things back on and pop along like a good girl, carry on at the Charm School, and learn as much as I could from all the wonderful teachers there. They had so much wisdom to impart about acting.

My feelings were indescribable, my misery overwhelming, and I still had to tell my parents. The full explanation I left till the following weekend, and then I only muttered something about them 'being concerned about my weight because I was so young'. My mother, naturally, was disappointed, for she too had imagined the news was going to be exciting. My father reacted in his usual manner.

'A man in that position wouldn't bother to speak with you for such a trivial reason', he said grimly. 'It's quite obvious you're not concentrating on your work properly. I hope you think seriously about what he said, for if they do drop your contract, *then* where will you be?'

Always ready to believe anyone else was right when it came to my behaviour, my father, seemingly despite all the success I'd achieved in so short a time, was preparing to wash his hands of me once again.

CHAPTER FOUR

LOVE SWEET LOVE

Jack and Jill went up the hill,
To fetch a pail of water.

The unhappiness and despair that followed my break-up with Guy Rolfe, and my disillusionment after the 'puppy-fat' episode, were finally quelled by my original mentor, Sydney Box, with the biggest screen role I'd ever had. It was in a film based on a family named the Huggetts, starring Jack Warner and Kathleen Harrison, and was inspired by their portrayals of Joe and Ethel Huggett in the comedy *Holiday Camp*, in which I had 'jitterbugged' one brief day.

In this, the first of what was hoped would be many adventures of the Huggett family, I was to play their flighty niece who comes to stay for a while and disrupts the household. The Huggetts had three daughters, Jane Hylton, Susan Shaw, and Petula Clark the 'baby'. Although only a year younger than me, Pet was still forced to cling to the child-star image that had brought her success mainly as a singer. And there were days when, seeing her in gymslips and ankle socks, with her hair in pigtails, I found it hard to believe she was actually fifteen. Especially as everyone, under the watchful eye of her dominant father, Leslie, treated Pet as if she really was about ten.

With me it was all so very different, despite Sydney Box's earlier memo. Besides, I was now sixteen, officially, and no longer protected.

In the film, the girls all had boyfriends: Jimmy Hanley was Jane's, Peter 'Pie-face' Hammond was Susan's, and a clever young boy called Anthony Newley, also under

contract to Rank, was Pet's. In real life, Jane was married
to film producer Euan Lloyd, Susan had many beaux, and
was about to meet the man who was to be her first husband,
German actor Albert Lieven. Pet, of course, had no-one —
her father saw to that — and nor did I, though not for the
same reason. Pet's schedule of personal appearances and
cabaret performances when she was not filming was very
demanding; little wonder that she eventually rebelled and
went off to lead her own life.

In *Here Come The Huggetts* I was teamed again with my
'jitterbug' partner from *Holiday Camp*, John Blythe, and as
we made quite an amusing comedy pair we were cast in the
follow-up, *Vote For Huggett*. I thought my career was riding
high at last, for I had a great deal to do in both films, plus
extremely good billings. But I made the mistake of going to
see the press preview of *Here Come The Huggetts*.

I'd invited my mother along, and together we roared
with laughter all the way through, both of us very pleased at
the way I had come out of it. But afterwards, half-expecting
the stone-faced critics to rush over and congratulate me, I
discovered, as they all slunk away without a word, that
success is a much harder nut to crack. In fact, they disliked
the whole thing, and after that I never went to another press
show of my own films.

Little did I know then that I was on the verge of the next
'backcloth tapestry' in my life, and I had no prescience of
what was to happen as I entered Gainsborough Studios for
an appointment with director Ralph Smart. A plump, jolly
man who seemed more like a games teacher than a director,
Ralph informed me he was making a film about cycling
clubs called *A Boy, a Girl and a Bike*, to be shot mostly on
location in the beautiful Yorkshire dales. I, of course,
was being considered for the part of the club's 'bad
girl', and would receive top supporting billing beneath the
stars, John MacCallam, Patrick Holt and Honor Blackman, a young actress who had recently signed with Rank.
'Shooting would commence', said producer 'Bunny'
Keene, who by now had joined us for the interview, 'in two
weeks' time, before which I'm giving a cocktail party at my

Chelsea home so that everyone can meet. I'd like you to come along too.' Needless to say I was very excited, and with enthusiasm set about preparing to travel to the north of England, where I had never been before.

Bunny Keene's party was quite thrilling, for he'd also invited a number of stars not in the film. It was there that I first met James Robertson Justice, complete with bushy beard and dressed in full naval officer's uniform. A fearsomely loud man who always spoke his mind and cared not a bit for anyone, James was just beginning to carve out an acting career, and I wondered what had prompted him to turn away from the sea, a life he obviously loved. When the party ended, Bunny asked me if I'd like to go night-clubbing and, as I'd borrowed a key from Daphne so that I could creep in whenever I liked, I accepted.

Away we went in his funny old motor-car, which looked not unlike Bunny himself – a left-over from the 1920s. The club we went to, The Gargoyle, somewhere in Soho, confirmed my opinion, for it was obviously a place once frequented by all those bright young things of Bunny's era. I didn't much care for it, with its tired atmosphere, its mirrored walls and its pillars, and I was almost glad to be dropped back home in the early hours.

The big day arrived for me to make my way, this time in a car hired by the studio, to King's Cross station where I was to meet up with Bunny, who was escorting Anthony Newley and me to Yorkshire. As the two youngest contract players in the Rank Organisation – there was a month between us – and both being important properties, we could not be expected to make such a long journey alone. Tony arrived with his step-father, and I wondered for a moment if he might be another Leslie Clark. But he waved us goodbye as the train eased out of the station, and we settled down to an eight-hour trip.

No bells rang for either of us at that stage, probably because Tony appeared too young to me. But I did find him different from other boys of his age, and remembered the touch of genius he had revealed in his portrayal of the Artful Dodger in *Oliver Twist*.

I was overcome by the magnificence of the Yorkshire scenery as we were driven to the Fell Hotel, near Grassington, to join the rest of the cast and Ralph Smart, whose wife Meg was there as a script consultant, but no doubt was also keeping an eye on her boisterous husband! The days that followed passed happily, and we'd be ready on the location by eight most mornings not to miss the sun. Filming still held an enchantment for me, and so I didn't mind the long hours or the weariness that follows a day's shooting. I could never understand why many of the bit-part actors were always moaning how tired or bored they were between scenes. But I soon became acquainted with their 'hanging around and hoping it would rain' routine. As most were on large daily rates, extra days meant extra money! To me, however, money was still unimportant, meaning nothing compared with the finer things of life like acting and stardom. My salary had now reached twenty pounds a week, and to me that was fine.

Some of the stars had their wives or husbands to stay; others, along with the camera crew and technicians, began playing the old game of flirting and teaming up with others on the film. Marital status was not always an inhibitor. In time, relationships formed as people away from their home lives found romance an easy flame to fan to create excitement or combat loneliness. Romantic dreams and pictures of what I, too, wished for flickered across my mind, without my really knowing who I was or what I wanted from life. What did I know of life anyway?

One of the actresses suddenly fell ill, but I could never discover the reason why she remained in bed so much. Or why, when we went to film in Halifax, the hotel manager there ordered her removal from the premises. Ralph and Meg Smart merely smiled when I innocently asked them what was going on and muttered something about her having a 'bad migraine'. As I wasn't too sure what *that* was, I figured I'd better stop enquiring. Quite why everyone was so secretive and treating the matter in such a peculiar way eluded me. Until finally an actor with whom I got on very well – he took an almost fatherly interest in me – explained that she had had an abortion on a recent visit to London and was trying to recover enough to cope with the rigours of filming. I was fascinated. The great problem of becoming pregnant had actually happened to someone at last. For my whole life up to then had consisted of everyone except me doing precisely what they wanted when it came to sex.

I asked Jimmy, for that was this actor's name, what I should do the next time I fell in love. Did men really think the worst of girls who slept with them? And was it really such a stigma, on one's wedding night, not to be found a virgin? He was very patient and understanding, and in a way he was the first person with whom I'd been able to discuss the mysterious world of sex. I had, of course, described my heartbreak over Guy, and it was a help when Jimmy carefully gave sensible explanations for what had been drilled into my mind as taboos.

'Things are not quite the same as they used to be, you know', he smiled. 'You're going to have dozens of men in your life; play them along for whatever *you* want out of it.'

His words had new meaning, for suddenly sex was not a dirty word or a forbidden act until marriage. It was something of which to be unafraid and, above all, to enjoy, not endure. Perhaps if I could have talked before to someone like Jimmy I'd have been spared all those months of frustration and fear. For here was a man of the world, almost urging me to go ahead and drink from the cup of life without inhibition. If his motives were ulterior, then he certainly never showed them to be so by making any kind of play for me.

On that romantic location, as I lay by the river between scenes, thinking of all the things Jimmy had said, I noticed for the first time a sun-bronzed young man, even though he must have been on the film from the start. Egil was Norwegian; tall, handsome and blond; quite different from the dark-haired kind who usually attracted me. He was one of the camera crew, and as I watched him moving around, stripped to the waist, I became aware of his gorgeous muscular body and long brown legs. Gil, as he was called, also happened to be the nineteen-year-old brother of Greta Gynt, who had presented me with my LAMDA trophy a year before, which made him even more interesting. Not that he needed anything further to enhance him as far as I was concerned! When a girl makes up her mind to have a man, *he* may think he's doing the pursuing, but it is *she* who determines the outcome.

I fantasised about Gil from that moment on. It mattered not that, compared with Geoffrey or Guy, he had rather a quiet personality, and lacked their sense of humour. Scandinavian and silent he may have been, but he certainly had no lack of sex appeal. Several of the girls on the film were eyeing him eagerly, but little by little we got into conversation and slowly something began to happen between us. Evenings after hot summer days of filming would find us strolling hand in hand through the long grass, and though I never had the courage to tell him I was a virgin, I believed that this love affair would triumph regardless.

Occasionally, to relieve the tensions that arise among people away from their families for any length of time, the film company would throw a shindig. One of these was held in the village hall near our hotel. I was dancing with Tony Newley when I noticed a young actress, who'd been ogling Gil for some time, pretend to faint so that he'd make a fuss of her and escort her home. Maddeningly he fell for the ruse, which drove me into such a jealous frenzy that I rushed from the hall and back to my room.

Tormented by thoughts that once again I was going to lose someone I believed I was madly in love with, to a girl who was obviously prepared to go all the way, I lay on my bed in a turmoil. Suddenly there was a knock at the door. It was Gil. At first I refused to let him in, but his protestations that he wanted me, and not some silly girl whose name he didn't even remember, convinced me that his feelings were as deep as mine. I relented and unlocked the door. If ever any moment was the right one, this was it. The time had come for me to venture into that unknown world of womanhood. No more the spectre of my parents, past taboos, fears of being pregnant or worrying what respectable people would think. I was ready to throw caution to the winds and give myself completely to the boy I desired.

It was all a terrible let-down! Gil was astounded to learn that I was a virgin and, given the choice, would probably have rushed back to the party – *and* that misguided girl. But it was too late for recriminations, and once the act of love-making was over I was left wondering what all the fuss was about. Sex and all its glory had been far from ecstatic for either of us! How awful, I thought, that once upon a time girls really waited until their wedding night. What if they then discovered they didn't like the man they had married, for better or for worse?

Perhaps they did as I did on the next few occasions we made love. Talked themselves into a state of ecstasy, or went on fantasising about the man so that, eventually, mind triumphed over matter to make the whole thing more pleasurable. Indeed, after a while, it really did begin to feel good. Gil and I were not tied in holy matrimony though, and the prospect of spending the rest of our lives together – 'Seeing the same face at the breakfast table', as my father often summed up marriage – was not our problem. It was, of course, there in my mind: Gil and me living happily ever after in a rose-covered cottage, preferably somewhere in the glorious Yorkshire countryside which I had come to love so much. Naturally it was all part of the romantic idyll of that memorable summer, and as the weeks went by love, and making love, had never been so sweet.

While we wandered in the wonderland which life offered us on such a perfect location, it never entered my head that one day it would end. I was in no hurry to get back to smoky, noisy old London, with all its conventions and life at the YWCA. I wanted to lie, as we often did, by the edge of the stream on silent summer evenings with only the sounds of fish jumping lazily out of the water to break our beautiful reverie. For the first time in my life thoughts of Hollywood stardom vanished; I envisaged only a life with Gil. But all dreams must end and the dreamer waken to reality. The company finished shooting and prepared to return home to do the interior scenes in the studios. My fantasy faded, giving way to panic. Gil and I would have nowhere to go and make love at the end of the day. No longer the peace and privacy of my hotel suite, with its view of the purple gorse-covered hills that we climbed to be completely on our own. Instead it would be a room shared with Daphne and two other girls; sleeping in a little iron bed and being roused by that shrill seven o'clock bell every morning. How could I go back to that after the life I'd become accustomed to?

An idea I'd been turning over in my mind now became a plan of action. I would find my own flat and have the complete freedom I had always craved. A frantic search produced a furnished one for five guineas a week in a large block just off the King's Road, Chelsea. Consisting of a small living-room, bedroom, bathroom and kitchen, it was not very elegant, but to me it was heaven. I held what felt like the key to paradise in my hand.

My parents were horrified that I was leaving the safe, secure hostel they'd arranged and was planning to live alone. Even my mother put up strong objections, but they were all to no avail. I was financially independent. I made it clear that I could not be expected to continue living in such a place as the YWCA. The real reason for this sudden decision to branch out on my own was left unspoken, but I was elated at the thought of being in charge of my own affairs. All the codes of proper behaviour set down by parents and others were finally a thing of the past. What price virginity now?

It never occurred to me during this frenzy of excitement at my new-found freedom that *I* was the one making all the arrangements for a love nest. I didn't even know where Gil lived! But none of this worried me the evening we went out to dinner in Chelsea and afterwards when I proudly showed him my new flat. Of course we made love, but somehow it wasn't quite the same as in Yorkshire. Gil was different. He was not married, as Guy had been, but perhaps there was another girl here in London.

No, he assured me, there was no-one. Yet gone were all the protestations of love he'd made so fervently all summer. Gone were the hopes and dreams shared as we walked hand in hand the way that lovers do. And gone, I could tell, was his interest in wanting to be with me, and me alone. Coldly and sensibly, like the Scandinavian iceberg he really was under that sun-bronzed exterior, Gil calculated that we should cool it for a while, leaving me in my little flat to wonder what had happened to our hot summertime romance.

Strangely, and for no particular reason, he was the first and last blond to whom I've been attracted. With hindsight, I doubt if I'd have noticed him had we not been thrown together on that idyllic film location, for he possessed few of the characteristics I liked, especially a sense of humour. Not that I was feeling much in the mood for humour the next morning as I reported to the studio for the remaining scenes of the film. I saw nothing funny in the fact that I had my flat, my freedom and was ready to play, yet had no-one to play with. Until Tony Newley confessed his love for me, that is.

In my infatuation for Gil, I hadn't realised that Tony was someone to whom I was suited. He was dark, talented, and brimming over with a strong personality, besides which he was an actor and that meant we had a far better understanding. He had grown up a great deal since that train journey we made several months before, but then so had I. And so it was that, with all the energy and optimism of youth, I forgot about Gil with his cameras and measuring tapes, allowing myself to believe I'd fallen in love with Tony.

Such behaviour seems ridiculous now, but at this time we were both sixteen, under contract to a major film organisation, and being paid the kind of money our fathers had never seen. I had once been told that you cannot put old heads on young shoulders, but I wonder if anyone in those golden days of British films realised what they were doing with teenagers like us. My old friend Jimmy the actor summed it up on the morning that Tony took twenty-seven takes to complete a scene. (There'd been a party at my flat the night before.) 'They can't pay these kids big money every week and then tell them to be at the studio occasionally when they want them. What the hell do they expect them to do with the rest of their time?'

Certainly, Tony and I were making the most of our time, living it up nightly in Chelsea where my flat had fast become the headquarters for fun. He still lived with his mother in Highbury, but at every opportunity he and his friends were at my place, making so much noise into the early hours that neighbours began complaining to the janitor, and rightly so! We, of course, considered it stuffy of them to behave like the conventional adults we thought they were, and took no heed of warnings that my six-month lease would not be renewed.

Chelsea, in those post-war days, was a fascinating place; perhaps a little too fascinating for youngsters like us with such vivid imaginations. We met alcoholics, criminals, drug addicts, pimps, and prostitutes, impoverished members of the aristocracy, writers, painters, cashiered ex-Army officers and con-men who would sell anything from a dozen pairs of nylons to somebody's house – if they could get their hands on the deeds!

The Connoisseur Club, a basement establishment which boasted a trio of musicians, was usually the centre of our evening's entertainment. With candles flickering on tables covered with red checked tablecloths and a colourful clientele, it seemed straight out of Toulouse Lautrec's Moulin Rouge. During the day we'd frequent a variety of interesting public houses, where we'd meet actors, lay-abouts, titled 'black sheep' and always heavy drinkers. For everyone, despite a lack of finance, could always manage to get a drink. Soon we were joining in with the rest, and though I'd never particularly liked alcohol, nor consumed great quantities like the others, I suddenly developed a taste for anything.

I began to wonder why, and how, no-one ever seemed to work, until gradually it became a chore for me to go to the studios, instead of the thrill it had always been. Rising at five-thirty and catching the workman's bus there, ready to put in a full day's filming, held no more enchantment. Why should I bother to make an effort? No-one else did; yet

everyone was happy. The Chelsea life was starting to interfere with my career; work was getting in the way of fun.

Tony's seventeenth birthday party at my flat was a riot.
But it wasn't such a riot one weekend later when, Tony
having borrowed the flat to hold another while I visited my
parents, the noise and rumpus reached such proportions
that the police were called and Tony ran all the way back to
Highbury for fear he would be recognised and caught.
However, when I returned on Sunday evening, to my
amazement the place looked neater than it had ever done.
Several Chelsea characters of somewhat dubious reputation had kindly cleaned it up after Tony's drunken guests
had departed. Indeed, two of them were still sitting there
when I walked in and, as they proudly showed me their
housework, they announced that another reprobate who
had helped, actor Denis Shaw, was waiting for us in the
Cross Keys. This was where most of the Chelsea 'set' hung
out.

Denis, an incredible character, must have been one of the
ugliest men imaginable, and one of the loudest too. Having
been sacked from some repertory company in years gone
by, he and his love of drinking found their way to Chelsea,
where he waited for his big chance to happen. 'I'm going to
be known as the ugliest bastard in British films', he would
boast. 'See this wart-covered mug of mine? I want it to be
the face everybody loves to *hate*!'

How he lived no-one knew, but then how did any of them
live? One of his tricks was to proffer an empty pint glass
around some pub after the poor old down-at-heel pianist
had finished playing.

'Money for the musician; show your appreciation', Denis
would bellow, thrusting it under people's noses. And in
would go pennies, sixpences and shillings. The unfortunate
pianist never saw his collection, for Denis would tip out the
contents and retire to the other side of the bar to buy himself
a drink.

My seventeenth birthday party was supposed to surpass
Tony's, and when the day came I was besieged with cards,
telegrams and flowers. Somehow I felt a little odd being

seventeen officially, after all the years of pretending to be
so, but I looked forward eagerly to the night's festivities,
especially as I wasn't on studio call that day or the next.
Perhaps it would have been better if I had been, for some
time during the day I got mixed up with 'Den-Den', as
Denis Shaw was called, plus various other characters, and
ended up at a strange club in Hampstead when I should
have been greeting friends at my party.

This was being held in the basement flat of a young
French artist named René, whose mother had just married
an American millionaire, Herman Rogers, a friend of the
Duke and Duchess of Windsor. René, however, preferred to
live the life of an impoverished Chelsea painter, existing in
near squalor. But there was always plenty of red wine to be
found at his flat, and it had a great atmosphere.

When I at last managed to get to René's, I found a very
upset Tony waiting for me with bedraggled, deep-red roses,
believing that I preferred to be with others rather than him.
We rowed, and I spent most of the night crying against a
wall with René and Den-Den trying to console me. But
most of my hysteria had little to do with Tony; it was more
the result of consuming too much alcohol that day, particularly gin.

I never fully understood Tony. He was a temperamental,
changeable person, and though we made love, talked for
hours on the telephone, and continued our wild ride
through Chelsea's underworld for several months after
that, things rarely seemed to go right for us. Yet professionally something very big was about to happen for
me – my first starring role. David MacDonald, a vibrant
director with a rough reputation for women and drinking,
was preparing to make the first British 'western', *Diamond
City*, with David Farrar, Honor Blackman and Jean Kent
as its stars. Honor was to play a Salvation Army lass, in
keeping with her fragile beauty, and Jean was cast in her
usual role of 'baddie', in which she had cornered the
market.

However, Jean Kent surprisingly announced she did not
want to portray yet another sexy, sleazy character, so they

tested me for the part of the hard-bitten saloon hostess who presided over the brawling miners in their rush for diamonds in South Africa. Looking like a little girl dressed in her mother's long clothes, my hair piled high and the make-up applied thickly to give a well-worn appearance, I sailed through a love scene test with David Farrar as best as I could, only to be embarrassed by the brusque director, well fortified by brandy, shouting to the entire set: 'There's no way she could have played that scene like that if she was still a virgin!' Obviously the Sydney Box memo had come to the fore in his somewhat befuddled mind and he beamed as though he had made a great discovery. Then he announced that the part was mine.

The prospect of working with David MacDonald did not worry me, regardless of his reputation. For I knew his marriage had broken up because of his affair with one of Mr Rank's leading stars, a lady publicly renowned for her sweet, innocent roles but who, in private life, was one of the film world's leading nymphomaniacs. She and the drink would keep him busy, I thought!

Diamond City was a great step forward in my career and some of the pre-Chelsea enthusiasm for work returned. I knew it would require discipline and would interfere with the parties and the good times, but once again I felt that my career as an actress was the most important thing in my life. The words of an elderly teacher at the Charm School came back to me: 'When all else fails, remember you always have your work.'

Not that anything had failed for me personally at the time. Things were the same with Tony and me, and there were two other Chelsea types I was seeing frequently, much to Tony's annoyance: Johnny Cussans, a character with long hair and a gold earring who lived by his wits, and James De la Mare, an ex-actor and descendant of the poet, Walter De la Mare, whose poems I'd recited and won medals for as a child. James had been married, but was separated, and like so many had gravitated to Chelsea for the excitement it offered. But I soon called a halt to our association when word reached me that his wife was suing him for divorce. Being cited as a co-respondent would not have been good publicity for a girl of seventeen poised on the brink of stardom.

With Christmas 1948 approaching, I received and accepted an invitation to spend it at my Aunty Kit's home in Cardiff. It was the first time we'd been asked there, as she and my mother had been at loggerheads for some years because of a disagreement over a cameo brooch that had belonged to Grandma Dors. It appeared that my fame had brought about a reconciliation.

I'd already had one dismal holiday at the end of the summer with my parents, the last time we went as a family to Weston-super-Mare. I suppose I was miserable then because I could think only of my summer sojourn in Yorkshire with Gil, but that holiday didn't make me look forward with bliss to Christmas with relations I hadn't seen for years. I was having too much fun in London. None the less we went, and Aunty Kit laid on a family-style Christmas with uncles, aunts and cousins anxious to be re-acquainted with someone who in their eyes was already a film star. I suppose it was to be expected, and somehow I was polite and tried to pretend I was enjoying myself. All I could really think about, though, was getting back to London, the flat, Tony and my new starring role in *Diamond City*. For this I was going to learn to dance the cancan, which meant lessons at a dancing-school in Hampstead.

New Year's Eve got under way at the Cross Keys in Chelsea, and it was there that I first saw Michael. There are moments in one's life when, as the song goes, 'You may see a stranger across a crowded room', and in the crowded, smoky, noisy bar that is exactly what I did. I glanced away from my friends to see a boy with the most disturbing eyes that seemed to pierce right through me. His dark good looks were almost beautiful compared with the characters and eccentrics around him. I half-smiled in his direction, but abruptly he turned away as if he hadn't seen me.

This was upsetting, for I was not used to being given a hard time by the opposite sex. Well, two can play that game, I thought, but ignoring him didn't work. It only made me all the more curious to find out who he was. Slowly I drew closer to his group, and in the general babble of conversation we began speaking, although I cannot remember what was said. It's odd that certain things, such as the first words you say to someone with whom you are going to spend a great part of your life, become lost in the mists of time. But I can still recall the rest of the scene.

Michael Caborn-Waterfield was courteously arrogant when I informed him proudly that I was about to embark on my new starring role in *Diamond City*.

'I'm off to Hollywood personally', he replied, and I detected the slightest of sneers at the corner of his aristocratic mouth. Ignoring my obviously silly question whether or not he was an actor, he went on to tell me that he was playing opposite Margaret O'Brien, a child star, in *The Secret Garden*. This spiked my guns completely. I couldn't lay claim to anything as successful as that, and suddenly my film at Denham seemed remarkably unimportant.

Having dispensed this piece of information, he abruptly turned away again to his friends and once more I felt slighted. But by this time I'd had enough. Good-looking he may have been, but I was not going to demean myself any more by trying to converse with him. Indeed I forgot all about him until much later that night when, at a party somewhere in Chelsea, he reappeared, this time rather the worse for champagne. We ignored each other studiedly, yet I remained fascinated and still wondered who he was.

Several times after that I would see him racing up and down the King's Road in various cars, usually in the company of a tall, golden-haired young man called Patrick Beresford. I learnt later that they shared a flat together, one much more elegant than mine, in St John's Wood. Eventually, and probably inevitably, we met again at the Cross Keys. Only this time Michael was absolutely charming as only he could be.

'Let's get out of here', he ordered, and so saying he, Patrick and I left the hurly-burly of Chelsea for smarter clubs in the West End. They knew them all, and most of the people who frequented or owned them.

Michael had an extraordinary, dynamic personality, a razor-sharp mind and unique good looks moulded by his Russian, Irish and Italian ancestry. I was to learn that his late father was the Count Del Colnaghi – Michael could now use the title if he so wished – and had been a Fleet Air Arm commander in Bermuda during the war. Michael and his younger brother, John, also strikingly good-looking, were brought up there as children. Prior to this his parents, great socialites in their time, had divorced, and the boys returned to live with their mother in England after the war. They had then been sent to public school, from which Michael ran away.

He reached his nineteenth birthday that New Year's Day, 1949, but already his life had been colourful and varied: a jockey in a large racing stables, living rough and starving here and there, attempting to become an actor. His story about going to Hollywood turned out to be more wishful thinking than fact, but he'd appeared in several films and a number of plays, having in his typically confident way informed the agent now managing his affairs that he was a genius! I had already had my fill of genius with Tony – and so, it appeared, had Michael. They had once worked together on the film *Vice Versa*, starring Petula Clark. Tony made it, Michael didn't! It was all in the luck of the game, but he was starting to discover that the film world could not be cracked by confidence alone. He and Patrick ran three cars, and gradually I concluded that Patrick's forthcoming inheritance plus Michael's various activities – which included selling anything at a profit and several well-paid film roles – enabled them to sail along on the crest of what looked like a wave of good fortune.

On our first evening out, after visiting all the better haunts where Michael seemed to have everybody in his pocket, including one or two peers of the realm, we went back to their flat where I met his brother, John. John was a complete contrast. Handsome yes, but brooding and lacking Michael's sophisticated zest for life. True, he was only seventeen, like me, but it struck me that he didn't really enjoy all the wild living in which his brother seemed to revel. Then again, The Honourable Patrick de la Poer Horsley Beresford was a different type of person, too.

At twenty-five – monstrously old to the rest of us – he was a very tall, gangly fellow with an off-beat sense of humour and fine, aristocratic good looks. For all that he allowed himself to be led by Michael most of the time, occasionally he showed a stubborn streak. I noted, too, that although Michael seemed to be the leader, Patrick occupied the master bedroom while the smaller one was Michael's. The reason given was that Patrick, being so much taller, needed more room, but I couldn't help feeling that it might have been because Patrick was the paymaster. However, in the enchantment of meeting Michael, money was the least important thing on my mind. Everything he did had such great style. Even the blocks of coloured ice over which he poured our drinks that first evening were not as garish at the time as they now sound in print. For garish is something Michael most definitely was not.

To say I fell immediately in love with him would be an overstatement. At seventeen, with my first starring role ahead of me and a growing trail of infatuations behind me, including the disaster of Guy Rolfe, I thought I knew what love was all about. Indeed, I thought I knew what life was all about. What I did not know was that I hadn't even begun to scratch the surface.

How often in the past had I asked what it was like to be really in love? How did one know real love when it happened? What was the difference between true love and infatuation? How could one be sure? I now made my first discovery; that to be *in love* with someone and *to love* unselfishly with all one's heart and soul are two different things.

In the early days with Michael it was all fun and excitement, a whirlwind tour of nightclubs and parties that went on non-stop round the clock. This was fine when I wasn't working, but even when the filming of *Diamond City* had started, the playing did not stop.

Tony had to be told the truth, too. I was still fond of him and always found him a fascinating, mixed-up criss-cross of emotions. But Michael had won my heart, and the day the three of us met to discuss the situation was not pleasant. Tony, ignoring common sense, blew up the infatuation that our affair had been, whereas I suspect Michael enjoyed playing the victor over someone whom he considered as a serious rival to his acting ambitions. He certainly conducted the scene with all the flair he was capable of displaying. And so the merry-go-round went on, for the adrenalin was flowing fast now: I was acting and I was in love. As a sign of my star status I had a stand-in, Oona, who was blonde and looked rather like me. Part of her job was to stand on set and let the lighting cameraman do his work. He was, I might add, having to call on all his resources as far as I was concerned, for the tell-tale signs of little sleep, parties and drinking were beginning to show in my face.

Michael and Patrick would arrive early in the evening, after filming was over for the day, and the four of us, now including Oona, would race in two cars back to London for another night's excitement that usually ended in some club. I hardly ever got to bed before four-thirty, and the limousine that picked me up each morning – no trains or buses now; I was a star – called for me at six-thirty. Little wonder I slept all the way to Denham and staggered into the make-up chair at seven-fifteen, with no eyes visible, muttering that I really would get some rest that night. Needless to say, when evening and my beloved Michael came I was ready to go out on the town again.

Finally, what with the heavy work schedule and the hectic living I'd been indulging in, I collapsed at the studios. Fortunately my role in the film was nearing completion, so the producers put me in a car and sent me back home to Swindon wrapped in a blanket. I'd no longer been going home so regularly at weekends, which made my parents worry about me, and as I was helped into the house, all their fears since I'd moved into my flat seemed justified. My mother nursed me for two weeks, during which time Michael, whom she'd never met, kept ringing. 'You've had her for seventeen years. I want her now', he told my mother one day, which did nothing to endear him to her. However, she laughed it off, thinking that this was yet another infatuation that would pass. How wrong she was!

Restored to health, I returned to London where I was stunned to learn that the lease on my flat was to be terminated, though it was hardly surprising after all those parties. It upset me that I'd have to find somewhere else, for I'd grown fond of the place after my early reservations. Not that I'd spent much time there since knowing Michael! Things weren't so favourable at St John's Wood either, as it appeared there was some hitch in Patrick's inheritance coming through and they could no longer afford the flat. Instead, they were thinking of buying an interest in a large funfair at Swanage in Dorset. Things seemed to be changing all round.

Feeling miserable about the way life was going, I took a depressing flatlet in Jermyn Street, just off Piccadilly Circus. The sky could be seen only by putting one's head out the window; it was so dark that the lights had to stay on permanently; and it cost more than my Chelsea 'paradise'. But it was all I could find in so short a time. Michael hated it, and perhaps it was just as well that he went to Dorset with John, Patrick and Oona, who was now living with Patrick.

Before they gave up the St John's Wood flat, where we had all enjoyed ourselves so much, we held a farewell party. And it was there, the next morning, that I sleepily answered the shrill-ringing phone to hear my mother's acid tones. 'So you're *there*! I thought so when there was no reply from your number.' She proceeded to berate me about my affair with Michael, whom she now hated intensely. 'We're going to get married', I protested, for we had discussed the idea of becoming engaged. Michael had even borrowed a cheap dress-ring from me to take to the jewellers for measurements, and I'd worn it on one of my visits home.

'Yes, that's another thing', raged my mother. 'Your father is furious about that ring. It is quite obvious this Michael has stolen it. Anyway, you'll be receiving a letter from him.' And with that she hung up.

There was nothing I could say or do. The moment had come when I was in the direct line of fire between my parents and the boy I loved and wanted to marry. Of course they meant well, but how could they possibly know what he was really like? They'd never met him, and I felt they were judging him unfairly. As promised, or threatened, my father's letter arrived the next day: a terrible one accusing Michael of being a thief, a liar and anything else he could think of. But it did close on a tender note. 'It is dreadful for your mother and me to have to sit back and watch what is happening to you, my dear. I can only liken it to seeing a child playing on the edge of a cliff, and we are powerless to stop you from falling over.'

Despite my father's obvious concern for me, I was filled with anger at his unjust opinions of my lover. How cruel and unnecessary to make such a fuss over a stupid dress-ring, when in all faith it was Michael's dearest wish to give me as beautiful an engagement ring as possible before he went to Dorset. It was all because, in my father's eyes, Michael did no honest work; he was not that 'decent sort of chap' he'd once envisaged for his daughter. Moreover, despite all their doubts, I did get my engagement ring; a beautiful topaz set in antique gold. And when Michael left for Dorset it was all I had to remind me of him.

The summer of 1949 was now on us, and I was glad to leave the stifling heat of the city for two weeks to appear with Barbara Murray in *The Cat and the Canary* at the Connaught theatre, Worthing. It was at that time the policy of the Rank Organisation to send many of their contract players there for a refresher season if they weren't filming – rather like the idea of the Charm School, which by now thankfully had closed. My mother joined me there and we had digs with a lovely family who lived by the sea. Clifton James, whose home it was, had once been an actor, but his most memorable role was being General Montgomery's double during the war. His striking resemblance to Monty confused the enemy on many occasions.

It was a pleasant two weeks, except for the times when

Michael telephoned and my mother immediately went into a rage about his character and intentions. No doubt she was hoping it would die a natural death while we were apart, but it didn't. And on my return to London I received the news that the funfair had floundered and they were all coming back. My father's prediction for that particular business venture was correct after all, but he wasn't required – as he sarcastically hoped he wouldn't be – 'to store a funfair in my back garden'.

I had missed Michael terribly and was thrilled to have him with me again as we began living together at Jermyn Street. He, of course, had no money, having lost it all, as had Patrick, but we got by on my weekly salary and life for a few months was fun, despite our dismal accommodation. Many hours were spent in the S & F grill, a restaurant near Piccadilly, where all the young actors and actresses hung out that summer, enjoying themselves while they waited for their big chance to come. And when that closed, around six in the evening, we would mostly gravitate to a small drinking club, The White Room, just opposite. Somehow there would always be a party to move on to from there. On days when it was so swelteringly hot, we'd find somebody with a car and rush off to the Ace of Spades swimming-pool on the Kingston by-pass, often to be treated to a free pool-side cabaret by a young Dickie Henderson. He was the sole one of our group working regularly – at the Latin Quarter nightclub.

It was about this time that I first met Michael's mother. Yvonne, only sixteen when she married his father, was then still only in her thirties: twice divorced, extremely well spoken, and to be seen at most of the sophisticated clubs in London. Michael had asked her to come up from the country, where she was staying with friends for the racing season, to meet my parents and try to placate them about our engagement. It was typical of Yvonne that she took my parents, at the time *en route* to Scotland for their annual holiday, to the most exclusive club she knew, The Garter in fashionable Curzon Street, and plied them with drinks as she endeavoured to improve their estimation of her son.

Sadly it had no effect on my father, who from that moment on referred to her as 'The Butterfly' and steadfastly refused to meet Michael.

This disappointment was alleviated by the chance to move to a better flat. Honor Blackman had recently married her first husband and was vacating a fairly pleasant place in Earls Court. It was more than we could afford but we took it. Anything to get out of Jermyn Street! Professionally life was very quiet, with no more films apparently coming my way. This, I consoled myself, was because producers and directors were waiting for *Diamond City* to be shown so that they could judge for themselves whether or not I had star potential.

The Rank Organisation, however, were not too happy about paying me money each week for doing nothing, so they insisted I accept the offer of a play that was going out on tour, with the possibility of eventually playing in the West End. It was a modest little musical comedy entitled *Lisette*, and I was to play opposite the male lead, a French singing star.

Rehearsals commenced at a seedy room in Soho, and it was planned that we'd open in Brighton before moving on to Margate and Eastbourne before, hopefully, hitting the big time. Which might have been pleasant if I had not made the frightening discovery that I was pregnant!

With so much happening in such a short time, I'd become quite oblivious of my original fears. And when, in the early days of making love, the dire consequences never eventuated, somehow I'd come to ignore the possibility. Now it was a horrifying reality!

My first reaction was to pull out of the play for, apart from the panic of wondering what to do – there was no way Michael and I could afford to have a baby – I was very physically sick. Indeed I'd never been so ill before. My pleas of not feeling well fell on deaf ears and I was told by the producer that I would be held to my contract. Moreover, if I did not comply, my parents and the Rank Organisation would be informed that I was expecting an illegitimate child. How he knew this was a mystery, but I was too sick and frightened to go against such an un-sympathetic and callous man.

Somehow I got through rehearsals and we opened at Brighton to lukewarm reviews. My parents, down for a matinée, noticed nothing to arouse their suspicions, and my father never knew the significance of his remark as he watched me removing my make-up afterwards. 'I don't know how she stands this life', by which I assumed that he still disapproved of my being in the theatre, remembering the days when he accompanied visiting artistes at the Swindon Empire.

The following week we played Margate, and then East-bourne, where Michael, came to join me in my digs – a strange house, with heavy, dark wallpaper and stuffed birds in glass cases. It was run by an old woman and her obviously homosexual son. But halfway through the week Michael, still seething over the blackmail threats and making his feelings known, was barred by the producer from coming to the theatre. I don't know whether he also said anything to the odd couple at the digs about Michael and me not being married, but the old girl threw a fit one day and ordered Michael out, saying she ran a respectable house!

On Sunday, 23 October, my eighteenth birthday, I returned gratefully to London, knowing Michael was waiting there for me. No further dates had been booked for *Lisette* as yet, so with any luck the wretched thing would come to an end and I could begin resolving my private problems. All the way home on the train I was sick and not even a porter's kindness was any real consolation for the way I felt.

The play did end its brief run there, as I was informed a week or so later, but any relief I felt was overshadowed by my pregnancy, which was now reaching a point where it could no longer be left in abeyance. Oona, living with the penniless Patrick at her mother's flat on Clapham Common while they waited for his inheritance, knew a woman who could help me. But it would cost ten pounds, a small fortune in those days. Michael and I had to live on the six pounds a week my father sent me after he had paid the rent of the flat and other expenses out of my weekly Rank cheque. We had nothing saved, and we certainly couldn't ask him for the money, so Michael decided to try his stepmother who was holding, he hoped, his inheritance due on his twenty-first birthday. This was still a year away.

Telephoning, he told her we were in desperate trouble and that he wanted ten pounds to pay for an abortion! I was astounded that anyone could be so candid with a relative, but she softened her usual stern position where money for Michael and John was concerned and sent the amount. Now came the moment I was fearing most and, as John and Michael drove me over to Battersea for my ordeal, I was trembling at the thought that I could possibly die at the hands of this strange woman. I'd heard so many terrible tales of what had happened to girls who'd had an abortion. And coupled with this I felt great emotional stress at having to abort the baby I was expecting, for in a way I was rather proud of the fact.

What followed after I had paid the fat, grubby little woman her ten pounds was a nightmare! Suffice it to say the operation was performed on a kitchen table, but the agony did not stop there. It took me many hours to miscarry my first child, and many months before I recovered mentally.

That Christmas saw Michael and me with only a bowl of soup for our dinner. It wasn't because I was broke, for I still received my twenty pounds a week from Rank. But somehow my money never stretched far enough. We were always without any by the end of the week. I had, however, had the thrill of seeing my name in lights for the first time. *Diamond City* had been released, to bad reviews admittedly, but they did not diminish the excitement I felt at standing in the middle of Piccadilly Circus and seeing DIANA DORS glittering on the sign there.

I was then contracted to Ealing Studios by the Rank Organisation for a film called *Dance Hall*, with Bonar Colleano and Petula Clark, among others, and Oona and I prepared to work together again. She needed the work more desperately than me, for at least I was under contract – and was receiving no more than my set contract fee anyway. Oona's situation reflected the irony of both our relationships, for at the time I introduced her to Patrick, he and Michael were a couple of playboys with plenty of cash to spare. Now we were both looking after them.

However, Oona's fortunes changed as we commenced the film. Patrick received an inheritance of £18,000, and now it was *her* turn to take me to the studios in a car. There were presents and parties, and Michael was filled with optimism at what our life would be when he came of age the following year. His inheritance, he estimated, would be far more than eighteen thousand.

Oona continued as my stand-in on *Dance Hall*, which said much for her loyalty, and I managed to get John and another friend of ours, Gaston de Chaleux, son of a Countess, jobs as extras on the big dance hall scenes. So for a time everything rolled on fairly well, although it was hard work, and cold too. That winter of early 1950 did not make it easy to rise early in the morning and put in a full day at the studio.

As my mother had never taught me to cook, I was now learning out of necessity and found I quite enjoyed preparing meals. I learnt a great deal from John, who was an excellent cook, for he lived with Michael and me most of the time. I always felt there was something very sad about both of them for they had known wealth and luxury until their father died but were now forced to wait in near starvation until coming of age and receiving the money that was rightfully theirs. Their stepmother made them each an allowance of two pounds a week, which John threatened to give back to her. But Michael restrained him, preferring to wait and see what would happen when he reached his twenty-first birthday.

That spring I was asked to appear in the play *Man of the World* for H. M. Tennant, being produced by Kenneth Tynan, a brilliant young newcomer down from Oxford. We opened at the Shakespeare Memorial Theatre, Stratford-upon-Avon, went on to the Arts Theatre, Cambridge, and then to London and the Lyric Theatre, Hammersmith. It was a serious, well-written play, and I received excellent notices for my role as the young mistress of the star, Roger Livesey, and was named Actress of the Year by *Theatre World* magazine. The wonderful cast included a young actor named Lionel Jeffries who had just left RADA.

My understudy was a blonde Canadian named Barbara Cummings, whom Michael knew well for she had married one of his reprobate friends, George Coburn. George had already achieved some notoriety by being sent to prison for stealing two umbrellas from Harrods and an errand-boy's bicycle during a drunken spree with Patrick, who managed to get away with it. George was unlucky and received twelve months, even though Barbara had married him in the hope that the sentence might possibly be lessened. Now he was out again, and one evening Barbara brought him round to our flat. He was just twenty, but I was soon to find out that 'Goldilocks', as Michael called him, was an inveterate liar whose word you could never know when to believe. Like many in that set he had had a varied career, conning his way around London, pretending to be Lord Carlton or some other member of the aristocracy. He and Michael decided to pool their resources, which were negligible, and start a carpet-cleaning business, securing a shampooing machine from somewhere and charging their customers twenty pounds a time. But things never really went well, and even a contract I arranged at the Rank couturier's salon in Mayfair was ill-fated. The machine ran away with both of them, breaking several valuable wall mirrors in the process.

Summer, after the play had closed at the Lyric, brought little professionally apart from appearing at a tiny theatre in Henley-on-Thames in a production of *Born Yesterday*, the American play in which I had seen Yolande Donlan on that unforgettable night with Guy Rolfe. I was required to do it under my Rank contract, but as we ran for only one week my life that summer was mostly a pleasant round of parties and good times at our flat in Earls Court. There, other out-of-work actors, like Digby Wolfe and Pete Murray, would spend most of the day sitting around talking.

As the weather was so warm and we all wanted to go swimming in the country each day, Michael decided it was time we invested in a car. The only way to do so was to put down a small deposit, which he obtained somehow, and buy an old, second-hand model on hire-purchase. This we did, committing ourselves to monthly instalments on a Ford V8 and continual expense. True, it *did* transport us to various swimming-pools around London, but it let us down more often than not.

Once, however, we drove it all the way down to Cornwall without mishap for a week's holiday in the beautiful village of Fowey, where we rented a picturesque cottage by the sea. But on our return to London the payments became too much for our limited income, we lapsed, and the company repossessed the car, leaving us without the only status symbol of our rather unsuccessful but optimistic existences. I say optimistic, but on reflection our future, apart from Michael's forthcoming inheritance, looked extremely bleak. Perhaps it was as well we had indulged ourselves in a car and a holiday in Cornwall, for black days were close at hand and the good times were rapidly coming to an end.

My parents went to Paris for their holiday that summer and called in to visit me on the way. Michael was conveniently out, but several other actors and actresses were there, loafing around, drawing from my parents the prophecy that they were just 'fair-weather friends'. Such words, of course, fell on deaf ears, for I firmly believed that they were all loyal companions. But I did wonder what my parents would have thought had they known how, on one occasion when none of us could afford to buy drinks, someone obtained some marijuana and we all sat round trying to get high. It was to no avail, though. We didn't know how to inhale properly!

Life was for living in those days, and the people I knew were exciting and stimulating. At nineteen, to enjoy was the main purpose of every day. This, and to experience everything, regardless of the cost. Many of whom I considered to be the smart set I had met at parties, and the faces of those carefree days come crowding back now. Edmund Purdom before he became a big star in America; Laurence Harvey; Harry Fowler and his subsequent wife, little Joan Dowling who committed suicide some years later; Tony Hubbard, whose Mayfair parties we left with bottles of champagne concealed under our coats; Maxwell Reed, who married Joan Collins; Caryl Coates, whose songs inspired Frank Sinatra to take him to Hollywood; and many, many others.

But those wonderful, shallow days quickly disappeared, along with the 'friends' I'd defended so strongly to my parents, the day I was summoned to the Rank Organisation's head-office and told that, because they were losing money to the extent of eighteen million pounds, all contract artistes like myself were being made redundant!

I could not bring myself to believe it. For some years now as I'd grown up I had been safely under their banner and, more important, drawing a weekly salary. Not much admittedly, but enough to live and get by on. Now, immediately, this was all going to end. I walked down Regent Street filled with a dreadful foreboding of what was to happen to me, and to Michael.

The first thing to do was stall paying the rent, which we managed to do fairly successfully for a few months, while we waited hopefully for Michael's twenty-first birthday and his inheritance. A part in a modest film, *Worm's Eye View*, netted me £275, a fortune then, but soon the well ran dry and there was nothing on the horizon. Patrick and Oona helped out, as did others with the help of postdated cheques which we kept writing until we owed money to almost everyone. But the crowd who had filled our flat, day and night, with their witty dialogue and clever ideas for living were all gone.

At last New Year's Day arrived, and Michael excitedly opened the envelope from his step-mother which he thought would contain not only her birthday wishes but also, he was sure, a fat cheque together with documents appertaining to his father's property businesses. Out fell a small note and a cheque for fifty pounds! The note stated that, as business affairs had floundered, it was the best she could do! She would of course continue the two pounds a week allowance for him and John.

To say we were crestfallen would be an understatement. All our dreams and ambitions were dashed that day. Our love did not die, but any possibility of building together the sort of life we'd envisaged vanished forever. Perhaps we would have married, bought a home, had a family and lived happily ever after. Perhaps not. That was the future, whereas the present saw us completely on the breadline. And as we were to learn, there is a great deal of truth in the saying, 'When poverty comes through the door, love flies out the window'.

The estate agents, to whom we owed rent, told us that we must leave immediately, and so, on a cold, wet day in early 1951, we began to gather our few belongings together. We had not the remotest idea where we were headed, other than to doss down for a week or so on the divan of a Chelsea friend. Just before we moved, John arrived unexpectedly at the door. The previous year, when he turned eighteen, John had been called up for National Service; but owing to injuries received in a car crash, when Michael nearly killed them both, he had been exempted on medical grounds after serving for six months at an army training centre in Yorkshire. Since then, we'd not seen a great deal of him and had often worried about his welfare or wondered with whom he might be associating. Now, it appeared, he too was broke, for he wanted to borrow my transistor radio to 'hock' it.

The absurdity of it all struck a humorous note as we were in dire straits ourselves and had already hocked the radio. Raindrops streamed down the window-panes almost like tears as I looked out at the miserable day and saw, parked near the entrance to our block of flats, a large, blue American convertible in which John had apparently arrived, driven by someone who was waiting for him.

'Whose is the car?' I enquired.

'Some guy I know called Dennis Hamilton', John

shouted as he hurried out, and moments later I watched as
he was swept away in a screech of tyres by the impatient
driver.

CHAPTER FIVE

ENTER SVENGALI

Little Boy Blue,
Come blow your horn.

During the next few months, as Michael and I drifted from
other people's divans to drab bed-sitters, borrowing a few
pounds here and writing more post-dated cheques there, it
would have seemed incongruous if anyone had prophesied
the vast fortunes we would make separately in the years
ahead. If only we could have accumulated all those millions
at the time when we were still in love and knew what we
wanted to do with our lives. There would no doubt be a
different story now. Suffice it to say that, forced to try to
exist on love alone, we did not find it easy to sustain the
burning passion we had once felt.

Finally we managed to obtain a bed-sitting-room at a
residential club in South Kensington. It was run by an
ex-Army major and frustrated part-time actor who, in
return for our promising to get him into films as a stunt
rider, allowed us to live there at a minimal rent. He also had
in his cocktail-bar a very useful pin-ball machine, for once
we had discovered its workings it netted us sometimes six
pounds a week pocket-money – when the major wasn't
looking!

At one point in the dark hours of despair about my
career, which seemed to have come to a complete halt, I
was approached about the possibility of going to Broadway
for a production of Ben Levy's play, *Springtime for Henry*.
This firework in my otherwise non-working life filled me
with the same excitement I'd experienced as a child. The

thought of getting to America at last. But after two agonising days of waiting by the phone for the American producer's decision, I was informed politely that my big chance was off. And so it was back to hanging around with our small set of friends, several of them actors, trying to keep ourselves amused.

Michael was trying all kinds of deals to make money, but nothing sensational happened until he got into some dubious business venture concerning a supply of perfume. By this time, though, Michael and I were growing further and further apart – we seldom went out together any more – and neither of us knew what the other was up to. Sometimes I would go out with our old friends, Patrick Beresford and George Coburn, Patrick now broke after going through his inheritance in a year and George having separated from my former understudy, Barbara.

It was on one of these evenings out that Patrick confessed his love for me, saying it had really been me he wanted all along and not Oona, who now had their child. Laughingly I told him it was a pity he hadn't declared his love when he had £18,000 to play with, but it was not truly what I felt. Money, even in those desperate days, was of no great importance for me, and I could never imagine myself making love to any man simply for the wealth or luxuries it might bring.

Also around this time George, in one of his many mad moments, persuaded Michael's brother to go with him on a rampage through the country dressed as Army officers, staying at the best hotels where they happily bounced cheques to 'pay' their bills. No doubt they had a hilarious few weeks as George lived like the aristocrat he always wanted to be. But, inevitably, the law caught up with them and they both ended up on remand in Strangeways Prison, Manchester. At the ensuing court case John's lawyer claimed he had been led astray and he got off, it being his first offence. But poor old George, having already done time for the umbrella-stealing episode with Patrick, got three years.

Quite without warning, my career took a turn for the

better and I was cast in a film being made at Shepperton Studios. *Beauty Queen* was all about that particular business, and hundreds of young actresses had been tested for the lead. But the producers finally decided on a complete unknown for the part. My role was that of a hard-boiled beauty queen who showed her the ropes! The salary was fixed at a miraculous sum of £800 and, so typical of the 'feast or famine' nature of show-business, another film followed.

For *The Last Page* I was to receive £450. But my elation at the prospect of working again, and the amount of money I was to earn, did not last for long. Michael got into problems over the perfume deal – the gist of which I never did understand – and was summoned to appear in court.

The case was still waiting to be heard when I commenced filming on location at Folkestone, where I met a beautiful young girl named Jane Hart who was playing a small role. We became good friends, and on the day we were due to return to London she offered me a lift with her boyfriend, who was coming to fetch her. Preferring her company to a train journey on my own, I accepted, cancelled my previous arrangements, and told Michael not to expect me back too late. But when the boyfriend arrived at our hotel I did not take to him at all: he looked devious and was something of a show-off. Before lunch he insisted that I go for a quick ride in his new sports car, and he drove around the country lanes at such speeds that I was terrified. Just as we prepared to leave for London, he turned to Jane and announced that he couldn't possibly give me a lift back. There just was not enough room for three of us. So off they went, leaving me virtually in tears, high and dry at the hotel with no more trains going to London for several hours. I never forgave him for that and often related the story when, in later years, he found fame as a slick society doctor among the jet set, being regarded as some sort of Prince Charming with women. My earlier opinion of him was confirmed in 1963, however, when Dr Stephen Ward died from an overdose of drugs after it had been revealed that he was behind the Christine Keeler affair that led to the Prime

Minister's resignation and the eventual defeat of the Conservative government.

Having started work in the studios on *Lady Godiva Rides Again*, as the film was now titled, I found myself late one warm May afternoon with nothing to do. I had not been called to Shepperton, so I decided to visit one of my old haunts, the S & F in Piccadilly. As usual the place was full to throbbing with semi-stars, young hopefuls and non-starters, and I was sitting in a booth, chatting to Jennifer Jayne, a young actress and ex-girlfriend of Tony Newley, when an extremely handsome young man at the next table leant over and asked for a light.

I had seen him there a few times before, but as I was usually with a crowd of people, nothing ever came of his efforts to strike up a conversation with me. He had, however, made some kind of impression, for I'd once asked John, whom I'd seen with him on one occasion, who the good-looking, vibrant character was. John had been rather non-committal, warning me not to bother with him and describing him as 'exactly like George Coburn!' As George was residing as a guest of His Majesty, I was now somewhat reticent about being drawn into conversation with this man, but I had to admit that he *was* extremely plausible and persuasive. He even insisted on paying our entire bill for tea after we'd been joined by five others.

That done, he demanded I go with him to collect some tickets to see Danny Kaye, who was appearing at the London Palladium. I didn't really want to leave the group, but there was a magnetism about him. His incredible ice-blue eyes compelled me to do just as he said.

'My car's over there', he said pointing, and I realised immediately that it was the same one I had seen outside my flat that day, months before, when John came for the radio.

'You're Dennis Hamilton!' I exclaimed, surprising myself how rapidly his name came back to me.

I remember that I was not swept off my feet, for although there was something attractive about him, I fought against it. Nor was he the type I normally went for – black curls and dark brown eyes. His eyes were a vivid blue and his hair, long and curly, was light brown. It was Dennis's personality which really bowled me over; and most other folk too, I came to learn. Added to that was a dazzling smile which charmed everyone, regardless of what they thought about him, his motives or his principles. Not that he had any of the latter, as I was to discover.

In May 1951 no-one had yet heard of American actor Paul Newman. But if he had made his début at that time, then Dennis would have qualified as his double, not only in looks but in the character of many early Newman film roles. As I learnt on that first evening out, Dennis Hamilton had been practically everything in his time, including a stand-in for Eric Portman during his time as a small-part film actor.

'Why did you stop being one?' I asked.

'I was useless', he laughed. 'Decided one day that I wanted to eat regularly!' This was his stock answer when anyone enquired why he'd never played the acting game, for everyone was convinced that, with his energy, looks and personality, he could have been a star. However, Dennis was one of those people whose own character is so much stronger than any he could ever portray. And oddly enough, for all his audacity to do anything, on stage or in front of a camera he froze!

After watching Danny Kaye storm the audience at the Palladium, we went on to a club that Michael and I frequented. There, we made the amazing discovery that we shared so many things in our lives. To begin with, we both lived in the same road – he in a flatlet at one end of Collingham Gardens and Michael and I in the major's club at the other. Our fathers' telephone numbers were exactly the same, though Dennis's parents ran a pub in Luton and lived a vastly different life from my parents. My mother and his father had the same birthday and so, even more incredibly, did Dennis and I! Perhaps none of this was of earth-shattering importance, but it all added to the fact that from the beginning there was some strange kinship between us.

Dennis was then twenty-six; born in Wales but detesting

any idea that he was Welsh. Indeed, as I was to find over the years, one sure way to send him into a psychopathic fit was to accuse him of being so. His life had been varied and strange. Somewhere along the way after leaving school, where once, in a rage, he beat up the headmaster, he caught the acting bug and began working in films as an extra or in small parts until Eric Portman took an interest in him. Eric insisted that Dennis work as his stand-in, and sometimes got him a minor role in his films, while at the same time keeping him as court jester and close friend at his home. Had Dennis been in any way homosexual, one could be forgiven for being suspicious of their relationship, but he was most definitely not. Nevertheless, they were so close that Eric actually took Dennis into a church one day and made him swear undying loyalty. After that he allowed Dennis to take as many girls as he wished back to the house, viewing the comings and goings like a tolerant, elderly uncle indulging a teenager's whim.

Before this odd relationship commenced, Dennis had worked briefly at many menial jobs; briefly being the operative word. On his first morning as a bricklayer's labourer he climbed a ladder and deliberately dropped a hod full of bricks on the foreman, who had dared try to order him about! As a commissionaire at the Blue Hall cinema in the Edgware Road, London, he ingratiated himself with the manager to such a degree that this misguided man entrusted him with taking the money for all the tickets. It wasn't long before he was 'earning' more than the manager – until the plot was discovered. (Many years later, this same manager walked forward to greet me at a Royal premiere in a West End cinema to which he had been transferred and, to his horror, saw Dennis behind me. 'My God, it's you', he exclaimed, going white as he remembered the bad old days at the Blue Hall!)

After his friendship with Eric ended, owing to some disagreement, Dennis drifted through several wealthy women and on to a firm which sold water-softeners. It was a shady sort of business for, apart from water-softeners being a quite unknown quantity, the models sold by this particular firm were bodged up in all kinds of ways to make them work – until salesman Dennis had made a deal. The hapless customer, having been hypnotised by his smooth sales talk, would often be stuck with a gadget that did not work properly. But by then it was too late. Dennis had roared off with his commission, and on certain occasions had left a housewife with more than just the loss of her housekeeping money to dwell on!

Naturally I did not hear all this on that first evening as we dined and danced and he whispered sweet nothings in my ear. Nor did I fall in love with him. Indeed I never fell in love with Dennis, nor loved him in the true sense of the word. Rather, I was the fly caught in the spider's web. Yet now that I'm older, and know more of the ways of the world, I cannot help wishing he was still here to look after me. In our time together, despite his outrageous satyric behaviour with other women, he put me on a pedestal in such a way as I have never been placed since, loving and worshipping me with all his heart. Cynics will say that I was just a meal ticket, and perhaps I was at the beginning. But there was something else about me that he needed. For although he conquered every one of his women sexually, he despised them just as Errol Flynn treated the opposite sex with contempt.

It is interesting to observe that both Hamilton and Flynn had strong mother-hate complexes that stemmed from childhood. When Dennis was a child, his mother had taken him with her when she went to meet her lover in a country lane, and now it was as if he wanted to hit back at every woman in anger at the child's hurt and betrayal. Maybe such men are basically frightened of women and use their tough approach to cover up their insecurities. But how, on that first meeting, was I to know how complex Dennis Hamilton was, or what a strong influence he would have on my life and my career?

Although I was not too concerned whether he contacted me again, I felt sure he would, even though he knew I was living with Michael. When he did call I introduced them both, and was not surprised that Michael was unimpressed. He was worried about his rapidly approaching court case and had no time to play games with anyone, least of all someone like Dennis Hamilton.

Several weeks went by, during which time Dennis subtly pursued me, always bringing along another girl to make it look as if he were more interested in her than me. Nevertheless, I knew he was sweet on me, having been told so by one of his friends, Jimmy Mellon, a young antique-dealer. Knowing it did not help, for I did not want to be disloyal to Michael, especially at this time, and yet Dennis disturbed me. For one thing, I never knew quite where I was with him. One lunchtime he arrived at the film studios with armfuls of flowers, striding down the long corridor near the dressing-rooms, smiling in his enchanting way and berating himself for being so stupid as to bring a girl flowers.

'What the hell am I doing?' he exclaimed, protesting at his own actions. 'I've never bought things like this in my life!' And he tossed the offending blooms on my dressing-room couch as if they were an indignity.

The day Michael's court case was heard, Dennis offered to drive me and some of our friends there. Yvonne was also present, ready to give evidence for her son, which helped to a small extent, but the judge decided that Michael needed to be taught a lesson, ordering him to be detained for two weeks so that he 'could see what the inside of a prison was like, and thus be deterred from any future temptations of making easy money.'

It was a terrible shock, and seeing Michael in a cell beneath the courtroom upset me enormously. I left the wretched place in tears, hoping that the next two weeks would pass quickly and uneventfully. How mistaken could I be!

Afterwards, in a small pub, we sat in a morose little group discussing the sentence and feeling sorry for Michael – except for Dennis, who behind my back made a pass at Michael's mother! But in the days that followed, he concentrated all his efforts to ensnare me while the going was good. When I returned from a day's filming, red roses would be lying on my pillow, together with little pieces of poetry he had written himself or taken from his collection. Dennis loved poetry, especially Rupert Brooke whom he thought was reincarnated in himself. And always, when we were together, he would make me laugh – that Achilles' heel where men were concerned.

Naturally I felt guilty about this whirlwind romance with Dennis, for a strong bond of love remained between Michael and me, regardless of the way our affair had come to a virtual standstill. So it hurt when, quite out of the blue, I met a girl who claimed Michael and she had been making love while I was out working. It was not jealousy; certainly not possessiveness. Simply a sadness that something that once was so beautiful had been ground by circumstance to such an end. Dennis, of course, could see the way I was feeling and took advantage of it to make his most decisive move. He asked me to marry him! In a confusion of lost dreams, bruised ego and romantic flurry I said yes, and we immediately set about making plans for the wedding to take place at Caxton Hall.

There were, however, some snags. Being a minor I had to obtain my parents' consent, but this was not the problem I had anticipated. Even though they had never met their future son-in-law, they readily agreed over the telephone to the marriage. No doubt it was sheer relief that I was getting away from Michael! Dennis's problem concerned a woman, older than himself, with whom he had been having a turbulent relationship. The police had been called even to quieten their disputes. Now, although he had managed to break off their liaison, he was being cited as co-respondent in her divorce. None of this came to light, however, until our wedding-day, when I was warned of the possibility of a discarded mistress committing suicide on the steps of Caxton Hall.

Michael was in a turmoil, powerless to do anything to prevent my marriage which he'd heard about from his brother. But, in a desperate attempt, he arranged for a friend to telephone the registry office anonymously, just before Dennis and I arrived, and tell them that my parents' signatures on the consent papers were not in order.

The morning of my wedding-day found me in a great emotional upheaval, for now that everything had been arranged I did not want to go through with it. I'd known this man for only five short weeks and did not love him as I loved Michael. It was no way to enter into marriage.

'Call it off. Don't go on with it; stop now before it's too late!' Such were my thoughts as I fought frantically with myself, right up to the time we were in a small drinking-club on the way to Caxton Hall. But Dennis and his friends were high with excitement and, just as I was to be led by the nose for the rest of my years with him, so I allowed myself to be led to the registry office. Outside we were met by a battery of newspaper men and photographers, plus a smattering of people who knew me as a film starlet. While inside we were greeted by a grim-faced official who asked the two of us to go into a private room. There were, he said, doubts about the certificate of consent. A telephone caller had claimed the signatures were forged, and if this was true there could be no ceremony.

I had seen slight flashes of Dennis's temper only occasionally over the few weeks I knew him, but now I was to witness the full extent of his rage. Grabbing the man by the collar, he pinned him up against the wall and snarled menacingly: 'You'll marry us or I'll knock all your fucking teeth down your throat.' I have often thought about this episode in my life. Has any bride ever had a wedding day like it? Certainly the Registrar who performed the ceremony in a falteringly nervous, almost petulant, manner had, I am sure, never conducted such a bizarre affair. Afterwards, as we had little money and nowhere arranged for a wedding reception, we and several of Dennis's friends went for a spaghetti and wine supper at a funny little Italian restaurant frequented by out-of-work actors who could never pay the bill. To this day I don't know if our bill was paid that night!

The days that followed did little to make me feel married, and each hour that passed brought nearer the dreaded day when Michael would be released. I knew I would have to face him, and was somewhat relieved when he called me from a mutual friend's flat rather than appearing un-heralded on the doorstep. But our tearful reunion, with so many recriminations, was interrupted by a telephone call from Dennis. He was obviously in a rage.

'You get back here at once', he stormed. 'You are *my wife* now!'

Everything, suddenly, had changed; the roles were reversed. Michael, whom I had loved and lived with for two and a half years, was now the 'other man'; I was married to a virtual stranger. It was so sickening that I began to hate Dennis almost as much as I hated myself for being so stupid. Nevertheless, back I went and tried to make the best of what looked, at that moment, a very bad job!

We moved into an elegant house in Beauchamp Place, Knightsbridge, though God knows how we figured we were going to pay the rent. Dennis as always was optimistic about selling his water-softeners, but it was just as well that I had started work on a film being made at Bray Studios. The star was American actor George Brent, and I will never forget the look of horror on his face the morning he arrived, fresh from Hollywood, to the little studio at Bray and saw the somewhat primitive methods being used. Remembering *The Spiral Staircase*, which had haunted me down those YWCA stairs so many dark winter mornings ago, I was still rather in awe of him.

Using the privacy of the studios, I still kept secretly in touch with Michael, for I felt so guilty over everything. The reason why, I now know, was due to a guilt complex, which I will probably have to my dying day. Michael had now decided that he wanted to get away from England and, perhaps so that I'd sleep easier at nights, I agreed to give him most of the £450 I was earning on the film to help him start a new life in France.

Life's ironies were to the fore again, for who should Michael go off to France with but his old rival, Tony Newley. The two had become fairly friendly over the years when Tony was living in the home of another mutual friend, Michael Jackson. A bit of an eccentric, who always carried a rolled umbrella no matter what the weather, Michael Jackson adored Tony and was convinced he was going to be a star. He was right, but before this happened Jackson's funds ran out and Tony went off with Michael to seek his fortune in Paris. An actress we knew there, Anne Valery – married to a Greek artist and with the most beautiful little son, Toffee – introduced Michael to many interesting and talented people on his arrival. (Many years later, Anne was living with a songwriter on a boat in the south of France and little Toffee fell overboard and was drowned. Perhaps to help compensate for their grief, Tony Bennett purchased and recorded a song the man had written called 'Let There Be Love'. Others later sang and recorded it, and the songwriter's fortunes changed from that day.)

When Dennis discovered I had given money to Michael he went into an uncontrollable rage. Never had I seen anyone turn from being a warm, amusing person into a screaming monster, but I was in for quite a few more shocks! His first blow sent me crashing across the room, and as one punch followed another he screamed that I was a 'faithless whore', which I learnt later was how he regarded his own mother! He also rang my parents – it was the middle of the night – and gave them a vivid account of my treachery with Michael. I had never experienced anything like this before, and my whole attitude towards him changed completely from then on.

Yet for much of the time Dennis was an extraordinarily amusing person, with endless energy and vibrant ideas. He drove himself on a tireless wave of dangerous, exciting emotion. And however much he terrified me, I could not hate Dennis for long. Certainly one could never be bored by him! His charm and his powers to make anybody do anything, even against their better judgement, were beyond doubt. Yet, if one analysed the situation, it all verged on hysteria, though this was something I was incapable of understanding at nineteen, held as I was in a web of dangerous fascination twenty-four hours a day.

Because of his satyric tendencies, which at that time I knew nothing about, he imagined that everyone else was sexually voracious, and so I was guarded at all times like a princess in a tower. The times he could not keep tabs on me, as when I was filming, he demanded to know each night who had said and done what to me during the day. The slightest compliment, in Dennis's mind, was taken as a preliminary to rape or seduction.

But the final straw for him was a nasty little cigar-chewing American producer at whom I would never have looked twice, even if I'd just emerged after twenty years in a nunnery. This producer wanted to put me under contract and take me to Hollywood – the object of everything I had worked for and dreamed about – but, he told my agent, there was one stipulation.

'She'll have to divorce that guy she just married!'

'Sir, we don't do things like that over here', my agent ventured, trying to sound British and stiff-upper-lipped.

'I don't give a damn what you do here', the producer replied, revolving his cigar from one side of his mouth to the other like a stick of gum. 'I wanna build her up into a big sex-symbol like Shelley Winters, and I can't do it if she's married.'

'Then what do you suggest?' asked my agent. Ten per cent of a Hollywood contract was slipping away fast.

'Let her divorce the guy then marry him again later. It'll make great publicity!'

When I dared relate the story to Dennis, having given careful thought as to how I should tell him, he flew into another frenzy – not at me this time, but at the audacity of 'some fucking American who thinks he can come here and dictate about my marriage'. He was right, I knew that, but I was dismayed at the thought of losing the chance of a lifetime.

No immediate decision was required, however, for the producer had returned to America on business. I finished filming at Bray, but with much of my salary having gone to Michael and the rest to cover our post-dated cheques, I was completely without funds. Even worse, Dennis's water-softener company appeared to be going broke. Despite his charm and persuasion, people were no longer buying the wretched things. The rent on our Knightsbridge house was now several months overdue, and other bills had mounted up, too. Even Dennis was worried, which was a new feeling for him.

Yet, as with so many things where he was concerned, even debt had its amusing side. One day an actor friend telephoned from a call-box at the end of the road to say there were five men in bowler hats waiting outside our front door. Dennis until then had preferred to lie low, knowing from past experience the sound of a creditor's ring! I thought the game must now be up, but I had not reckoned with the full force of Dennis's personality. Suddenly throwing open the door, he exclaimed with a devastating smile to the five astounded men: 'All right, gentlemen, you've got me cornered. Come on in and have a drink.'

To my amazement they did exactly as he suggested, and before long I heard him dispensing drinks and setting them all roaring with laughter. (I was hiding upstairs.)

'Well, we have a most interesting situation here, gentlemen', he told them cheekily. 'You all want money from me and I cannot pay. So what the hell are we going to do?'

No-one actually replied, and Dennis chuckled.

'Well, no hard feelings. Let's all have another drink.' I heard him topping up their glasses and for a good half hour he kept them entertained until, apologetic for having disturbed him in the first place, they put on their bowler hats and almost bowed out of the house.

It was now quite apparent that we had to move, but where to go and what to do? The water-softener company's creditors had repossessed Dennis's blue car, so we arranged to borrow a little one from another salesman who was holding on at the office for a while. As we went to collect it in a taxi, we both suddenly realised that all the money we had in the world was one pound, some of which would go on the taxi fare. How strange, I thought, that every time I met a man who appeared to have plenty of money and behaved like a playboy, he went broke once we got together. It had happened with Michael, now with Dennis; and it was to happen again.

The borrowed car was by no means a luxury, it was a necessity. For Dennis had decided we should move out of London. He had found a beautiful house in Dunsfold, Surrey – the rent was much smaller than anything in London – and I became aware for the first time of his great love of the country. Personally, I was appalled at the idea of leaving London, where I had lived since I was fourteen. Who in their right mind would want to live in isolation, miles from friends and away from clubs, restaurants and the old haunts where everything happened? A life buried in the country with no theatres or cinemas, not to mention parties, held no appeal for me. My mother, who had by now met Dennis, summed up the whole thing shrewdly: 'He wants to get you away from everyone, darling. Out there in the middle of nowhere he has you to himself, and as he's so jealous it suits his purpose well.'

This was no doubt true, but then my mother did not know the full facts of our financial circumstances and that creditors were hounding us. At least the country was a good place to lie low for a while. Although she and my father had not been too impressed with Dennis, despite his many charms, they at least thought he had a steady job. Perhaps it was the malfunctioning water-softener he'd unloaded on my poor mother! But whatever Dennis did, in their eyes it was better than my being with Michael. Still owing rent on what had been a perfect home in London, we piled our few belongings in the back of the borrowed car and drove south. The next few months were grim, with Dennis occasionally obtaining water-softeners from various contacts and filling them with sand so that they'd at least work for the demonstration. But sales were few, and we lived on credit at the village shops or borrowed money from Jimmy Mellon who sometimes came to stay. We were in debt to the local garage, too, for we'd somehow managed to make a down-payment on an old American car that frequently let us down.

I was terribly depressed about my career, which had once again come to a halt, and clung to the thought of that Hollywood contract. Dennis never mentioned it, but the threat hung over him like a cloud. He could not have stopped me going, and he knew it, so his delight was as great as my distress when my agent phoned with the news that the contract was off. The producer had fallen foul of the Screen Actors' Guild.

For me this really was the end, and I sobbed uncontrollably for my lost dreams and for myself.

'Dors', said Dennis kindly but firmly. 'You think you're a has-been before you've ever been anywhere. But I promise you this now. I will build you up to be the greatest star this country has ever known.'

'How can you do that?' I howled. 'I'm finished. No-one wants me, and buried out here I'll wind up forgotten.'

His eyes flashed excitedly as ideas piled up in his mind.

'You are going to be the female Errol Flynn, always in trouble. I'll see to it that you receive more publicity than even he's had. And we'll start by announcing to the press that *you* have turned down a Hollywood contract to stay in England, the country you love.'

To be known as a female Errol Flynn was not what I wanted at all. I wanted to be a serious actress. Moreover, what would my parents think if I got involved in scandals like Flynn?

'The press would never believe that I turned down Hollywood', I said cautiously.

'Oh yes they will! They'll believe anything I tell them', he answered triumphantly. 'Come on, Dors. What the hell do you want? The bastards to print that you've had the contract cancelled by that cigar-sucking idiot. Fuck him, and the press. We'll begin the campaign now.'

Terrified as to how he was going to follow through with what seemed to me a ridiculous plan, I heard him telephone each national newspaper with the sensational story. That Diana Dors was the only star in England to hold the distinction of turning down a Hollywood contract because she wanted to live and make films in her own country. (That was an even bigger joke. I wasn't wanted for *one* home movie at that time!) And yet, like everything he did in the future, it worked. The press lapped it up and for a while I basked in the publicity.

'You see, Dors, I told you I would do it'.

'Yes, but what now? What happens next?' I did not have his enormous confidence.

'The offers will come rolling in', was his firm reply.

But they didn't, and more depressing weeks followed while we continued to live on credit.

Suddenly one day I had a call from an unexpected source, the BBC, enquiring if I would care to take part in a television comedy series with Terry-Thomas, who was then fast making his mark in this medium. Television was still very much in its infancy, though. I had done a play about a year earlier at the old Alexandra Palace. It was transmitted live, which was a gruelling experience after the security of filming, in which mistakes were immediately covered up by another take. In addition, it was uncanny to think that people all over the country were watching you and yet were invisible to you. The series was called *How Do You View?*, and we worked out that the whole job would bring me about £250. Naturally I jumped at the chance.

Because the American car was too unreliable to get me all the way to London for the shows, we sold it and used the money to buy an old rickety Opel which would get us about provided we didn't expect it to trundle along any faster than thirty miles an hour. But the cheque we'd received for the Oldsmobile bounced! So too did the buyer until he gave Dennis the money he owed him, and once again I saw what Dennis was capable of when angered.

During rehearsals, for which Dennis would drive me up to London and wait until I was finished, I received a call from my agent to say that Burt Lancaster was in town preparing a film called *His Majesty O'Keefe*. He wanted to meet me with a view to testing me for the lead part, that of a native girl in the South Sea Islands, but it seemed highly unlikely that, even with a wig and make-up, I could play the part. Still, with the optimism of youth, plus Dennis's determination that I was going to be an enormous star, I went along to Claridges to meet Lancaster. Dennis, needless to say, drove me there and waited outside.

Burt greeted me warmly. He was one of the most handsome, gorgeous specimens of manhood I had ever seen! Nor could I help feeling, although he was perfectly serious about the film and discussed the entire story in detail, that there might be more to my securing the role than merely testing for it. To date, as far as my career was concerned, sex had never entered the picture, despite my father's early warnings about success being achieved behind the bedroom door.

For that matter sex played little part in my personal life at that time. Indeed survival was the keynote! There had been sexual scenes with Dennis and Jimmy Mellon arranging orgies so that they could spy on their friends' performance with unsuspecting women. Both, as I soon discovered after our marriage, were fervent voyeurs, and on several occasions I was unwittingly dragged into a cupboard with them on the grounds that nothing would happen if I was seen around the house. Apart from finding the whole thing stupid, if amusing, I experienced a feeling of disgust at what happened when others spied on two people in the sexual act.

Being alone with Burt Lancaster in a magnificent suite at Claridges was a vastly different setting, however. And as the evening went by, it was inevitable that he should try to take advantage of it. But, desirable and attractive as I found the American star, the spectre of Dennis waiting below spoilt the entire scene as far as I was concerned. Already his spell had been cast over me to such an extent that I believed he would know everything that happened between Burt and me in that private suite, and so I did not dare allow myself to succumb.

'How did it go?' Dennis asked when I got into the car.

'Fine. Hecht-Lancaster, the company he owns, are going to test me', I replied, wondering what he would have said, and done, had he realised what nearly happened. Yet, oddly, this was one occasion when Dennis did not jealously demand explanations. Perhaps he knew and turned a blind eye? I doubt it, but in those hard-up days it could have been possible.

A few months later Burt was as good as his word and, dressed and made-up to look as much like Dorothy Lamour as possible, I did a screen test. It was a failure from the start and Joan Rice, who had been discovered working as a waitress in Lyons Corner House, got the role. I, meanwhile, remained buried in the countryside, broke and with Christmas fast approaching.

Dennis often took me to Bedfordshire to see his parents in their little pub, and then we'd go on to an old schoolfriend whom his mother for some reason detested. This wasn't too surprising for David was an eccentric with even more eccentric parents. His mother was a relative of Hollywood star Gary Cooper; his father, a retired major, poached rabbits for a living and drank for his pleasure. David, if rabbits were in short supply, would knock off anything that was available.

He and Dennis had once raided the home of an eminent film producer named Brian Desmond-Hurst, a well-known homosexual in his day, who had made the mistake of inviting Dennis to his country home for the weekend. The next time he was away directing a film, Dennis and David had returned and emptied the place of most of its valuable contents. Brian, being the lovable and kind old rogue that he was, eventually forgave Dennis, so irresistible was that Hamilton charm!

On one of our visits there, David welcomed us with the news that he knew of a farm where there were some chickens to be had for the taking. It wasn't as if they needed chickens, for David's mother kept a good table, but neither of them could resist the scent of danger, and so away we went in our funny little Opel, David directing us through a blinding rainstorm.

Once there, I waited outside while the two of them went with a sack to obtain their booty. But when they got back to the car, soaked to the skin and with five live hens in the sack, the Opel refused to start. The farmer, hearing the grinding noises, came out with a lantern to see what was happening, whereupon Dennis wound down the window and, with a beaming smile, cheekily asked him for help!

Obligingly the unsuspecting old farmer put down his lantern and in the pouring rain tinkered with the engine. All of which would have been embarrassing enough, but was made even worse by the fact that his hens had struggled free and were now flapping about inside the car, clucking with anger. Mercifully they couldn't be heard above the sound of the storm and eventually their rightful owner finished the repair job, was tipped a few shillings by Dennis and we drove off. That visit we also managed to 'acquire' a magnificent Christmas tree, and again the Opel tried to land us in trouble by getting stuck in a ditch as we made our escape. So hard up were we that Christmas that we used coloured milk-bottle tops to decorate the tree. But what the heck! We weren't paying the milk bill either.

Whatever else we did not have, at least we ate well, for Dennis got to know a grocer in Guildford who allowed us an unlimited supply of everything, regardless of the need for ration books to purchase groceries and meat. No doubt he put an enormous mark-up on his wares, thinking with Dennis's encouragement that we were loaded with money. But by early 1952 things were becoming too hot for us in the Dunsfold area. Tradesmen would not go on permitting credit forever, and the local garage, the landlord, and the Guildford grocer were beginning to press their accounts. It was time to move on!

To complicate matters further, I discovered I was pregnant! There was no question as to whether or not I should have our child, for to Dennis it was an obstacle that would stand in the way of every glittering plan his mind held for both of us. He immediately made arrangements for me to visit a well-known show-business doctor who, for a fee of fifty guineas, would perform an abortion, though where the money would come from he had no idea. Our immediate problem was to get out of Dunsfold.

At dead of night we left with our few belongings piled in the back of the Opel. These now included a beautiful golden Labrador puppy named Topaz, given to me by Dennis as a present. This was the man I married: a great sentimentalist who adored poetry, the countryside, classical music, animals, me. But children were out!

Our next home was an attractively furnished one in Esher, which at least was nearer London and would reduce our petrol bills; that is if we ever paid any. Luck was in Dennis's corner again, for soon after we moved he received an offer for me to model a chess table at a furniture exhibition – for fifty pounds. So we had the money for the abortion. Other expenses were taken care of by accounts with unsuspecting tradesmen and shopkeepers in Esher.

Having experienced an abortion before, I was more than terrified this time, but Dennis was adamant that it must be done. So on a cold February night he drove me to London, where the operation was performed at the doctor's private house with his wife and Dennis in attendance.

The depression any woman feels after such an ordeal is indescribable, but as always I was swept along by Dennis's whirlwind and not given time to feel sorry for myself. And with his friends coming to stay at the house frequently, there were plenty of laughs and action to be had.

Dennis never tired of playing jokes on either friends or strangers and would often sit among his followers and dial telephone numbers, inventing the most absurd hoaxes with which to confuse and annoy.

'When you die, Dennis,' Jimmy Mellon remarked one night, 'they'll write on your tombstone "Here lies Dennis Hamilton. Respector of neither time, person nor place."'

There are certain days when something happens to alter the entire course of life, and for us it began one spring morning with the ringing of the telephone. A theatrical producer wanted us to go to London to discuss a revue he hoped to stage at the Comedy theatre. We agreed, trying not to sound too desperate, and were trundling on our way there in the Opel when Dennis saw, in a garage with several cars for sale, a large, sedate black Rolls Royce.

'We're going to buy that!' he announced, pulling to the side of the road.

I imagined that the news of a possible job for me, with a regular salary, had driven him a little mad. How, I enquired, were we going to buy it when we were already up to the hilt in debt?

'Leave that to me', he replied confidently, and before I knew what was happening he was in the manager's office. Ten minutes later he emerged triumphantly with the papers in hand and ordered me to get out of the Opel. We were now the proud owners of a Rolls Royce.

'How on earth did you do it?' I gasped.

'Just gave the man some chat about you starring in a West End show, traded in the old car and signed the hire-purchase papers.' Saying which he tossed the bundle contemptuously on to the floor of the Rolls Royce.

'But what's it going to cost a month? How can we pay the instalments?' I protested.

'We'll manage, Dors. Have I let you down yet?'

'I may not even be doing the show', I retaliated. 'They haven't cast me for sure.'

'They'll cast you, and one of the reasons will be that you're going to arrive at the theatre every night in a Rolls Royce – like a star should. I'll make it known that at twenty you're the youngest owner of a Rolls in this country. That'll amaze the bloody press. I tell you now, Dors, this car is going to be our lucky mascot. From here on we'll be in the big time!'

I wasn't reassured, and it was with a sense of foreboding that I journeyed on to meet the producer. But, as Dennis had predicted, he not only cast me in his revue, but felt bound to offer more money when he saw us drive up in such an opulent motor. My doubts about Dennis's plans flew out of the window.

The show opened in Brighton after a few weeks' rehearsal, and to say I scored a great personal success would be an understatement. One of my numbers, 'I Want To Be A Gangster's Moll', for which I dressed as a little girl in gymslip and pigtails, was a show-stopper. On the opening night I was already back in my dressing-room when Dennis rushed round and dragged me back to a cheering audience who would not stop applauding until I took another bow.

The reaction was the same when we opened in London at the Comedy. Hard-boiled critics, producers, fellow show-business personalities and public all praised my performance as something the West End had not seen for many a year. Kenneth Tynan, by now a theatre critic for the *Evening Standard*, wrote about me in glowing terms; all Fleet Street marvelled. Part of the incredulity came from the fact that, in so many of my films I had played dumb blondes. Now, in addition to the fantastic body on display in a black bikini, which sent the male members of the audience wild, I was displaying other talents, singing satirical songs and showing a fine sense of comedy.

During its short run, *Rendezvous*, which did not attain great notices itself, saw just about everyone in the theatre and film world applauding me personally. I enjoyed success such as I had never known; Laurence Olivier was one of many stars who came backstage to compliment me. London was truly at my feet, and offers of films, plays and cabaret came rolling in. As Dennis had predicted, the Rolls Royce, apart from creating and attracting publicity, was proving to be a lucky mascot.

Having to choose which job to accept when the revue ended was a most unusual problem for Dennis and me. Olivier wanted me for a film, *The Beggar's Opera*, and various plays were in the offing, plus a summer season at Blackpool with Bebe Daniels and Ben Lyon in *Life With The Lyons*, for which I was offered the unbelievable sum of £100 a week! There was also an idea put to me by a variety agent, who guaranteed £135 a week for each week of the year if I performed a twenty-minute variety act around the music halls.

'It's all very well now. You may have conquered London,' he warned (and later was proved right), 'but there will come a time when this whole show and your success will be forgotten. You have to decide whether you're in this business for the money or the glory. And you can't eat press-cuttings!'

Courteously I informed him that I was primarily an

actress and, although money was important, I could never envisage myself standing on a stage without other actors.

'Just remember the offer is always open', he smiled. 'Get a cabaret act under your belt and you'll never go hungry again.'

Following the show's close I appeared in a film called *My Wife's Lodger*, a modest little romp which oddly enough had been performed in its heyday at the Comedy. Then, having accepted the Blackpool season, Dennis, Topaz, a poodle named BaBa and I headed north with our belongings piled high in the Rolls.

Blackpool was a gusty place to which I'd never been before, and I did not really like it. But the thought of £100 a week, despite the fact that it was a heavy work schedule – two shows a night – made the prospect of three months there easier to bear. Dennis began meeting theatre producers and all kinds of show people, gradually learning about percentages, fees and show-business know-how. My hard-earned hundred a week, he told me, was peanuts compared to the vast percentages artistes were receiving in variety shows. Some were getting as much as £1,500 for a week's work! But what Dennis also got up to, with other characters he met and with the local girls, everyone knew about, it seemed, but me.

During that summer spent suffering the ardours of working with the Lyon family – not always the happy-go-lucky, loving group of their public image – I heard news of Michael from America, where he was projecting himself as a British dandy, wearing the most elegant velvet-collared coats and Edwardian-style clothes. It earned him the name by which he is known to this day – 'Dandy Kim' Waterfield – and also started the Teddy Boy dress cult a couple of years later in England.

I had no idea how he managed to attain such notoriety in New York, for it appeared that he was moving in the best social circles there and in Florida. Patrick Beresford was out there, too, now married to a cheese heiress, and between them they had five Rolls Royces, an island near Bermuda and their own seaplane. Nights in New York were spent at El Morocco; days began in the late afternoon, always with champagne, and when the 'cheese wife' moved out and left Patrick a large settlement, hunting down other heiresses was their main preoccupation. How different it was from our life together in Earls Court, with a hire-purchase car, no money and only dreams to exist on!

The Blackpool season over, Dennis and I returned thankfully to London, where we rented a small house in Chelsea. I began another film, *The Great Game*, in which Dennis even had a small part as my boyfriend, for producers were constantly trying to persuade him to go into films. But Dennis, though he looked good, knew his limitations as an actor and wanted fame solely for his 'Darling Dors', as he called me. 'There's only room for one star in this family', he would say. He revelled in it when the press continually referred to him as 'Mr Dors' every time he made the newspapers for speeding offences and the like. To Dennis it meant that they were spelling *my* name for the world to see. And that was fine with him!

Whatever occurred with women when I was working did not stop him thinking for me, about me, and because of me. I was like a bird in a gilded cage; spoilt, cosseted and cared for in every way, treated like a child who must be sheltered from outside worries and responsibilities. I came to rely on him for everything, even to post my letters. If, that is, I was ever allowed to write one!

As we went from strength to strength professionally and financially, people saw in me a young woman mesmerised by this dominant man. A blonde glamour machine who went through the motions of film acting or performing on stage as if propelled by his dynamism. On the face of it, we made an incredible couple, for when we walked into a room we had magic; our success was the envy of many. But beneath the whole facade I felt stifled and cornered like the cat's captive mouse. Dennis still frightened me with his violent tantrums, and at twenty I was too young to appreciate so many of his good points. I had a continuous desire to run away, to be free and to find someone with whom I could fall in love before I grew old.

An offer of another West End theatre venture, a play which had run on Broadway, came to me through impresario Jack Hylton, and Dennis, even though I had an agent, negotiated a weekly salary of £175, a great deal of money for a straight play in 1952. It was during rehearsals for *Remains To Be Seen* that I celebrated my twenty-first birthday, and as it was Dennis's birthday too, he decided to have a big party and turn our house into a grotto of lights and decorations. He had great flair for interior decoration, developed in the days when he and his brother-in-law used to buy broken-down country cottages, smarten them up and sell them at a heavy profit. Where those profits had gone I knew not, for it was all before my time.

For the birthday party no expense was spared, and that night some eighty people crowded into our tiny Chelsea house to revel in the beautiful atmosphere Dennis had created and to feast on the sumptuous buffet supper he had prepared without assistance. But not even a night as wonderful as this could go by without incident if one was married to Dennis. Already in bed, for I had a rehearsal in the morning, I heard a terrible argument below and got up to peer down the stairs. There was Dennis in full swing, physically and verbally, against a friend of his who was well fortified by alcohol. They knocked each other from one end of the hall to the kitchen and back, but it wasn't the bruising battle that upset me. I had seen Dennis in many of those and knew he could look after himself. No, what troubled me were the words his opponent was screaming between blows.

'I'll tell Dors the truth about you! I'll spoil your meal ticket!' But that was as far as he got. Dennis silenced him with another punch to the mouth.

Disturbed by what he could mean, and yet never daring to ask, I never fully allowed myself to believe he was refer- ring to the number of women Dennis played around with in my absence. Like all the best partners in marriage, I turned out to be the last to know.

The play toured for a few weeks, to lukewarm reviews, and naturally Dennis was at my side all the time. But he had no cause for concern. The male cast consisted mostly of middle-aged Americans, and my co-star was old friend Dickie Henderson, who used to swim with Michael and me in the hot summer of '49. Then it was back to London, where we opened with much publicity at Her Majesty's theatre in the Haymarket, the first-night crowds increased by pickets protesting at the current anti-Communist purges in America. The play was slated by the critics and we closed after just five nights. It was almost Christmas, and Dennis was actually in tears as he watched me packing in the dressing-room. 'Oh God, darling,' he cried, 'you've worked so hard and deserve much better than this.'

It was true, I had worked hard, and I'd received very good notices for my performance. But now it was two personal successes in two not-so-good West End shows in one year. As actor Bonar Colleano, a great character around town, quipped: 'When is Diana Dors going to be a flop in a success?'

Now it was time to look around for something else. The agent who had forecast, during my revue success, that the press and public have short memories was now being proved right. No-one was battering down my door with offers any more! Dennis, none the less, remained as optimistic as ever, and driving around Sloane Square one day he grabbed my arm excitedly.

'Look, there's Sir Carol Reed! One day, Dors, you'll do a film for him, I promise, and that will make them all sit up.'

Rather like the time he prophesied I would be the biggest star in British films, I took his statement to be a boost for my flagging morale and shrugged my shoulders. How was I to know then that Dennis's dream *would* come true; and through none other than Reed himself?

Dreams were one thing; money was another, and we were getting short of that again. I needed work. A shrewd agent – not the one who suggested I try a variety act – offered me a five-week booking at the largest variety theatres around the country, though it was obvious he didn't give a damn about my inexperience. Or my nerves! For he headlined me at the Empire, Glasgow, a fearsome place for English artistes where even seasoned comedians like Max Miller refused to appear. The Scottish audiences reserved their thunderous applause for their own performers, or for American stars like Danny Kaye, Judy Garland and others who had topped the bill there. But I knew nothing of this as Dennis and I walked in on the first morning for band call, armed with music arrangements for numbers I had done in the revue.

Needless to say I died the death of all times, and yet when the manager came at the end of the week with my percentage salary, it was £250, more than I had earnt for a week's work in my life! This gave Dennis the incentive to drive me to Brighton the following week. Having rearranged most of my act, I was better received there, and then it was on to Birmingham, Portsmouth and Hull, with me gaining experience twice nightly and Dennis gleefully counting the cash!

'This is the game, Dors', he chuckled. 'To hell with all that acting rubbish; it's for the birds! In variety we can make real money. And I like the people better; they're more down to earth than all those boring actors.'

But to me it was just like being driven around the Wall of Death!

With our weekly takings and the promise, from a different agent, of many more bookings, Dennis began eyeing a most attractive house just round the corner from where we lived. For a long time now he had been saying that we should buy property and not throw money away on rents. 'Consolidating for the future' was a term he would often use as our fortunes grew. And so, using a fairly large part of my variety earnings, he secured the house on a mortgage and announced happily that at last we'd be paying for something that would one day be ours. The house needed a great deal of work, but while I went off to theatres around the country, Dennis set about decorating our new home. With the money I now seemed able to make we began buying pieces of antique furniture, about which Dennis taught me much, and life took on a new, exciting air.

To add to our increasing bank account, a photographer

approached Dennis with an idea for a book of photographs to be called *Diana Dors in 3D*. Three-dimensional viewing was the rage at the time and so, in various bathing-suits or with discreet pieces of white fur draped around my other-wise nude body, I posed in our luxurious-looking house and on the patio with its cocktail bar and fountained goldfish pond. We were paid a straight fee of £175 for this booklet, but if we'd known how successful it was going to be, we would have demanded a percentage.

We were now sailing on the crest of a financial wave, and all the while Dennis was obtaining publicity for me, the like of which had never been known before. He formed a company, Diana Dors Ltd, to deal with our future affairs and spun a rumour that, as we were extremely wealthy owing to astute property investments, I lived like the old-time Hollywood stars in complete luxury. To the war-weary British, grown accustomed to austerity, this sort of thing was like manna from heaven and they lapped it up! I was supposed to have my own private plane, in which I'd flown myself to a premiere in Blackpool the previous summer, and to be the youngest pilot in the country. This followed Dennis's other gimmick about my being the youngest Rolls Royce owner, but this time I thought he was going too far. Yet, incredibly, the press and public always believed the stories; to such an extent that I was the subject of a question in the House of Commons. Some MP wondered how I could live so affluently, with income tax as it was.

Such publicity stories, plus a large piece in the *Daily Mirror* by gossip columnist Donald Zec about my palatial, gold satin bed and the tiger skins thrown nonchalantly over the floors (all of which had been picked up cheaply by Dennis) brought the taxman himself to the house to see how I managed to live so extravagantly. He did not believe Dennis when he explained that the tiger skin in the hall had been purchased for a mere three pounds ten shillings at a junk shop in Bournemouth. But as he was drinking a large whisky from a crystal glass worth at least five pounds, he had good reason to be dubious.

A break from variety came with work on another film, *Is Your Honeymoon Really Necessary?* with Bonar Colleano. Dennis kept a wary eye on him for Bonar's reputation with women was notorious. But Bonar was too busy with his new love, starlet Simone Sylva, to worry about me. Furthermore he was still married to Susan Shaw, so he had his hands full! Simone Sylva later won notoriety by stripping to the waist at the Cannes Film Festival, but by doing so she ruined her chances of ever becoming a star.

Marilyn Monroe was the hottest sex symbol to come out of Hollywood around this time. When she had first appeared in *Asphalt Jungle* as far back as 1950, a British film magazine had written: 'How much like our own Diana Dors this new Monroe girl is.' Now Marilyn was making films like *Gentlemen Prefer Blondes* and *How To Marry A Millionaire*, while I struggled along in anything I was lucky enough to get. Hardly guaranteed to give Monroe or her Twentieth Century screen bosses sleepless nights!

Dennis geared all my publicity to make me Britain's Marilyn Monroe, however. It was not easy when one made film comparisons, but the press and public loved the idea of England having a blonde bombshell who could compete with Hollywood, and it certainly made me a household name. However, I was still way down the list when it came to big money; nor was I well known to American producers who arrived in London to cast their films.

Director Joseph Mankiewicz was one of many, when preparing *The Barefoot Contessa* with Bogart and Ava Gardner, who compared me with Monroe. And after a while, especially when I did not get into any of these epics, I began to resent the references they always made when I arrived at their offices. Instead of telling me about the film, or giving me a chance to show what I could do, they spent most of the interview discussing how they had discovered Marilyn. It would have been comical if it hadn't been so serious for my career. Every director I met laid claim to being the one who found her.

An offer of £1,000 to appear in a film being made in

Manchester was a far cry from Monroe's Hollywood, but it was either that or the inevitable variety work and so off we went. Starring Northern comedian Frank Randle, the film was an utter shambles, for Randle was mad – and usually drunk into the bargain. But, as he owned the film company, we had to put up with him shooting guns at the dressing-room wall or dragging his girlfriends by the hair along the corridors.

On one occasion, when he had gone on a drunken binge and locked himself away, refusing to work at all, Dennis and I took off for Blackpool to look up some friends made while I was working there the previous year. Owing to one of Dennis's now-infamous practical jokes, we and another man named Freddie Markell landed in trouble by breaking into the flat of his friend and relieving his cocktail cabinet of a couple of bottles. The joke was that we were going to invite him to drink them later at a party Dennis had organised, for this mean man never bought a drink for anyone. The joke went sour, though, when he made a charge of housebreaking, not knowing Dennis, Freddie and I were responsible, and once the police were involved the whole thing got entirely out of hand. We were charged and subsequently taken to court, where Dennis and Freddie were fined and I was given an absolute discharge as it was my first offence.

The publicity generated by this appearance in court was astounding, and Dennis found much satisfaction that his original idea for me to become 'a female Errol Flynn' was coming to fruition thanks to this and similar scandals. For scandal it was, and I hated the whole thing! Not for myself but for my parents. 'Diana Dors on Housebreaking Charge' and 'Starlet Arrested' upset them terribly, as did the anonymous caller who took obvious delight in phoning – before the news reached the papers – to inform my father that his daughter had been arrested in Blackpool. Finally, however, it all blew over, filming in Manchester finished, and we happily returned to Chelsea.

For simply being involved in a joke which misfired, my fame spread even further, and when I next walked out on to a variety stage, I quipped, 'It was difficult getting the handcuffs off, but I made it,' which filled the audiences with glee, but did not do too much for any serious aspirations I had as an actress.

Ironically, in keeping with my 'criminal record', a film about life in a women's prison came along. *The Weak and The Wicked*, starring Glynis Johns, was set to commence at Elstree and I was cast as her friend in the prison, a young girl who is led astray. The author of the story, Joan Henry had herself been jailed, was now cashing in on her experiences and, as she told me while we were making the film, was in the process of writing another story, this time with the grim theme of a woman's last days in the death cell for murder. She and director J. Lee Thompson were considering me for it, she said. This was a very exciting prospect, and I hoped it wouldn't fall through like so many other film ideas. However, I was earning another £1,000 for *The Weak and the Wicked*, so the future looked bright.

Looking not so bright at that time was Michael's future. Now famous as 'Dandy Kim' Waterfield, he had just hit the headlines for some escapade at film magnate Jack Warner's villa in the south of France and relieving him of £25,000. Kim was engaged to Warner's daughter, Barbara, and had, it was rumoured, coaxed her to open the safe and give him the money which he and our old friend Bobby McKew had got to England with help from an extraordinary Catholic priest well known in show-business circles for his work in boys' clubs. The French police were trying to extradite Kim and Bobby, but for the moment Kim was to be seen driving a beautiful white Rolls around London. How long they would be safe in England was uncertain, and I worried for Kim, wondering how long his 'star', if that was the appropriate word, would last before it waned. Of Patrick Beresford and his heiress wives there was no word.

At the end of the film, and between variety engagements, I was asked to do a radio series, *Calling All Forces*, which broadcast endlessly after the war. Indeed, I had appeared on it from Germany the previous year.

Bob Monkhouse, along with partner Denis Goodwin,

was engaged as a writer for this latest series. There was
something about him that reminded me a good deal of
Tony Newley: his humour and his intelligence. And
because I always had a weakness for writers, he attracted
me enormously. Certainly I was vulnerable to someone
with sensitivity, for my life then seemed to be no more than
a continuous round of work, work, and more work. Love,
excitement, thrills were non-existent; the only laughs were
when Dennis played his jokes or verbally amused the
people who came to our house. And as I'd been listening to
his patter for a couple of years, this was now beginning to
become less interesting to me.

Between Bob and me there grew a mutual attraction
which was fanned on Sundays at the Garrick theatre where,
broadcasting the show, we worked together for a whole day
and I was free of Dennis's suspicious attentions. But I
should have known nothing remained secret from Dennis
for long. During a dinner party at our home, not long after
the show had ended, he threw a fit and smashed to pieces
most of the contents of our new house, accusing me of doing
all the things with Bob I only wished I had done. A few
weeks later there was more violence when, arriving in
Bournemouth to do a pantomime, I received an enormous
basket of flowers with a cryptic, loving message from Bob.

Dennis's brainstorms were now becoming more common
by the week and could no longer be put down to being
jealous fits. He often became extremely hot when everyone
else was cold, throwing open windows regardless of others'
shivering. Other times he would complain of being able to
see only half an object! Yet to all outward appearances he
was a very healthy man and so no-one, least of all myself,
paid much attention to these symptoms, believing that it
was because he drove himself along at such a pace. Much of
his behaviour was irrational, anyway – as 'Wee Georgie'
Wood discovered when, during the pantomime season, he
'forgot' to pay me two weeks' salary. Dennis threatened to
hang him on the wall by a coathanger and leave him there
until he found the money.

Dennis was appearing in the panto too – as a Chinese

policeman. But he spent most of his time hoaxing Wee Georgie and other members of the cast, or raising havoc at the hotel after the show. Anything to relieve the monotony! It was all hysterically funny, especially to his new-found disciples, but though I laughed along with the rest, there was an empty feeling inside me because I knew there was no future for Bob Monkhouse and me. We could have made a good team, Bob writing scripts for both of us to appear on television or in films.

Early 1954 saw me not doing a double act with Bob, but slogging along single in variety theatres dotted around Britain. With the advent of more television, music halls were on their last legs and this was the time to cash in. Dennis toured with me, of course, and more and more I felt like a trapped butterfly whose sole purpose was to spread its wings for an hour or so each night and then be locked away in a box. I wondered how Marilyn Monroe would have coped with my life: grubby theatre dressing-rooms in places like Huddersfield and Wolverhampton instead of a beautiful suite at Twentieth Century Fox while making technicolour movies. The sort of films I was making had titles like *Miss Tulip Stays The Night*, small budget with stories as silly as the names. (*Miss Tulip*, much to my embarrassment, was later shown in America as *Dead By Midnight!*) Our lives were so different, yet all the time I had to live up to the Monroe image. I was not jealous; I just felt it was so unfair. But my chance was coming.

Sir Carol Reed was preparing to film *A Kid For Two Farthings*, by Wolf Mankowitz, and I was one of many young actresses interviewed for the starring role. My confidence at this time was considerably low, but the news a week later that the great man had chosen me sent my spirits soaring. Dennis's prophecy that day in Sloane Square had been confirmed. My professional stock rose overnight. To be selected as Sir Carol's leading lady was a far cry from being the sexy blonde who toured variety theatres, lived by sensational publicity and was compared, despite the cheap films she made, with Hollywood star Marilyn Monroe.

Things were looking up in other respects, too. For although my fee for the new film was only £1,700 – I would have done it for nothing – Dennis bought the house next door to ours, for £1,000, and was decorating with a view to selling it profitably. This he did and, having found a buyer for our house, persuaded me to move out of London to a beautiful place on the river at Bray. Misgivings about being buried in the country for a second time quickly disappeared when I saw the house and its setting, for it was very different from Dunsfold. For a start this was a five-bedroomed house with a tennis court, and a boathouse with river frontage. It cost us exactly £7,000, and to us then that was a fortune.

We moved to Bray during filming, taking with us Mrs Sholl, our cook-housekeeper, a Hogarthian type of woman we'd found in Chelsea. For two pounds ten shillings a week, and no time off, 'Sholly' cooked fantastic meals and put up with Dennis's outrageous behaviour, being a constant butt of his ridicule. But secretly she enjoyed every moment of it.

She was also sending food parcels back to her idle husband in London, doing so by juggling with the money Dennis gave her for household bills. A dangerous game! This must have been going on for several months before it came to light accidentally. We were sitting in the drawing-room with actor Peter Reynolds and his brother, Bob, both regular guests, when we noticed a little man outside holding aloft a chicken on a plate. On enquiring what he was doing, Dennis discovered that the poor fellow had been delivering chickens to the house every week since our arrival but could no longer afford to, he added apologetically, because his bill hadn't been paid for months.

That afternoon Dennis threw an entire dinner-service at Sholly, Peter, Bob and I listening with horror to the smashing and screaming emanating from the kitchen. Nevertheless that evening she prepared dinner in her usual excellent way, despite the cut on her nose and a rather sullen expression. To Peter and Bob she later sniffed: 'That husband of mine always gets me into trouble. Why, Mr

Hamilton winded me once on Good Friday! He's raving mad, you know!'

Other than a hint of jealousy over Joe Robinson, a handsome muscleman who played my boyfriend in the film (our off-screen relationship never went beyond holding hands), Dennis now had little to distract him from his favourite pastimes. He built an aviary in the grounds, for he was passionately fond of birds, and he soon got to know – without my knowledge, but certainly with Sholly's – many of the human variety around Bray! Another interest was a beautiful river launch, and in addition to busying himself with this he decorated the boathouse with Italian-style raffiawork and wine bottles.

Those early days at Bray were to prove our happiest together. Away from the frantic atmosphere of London we came to know peace. Money was plentiful, we had our first real country home and my career was flourishing.

Only one thing happened to threaten my new-found success and status. *Diana Dors in 3D*, that innocent little book I had once modelled for, was suddenly declared obscene by magistrates in Halifax. Then, before pronouncing judgement, they retired for a month to have a really good look, during which time they decided that it was quite mild after all and not offensive. But by then the damage had been done. 'Halifax Magistrates say Diana Dors is Obscene', and headlines like it, did not please Sir Carol Reed when he was hailing me as his leading lady. It did not please *me* either, but eventually the whole thing blew over. And to make up for the unhappiness it caused me, Dennis decided that, as I had never been to Paris, he would take me there for our birthday.

With 1955 came one of the most successful years of my career, beginning with a starring role in *Value For Money*, with John Gregson, for J. Arthur Rank. My fee was now £5,000! And that was just the beginning. The Rank Organisation, now very much 'in the black' since the days when they dropped me, invited Dennis to lunch to discuss another contract – this time on my terms. No doubt the producers had in mind a typical contract which would permit them to have permanent call on my services. But they reckoned without Dennis's smooth-talking ways and shrewd business sense. He came away with a five-year agreement, and no options, whereby I would be paid £7,000 a year to make only one film per year for Rank. Nor was that all. He obtained a contract for himself too – as a producer for Rank films!

As with so many things, he never followed this through. It wasn't just that he knew his limitations were confined to promoting publicity stunts or making property deals. He could never concentrate on anything for any length of time. Comparing him to a clock, it was as if the hands went round until they reached ten minutes to the hour, then stopped permanently.

While filming *Value For Money* I was invited down to the exclusive Poole Harbour Yacht Club in Dorset to help judge a fancy-dress contest. My fellow judge was a woman whose luxury lifestyle beat mine hands down – and Lady Norah Docker's was for real! But it was not because of Lady Docker that this visit was memorable. It was the first time I discovered Dennis's infidelity. He had taken off in our car with some model when he thought I was asleep, but I heard him go. I had had my suspicions ever since that birthday party in Chelsea and now, as I waited at the bedroom window for him to return, I felt they were about to be confirmed. An hour later the car pulled up and I watched Dennis and the model get out, quite obviously having used it to enjoy each other's physical attractions.

When I challenged him we had a terrible fight. But there was no way he could deny what had occurred, and in his rage he punched me in the face. It was one more nail in the coffin of this marriage that I often hated so much.

For days afterwards he tried to win back my affections with charm, flowers and presents. But all the toy animals he placed around my bedroom, the household pets or the day-old yellow chick hatched by one of our hens, could not suffice! It was no good treating me like a child whose nursery must be filled with playthings. I was not a child. And yet I didn't feel like a real woman either!

My anger at Dennis, though, was nothing to the great emotional shock I experienced some weeks later. My mother, who had been in hospital for a short while, suffered a sudden heart attack after an operation and died. I was shattered. I had not been so close to her since my associations with Michael and Dennis, but all the earlier memories were there in my mind, never to be erased. It was April, my favourite month. But this spring even the primroses looked sad. My father was inconsolable, and the wreath he carefully worded read simply, 'From your Peter, and our Diana'.

Work gave me little time for mourning or remorse, however, for I was soon journeying to Pinewood Studios again, this time for a comedy entitled *An Alligator Named Daisy*. The director was J. Lee Thompson who, I was hoping, would remember what he'd said when he came to casting the death-cell story, *Yield To The Night*, later in the year.

Trying to forget the sadness I felt over the loss of my mother, I threw myself into filming and pretended to show enthusiasm over Dennis's latest project, a coffee-bar in Maidenhead. The coffee-bar craze of the time made business very competitive, and in order to make his place unique, Dennis flew in two large toucans from South America. The birds sat in an exotic bamboo cage, and I remember thinking how those birds were not unlike myself. We all served his purpose in a business venture.

Two important events occurred for me that summer, the first being the Venice Film Festival. Instead of flying there with the other Rank stars, at Dennis's suggestion I arrived in our new, powder-blue Cadillac convertible. As he predicted, this caused quite a stir with the Italian press who singled me out from the other British stars photographed in military line-up beside the plane in which they'd flown to Venice. But even my arrival by Cadillac paled into insignificance when I travelled down the Grand Canal in a mink bikini! The photographers went wild, nearly toppling into the water to get the pictures that would be published all around the world, and the following year a musical show,

Grab Me A Gondola – based on my adventures in Venice – was produced in London.

Dennis, too, had an adventure during the festival, with actress Mary Ure. On the evening of the British film, and subsequent party, he made a breathless entrance just before I arrived at the reception, excitedly informing everyone in earshot that Mary was his latest conquest. No doubt they were highly amused by this outrageous man, and sniggered when they thought what might happen if I found out. By the time I did, it no longer mattered.

On our return to England we learnt that I had been placed as the only woman among the top ten box-office stars, and that *A Kid For Two Farthings* had received wonderful notices artistically. Its premiere had been a splendid affair some months before, with Sir Laurence Olivier congratulating me on my performance. So now Dennis's prophecy and promise about me being the biggest star in British films had come true, and my next milestone was being presented to Her Majesty The Queen at the Royal Command Film Gala.

'How sad', said one of my mother's friends to Aunty Kit, who was now housekeeping for my father. 'How sad that Diana's mother never lived to see the success she achieved.'

After all the years of dreaming, planning and hoping, her death had come just too soon for that happiness to be fulfilled. There was only one wish I now desired; that she could not look down and see the kind of existence I led with Dennis. She had a vague idea during her lifetime, but at least she never knew the whole truth.

J. Lee Thompson was as good as his word and a contract was negotiated for me to star in *Yield To The Night*. Although everybody later thought that this was the real story of Ruth Ellis, the last woman to be hanged in England, it was actually written two years before she committed her crime. But the plot was uncannily similar. I loved playing my first serious dramatic role, not finding it at all as sinister as everybody, including the Queen when I met her at the Royal Command Performance, thought it would be. And at the end I sat back and waited eagerly for its release, knowing that I had given a good performance and that it would surprise many people who still thought of me as the 'dumb blonde' Dennis had created.

In a strange way, Dennis's Svengali reign was coming to an end, for no longer did I need his publicity gimmicks to make me a household name. Perhaps Dennis, too, felt his grip loosening, for while he was thrilled with the fame and money my success brought, he was experiencing a fear of being left out in the cold; no longer needed. This was especially so when, early in 1956, I was awarded the highest possible accolade by the Variety Club – 'Show Business Personality of the Year'. One film columnist present at the ceremony later described Dennis as a 'Suede-shod Svengali'; of me, the columnist wrote 'I watched the expression on her face when he was not looking. She seemed so sad.'

'How dare that bastard call me a Suede-shod Svengali', stormed Dennis during a dinner party at our house some evenings later.

Sholly, serving him more red wine, warned him in her usual forthright manner.

'Now then, Mr Hamilton, you've had enough to drink. I can see by your eyes.'

He had already thrown open the window that cold spring night, irrespective of anyone else's comfort, for one of his hot attacks was coming on. And we all knew he was spoiling for an argument, either because he was bored or because he had drunk too much wine. Of late the brainstorms, as everyone who knew him well described them, were occurring more and more frequently.

Up to then it had been a good party, and no-one wanted it ruined by getting punched on the nose or having the house smashed to pieces. Dennis, however, paid no heed to anyone's pleas, drinking more wine and accusing me of various infidelities that were entirely a figment of his imagination and growing paranoia. As the night wore on I became tired and angry with him, and to avoid any more unpleasantness I went upstairs to bed. Dennis remained downstairs with a few friends, when around midnight there was a ring at the front door. Two newspaper reporters, somewhat the worse for drink, were demanding an interview with me. Probably, knowing Dennis's reputation for hospitality towards the press, they were also hoping to be invited in for an all-night drinking session.

'Dors!' he shouted up the stairs. 'Get down here. There are two pressmen who want to see you.'

Infuriated beyond belief at everyone's drunken behaviour, I called out that I saw no-one at midnight, especially when they arrived unexpectedly! What sounded like a raging whirlwind ascended the stairs and there at my bedroom door stood Dennis, white with temper.

'You'll do as I say and come down to see the press', he shouted, grabbing my arms and propelling me towards the landing. I struggled without success to free myself, and at the top of the stairs he gave me a violent push which sent me tumbling to the hall floor, where I lay motionless. The dressing-gown I wore spread open, displaying my naked body to the aghast pressmen.

'Now fucking interview her!' ordered the man who created a myth known as Diana Dors.

CHAPTER SIX

THE IDOL HAS FEET OF CLAY

Twinkle, twinkle, little star,
How I wonder what you are!

Many people still ask why I never left Dennis, or how it was that I didn't know about his other women for so long. The answer to the latter is simple. He was unfaithful when I was at the studios filming. And with regard to the former? Because of his great love for me – despite his need to conquer physically every woman he met – he steadfastly refused to move out of my life, even for a day! Many were the occasions when I pleaded with him to let me go free.

'What the hell would you do without me, Dors?' he used to ask laughingly. 'There's more to life than driving around in a car, you know.' This followed one of my pleas to be allowed to learn to drive. As with all other things, driving was taboo; as were making telephone calls or shopping for clothes.

'You couldn't get as far as the garden gate without me', he often said. And brainwashed as I was, I felt this was probably true.

To write of the great love Dennis felt for me must seem strange in the face of how he behaved at times. And the cynical would be justified in thinking that his reasons for holding on to me were strictly mercenary! Yet even today I do believe that, in his own way, Dennis did love me obsessively. I was the only woman in his life to whom he gave his heart, for basically he hated women and often spoke of his contempt for them.

Anyone reading of the astonishing and sometimes ter-

rible incidents that took place during my marriage to
Dennis must also remember that we enjoyed weeks, months
often, when everything was smooth, successful and hilar-
iously happy. The only discord was the frustration *I* felt at
being tied to someone I could neither appreciate nor love at
that time.

To try to compensate for that dreadful night with the
pressmen, Dennis embarked on an all-out effort to prove
how sorry he was. My first treat – driving lessons! Followed
by a test, which I passed, and the new-found freedom of
being allowed out on my own in the car. But all my pleas for
a mink coat, an item I had always longed for, fell on deaf
ears. 'You look like a whore in a fur coat' was his stock
reply. 'Property', he reiterated over and over again, 'is the
thing to invest in'. And with the coffee-bar ticking along
well, he set about finding new business ideas.

One day I was dragged off to see an old Victorian
property he'd found on the river at Maidenhead.
'Woodhurst' stood in several acres of ground, empty but
proud! There were two small lodges, a stable, indoor
squash court, two tennis courts, a 'Roman' marble
swimming-pool (with a roof, three walls and pillars),
twenty-three bedrooms, servants' quarters, and the usual
domestic rooms, such as library, breakfast-, dining- and
drawing-rooms, that eminent Victorians found so essential.
It was now up for a quick sale, the previous owner having
been killed in a car crash.

With the luck of the devil that Dennis enjoyed all his
life – until the devil played his last diabolical card – he
managed to buy the whole place for £12,000; a lot of money,
but our finances looked healthy on paper, thanks to my
Rank contract. Dennis's plan was to convert the house into
fifteen flats, an operation which would cost us a fortune and
frightened me even to contemplate it. However, as always
he was highly optimistic and set about engaging builders.
The stable he converted into a small cottage, and he himself
began decorating the two lodges with a view to selling them
privately. (It was interesting that, while all this was going
on, he never had the desire to chase other women.)

One March evening, as we walked around 'Woodhurst', both Dennis and I were inspired with an idea. The swimming-pool had a roof and was solid. Why not, we thought, having climbed on to the top, build a beautiful house to our own specifications above it? From that moment all Dennis's energies were directed towards this exciting new project. The flats were left, so were the cottages, while he designed the dream home fit for a movie star. He finished the project in just eleven weeks!

During all this activity it was revealed that *Yield To The Night* was the only British film to be chosen for the Cannes Film Festival. It was to be the most glittering, successful week of my life. I stayed at the luxurious Carlton Hotel, was courted by the press, photographed leading the famous flower festival, competed with Susan Hayward and Doris Day among others for the Best Actress award, and received a standing ovation after the film premiered. I remember looking down from the balcony of my hotel suite that evening, seeing all the lights twinkling along the Croisette, among them my own name, and hearing the roar of the crowd below. 'This is my night', I thought breathlessly. 'Whatever happens to me in the future, no-one can ever take it away.'

The moment I had lived for had arrived. From then on there was no need for gimmicks and sensational publicity. My reputation as an actress could have taken over. But Dennis had gone too far to stop now. His powers as the fast-talking manager, the man who 'built' Diana Dors – just as he was now building our dream house – were all the time magnifying in his mind. And the delusions of grandeur began to display themselves even further. I had to call on close friends like actor Peter Reynolds and hairdresser 'Teasy-Weasy' Raymond to restrain him from now buying a castle in Wales! Another time he was going to make a bid for Fort Belvedere – the one-time home of the Duke of Windsor before he became King of England! It mattered not to Dennis that the place wasn't even on the market.

King Hamilton's empire was expanding regally now.

And regal were his choice of furnishings for our new Penthouse, as it was called. Chairs that looked like thrones, magnificent mirrors, tapestries and king-sized sofas filled the interior. It was little wonder that everyone believed, as Dennis did himself now, all the razzamatazz about the vast fortunes he had made from property deals. Only I kept thinking that all we really possessed were an awesome mortgage and a reasonable Rank contract.

My father, too, expressed an opinion about the extravagant lifestyle we had adopted, but as usual I paid no attention to his moderate views of life. Indeed, I was finding *his* behaviour somewhat outlandish just then, for he had come to see me 'to discuss a serious subject'; to wit, and to my amazement, what I would think if he married my Aunty Kit? I was stunned. My mother had not been dead for a year. And though I appreciated his need for someone to care for his creature comforts, I could not accept the reason he gave as anything more than nonsense.

'There is nothing to it, my dear, other than the fact that I have found your aunt to be such an unselfish woman. When I die, I want her to have some security in the way of a widow's pension', he carefully explained. Well, I couldn't help thinking, he'd been preparing to do that all through my lifetime, yet it was my mother who passed away first.

'I hope you don't expect me to come to the wedding', I said harshly, and that was the last I ever heard of the matter.

Dennis made one last property bid while curbing his impatience at waiting for the Penthouse to be finished. He was restless and irritable, for there was nothing he could physically do other than hound and harass the builders daily. This particular day, he, Jimmy Mellon, and I were out driving near Cookham, when we spied a lovely, white Georgian house set back from the river. In his usual, bombastic way Dennis headed straight up the drive and demanded to see the owner.

Lady Guinness turned out to be a charming person who, like most others, seemed mesmerised by this polite, affable young man and invited us all in for tea. Whereupon Dennis stalked around her drawing-room offering prices for various statues and ornaments which were dotted about. Anyone would have thought the poor woman was conducting a jumble sale of her belongings. And yet, to my amazement, she accepted his audacity, agreeing to let him purchase different objects for a few pounds. But the real shock came when he made her an offer for the house itself. Without blinking an eyelid, she accepted!

'This must be the first time you have had someone here for tea who wound up giving you notice to quit!' laughed the irrepressible Dennis from behind her silver teapot. How he was going to pay the woman I did not dare to think.

Whether she would change her mind after he left, and the spell was broken, neither Jimmy nor I knew. But we'd seen Dennis in action before, and his effect on people was staggering. There had been one occasion when he knocked Bob Reynolds down a flight of stairs during an argument and Bob had grasped him warmly by the hand, saying 'Thank you, I deserved that'. This sort of scene could not be compared with what had just taken place at the Guinness household. But it was possible for Dennis to go into a complete stranger's home and buy some of his belongings, plus the house itself, without his 'victim' thinking there was anything odd about the situation. Sell the house Lady Guinness did! Though how he bought it I still do not know. I do know that he managed to sell it, and I'm sure it was at a profit.

When the day came to move from Bray to the elegant new Penthouse I was inordinately sad. Somehow I felt that this dream house, for all that it was the fulfilment of our own inspiration, would not be a happy or contented home, as Bray had been.

Bray was our first country cottage, and had exerted a quieting influence on Dennis. Now we were to live in splendour above an exotic swimming-pool, with an enormous stone fireplace in the drawing-room, regal furnishings and a king-sized ornate bed raised on a dais. We had most of the grounds, which had been divided off from 'Woodhurst', including a tennis court. And the squash court had become a private cinema with leopard-skin seats, a fountain rock-pool and giant, framed photographs of me in various glamour poses. On one of the stones inlaid among the gold stars scattered around as decor was inscribed the message: 'I love Diana.' It was signed, 'Dennis, May 1956'.

The British premiere of *Yield To The Night* took place in London, and as I arrived in our powder-blue Cadillac, wearing a fabulous gown, police had to restrain the thousands of screaming fans who lined the Haymarket. The cinema was just a short distance from the theatre where, what now seemed like a hundred years ago, my ill-fated play *Remains To Be Seen* had flopped after only five nights! How our fortunes had changed in just a few years, I reflected happily.

After the premiere we held a party at the Penthouse, where many friends floated in the pool, drinking champagne, and feasted on Sholly's marvellous celebration supper. Parties were regular occurrences now, for Dennis was never happy unless he could entertain multitudes of people, show films in the cinema, wine and dine them or persuade them to go swimming in the heated pool at whatever time of day or night took his fancy. Film stars such as Rex Harrison, Anna Neagle, Kim Novak and Roger Moore, producers and directors such as Otto Preminger and John Houston, were among the many who enjoyed our hospitality; as of course did old friends Jimmy Mellon, Peter and Bob Reynolds, the 'Teasy-Weasy' Raymonds, Patrick Holt, Sandra Dorne, Jon Pertwee and his actress wife, Jean Marsh. We seldom went out to parties ourselves. Why should we when there was so much pleasure for everybody at our house? Moreover, Dennis could choose the cast list. It was important to him to select the male guests because he was increasingly paranoiac about any man taking away his 'Shiny Doll', which was what he affectionately called me. On one of the rare occasions when we did attend a show-business party, Bob Monkhouse and his wife arrived. It was the first time in three years that I'd seen him, and it was only to be for a moment. Dennis flew across the room and pushed him threateningly out the door.

Another paranoia which he seemed to be developing was that people lied to him all the time. There had never been direct proof that any of his 'courtiers' did so, but an obsession that they were plotting against him became more predominant in his mind.

Despite the success of *Yield To The Night* I had not worked for nearly eight months, apart from a Bob Hope NBC television spectacular that had been filmed in England. The only offer of a film from Rank Organisation had been dismissed by Dennis as 'rubbish'. A Norman Wisdom comedy, it was hardly the kind of follow-up to the dramatic role I was so acclaimed for, and the part went to Belinda Lee.

No-one could understand the slowness of British film producers to find another vehicle for me. It was as though they were still frightened of my publicised image and did not know what to do with my talent. The *Daily Mirror* gave me the largest 'spread' any actress had received at that time: three entire pages, including the front, were emblazoned with the headlines 'BLONDE GOLD MINE'. Stories of Dennis's shrewd business brain, clever property deals, and subsequent wealth excited the awe-struck British public, as well as Dennis himself!

And then, in the midst of 'everything and nothing', Hollywood beckoned! The Bob Hope television show had shown them a British blonde who appeared to have imitated Monroe and could deliver comedy lines with Bob. RKO films, once controlled by Howard Hughes but at the time financed and owned by General Tyres of America, offered me $85,000 to appear in a film called *I Married A Woman* with a comedian named George Gobel. He was the biggest comedy star in America but had yet to be seen in England. Their plan was to team him with Britain's biggest sex symbol and so make the film a viable proposition over here.

At last I was on my way, and this time it was *really* happening. Not some shady deal with a small-time cigar-smoking producer who wanted me divorced first.

As we prepared, a trifle regretfully, to leave our beautiful new home for the unknown world across the ocean, it was announced that Marilyn Monroe was coming to Britain to do a film with Sir Laurence Olivier. One of her representatives telephoned to enquire if he could inspect the Penthouse with a view to their renting it for her while she was filming. He arrived a few days later, gasping with delight and saying it was perfect for a star of Marilyn's calibre. But shortly afterwards, because of her shyness and preference for privacy, he had second thoughts. It was right on the river and already hordes of tourists on organised trips were having Diana Dors' home pointed out like Windsor Castle as they floated by.

We left for America on Midsummer Day, and while I took one last wistful look around the great drawing-room I couldn't help wondering what was in store for us. What would happen before we saw it again?

Because Dennis had a terror of flying, it was arranged that we sail on the *Queen Elizabeth* from Southampton to New York, but from there we *would* have to fly on to Los Angeles. Our farewell party in the state suite of that great ship was a splendid yet sad affair, saying our goodbyes to all the friends who had come down to see us off. And unexpectedly the fear of visiting new territory, and the loneliness we would feel being so far from everything familiar, overtook the grandeur of the occasion; the baskets and bouquets of flowers, the chattering people, the stewards in their white jackets and the bubbling champagne. I would have preferred to be sitting in the Penthouse gazing at the Thames, not crossing the Atlantic.

I hated the five-day journey, partly because I was anxious to get to America but also because I felt claustrophobic on the ship. However, the big day arrived, and as we were approaching New York harbour we looked in wonder at Manhattan's magnificent skyline and the Statue of Liberty. No sooner had we berthed, it seemed, than photographers swarmed all over the decks, taking pictures of 'Britain's Answer to Marilyn Monroe' as I was now to become known permanently. It was a label I grew to detest!

RKO assigned ten public relations men to look after us. We had large limousines at our disposal, tickets for every Broadway show including *My Fair Lady*, the hit of the decade, and our every wish and whim was pandered to. An enormous press party was held in the Crystal Room of the Sheree Netherlands Hotel, where we had a sumptuous suite, to introduce me to the American press, and I did my best to describe who I was, and had been, in England – long before Monroe was even heard of. But all the time her name kept coming up, for nothing I had done – apart from the Bob Hope TV special – meant anything to these hard-boiled American reporters. So different from the ones we left behind at home! *Yield To The Night*, the Cannes Festival, films, plays, variety – it all meant nothing as they compared me with her.

This made me feel extremely insecure. For the first time in my life I experienced the sensation of people thinking and implying I had copied someone else to attain success. In the minds of the American press, and soon the public, I was merely some British blonde without any talent who had jumped on Monroe's band-wagon. Even worse, to them I was a beginner in show-business!

Apart from this stumbling-block, though, everything else went fantastically, and the newspaper coverage I received on both sides of the Atlantic was tremendous. Another blonde, Jayne Mansfield, was making a terrific bid for stardom at this time, but even her extraordinary penchant for publicity was eclipsed temporarily by my arrival.

After several days in New York, we flew on to Los Angeles – and Hollywood. Once again we were greeted by pressmen and photographers, plus more studio-hired managers, public relations men and so forth. The head of RKO, William Dozier, was also there to welcome us, and we were booked into the exclusive Beverly Hills Hotel where, on our second evening, another large press reception was held. All Hollywood had been invited, it seemed!

Heading the columnists were the two high priestesses of the film world, Louella and Hedda. Everyone was terrified of them because they literally governed the place. Louella Parsons, a wrinkled crone with voice to match, supposedly held fervent beliefs regarding Catholicism, but the acid she dished out in her columns, causing most stars great unhappiness, was hardly Christian! Hedda Hopper, her rival, was a former movie actress with fascist political views, a sharp tongue and an evil eye fixed on everybody.

Dennis got off to a bad start with Hedda, something he had never experienced before with the press. In his usual way he turned on the charm, trying to melt her icy exterior by telling her that he did not see, having now met this lovely lady, how she could possibly deserve the reputation of being unkind to anyone.

'Okay Hamilton,' snapped Hedda, the flowers on her hat spilling over like an overstocked florist shop. 'Don't overdo it!'

Taken aback by her bluntness, Dennis was thrown completely. This was an entirely new type of behaviour, particularly from a gossip columnist, a breed he had always been able to win over successfully at home. And he never got used to it during his stay in America.

RKO were beginning preparations for the film, and I was driven to their studios on Gower Street, next door to Columbia Studios, met all the people concerned and underwent a series of make-up and dress tests. The care and trouble everyone went to for perfection astounded me; the professionalism was something I had never known. It was as if in England we only *played* at making films.

Dennis found a beautiful little hilltop house for us to rent, and so the pattern began exactly as it had been at home. I worked at the studios, he managed the domestic scene. Not that there was anything else for him to do, other than swim in the pool or drive around Hollywood. All his business ventures had been left in abeyance back home. So too, as he was to discover, was his hold over me and his ability to dictate my affairs.

We were dining one evening with William Dozier and his wife, former actress Ann Rutherford, and it came out during the course of conversation that I had no mink coat.

'No mink! Why not?' cried Ann.

'Dennis hates the idea', I replied, which he confirmed by adding, 'Dors looks dreadful in a fur coat'.

'But every woman should have a mink', persisted Ann, wincing at his reference to me by my surname. Indeed, no-one in Hollywood liked the way he called me 'Dors'. The Americans felt it was not respectful to a woman, especially one's wife. Next day at the studio I was summoned to Bill Dozier's office and there, laid out on a sofa, were three beautiful mink stoles.

'Which one do you like best?' he asked.

I pointed to a breathtaking silver-blue model.

'Then it's yours', he said, smiling. 'A present from Ann and myself. Frankly,' he said, placing it around my shoulders, 'I don't think you look dreadful in it at all'. I thanked him excitedly and went home wearing my first mink, feeling like a princess.

Dennis froze when he saw it, and a strange expression came over his face when I told him Bill had given it to me as a present. But he said nothing, possibly wondering what Dozier's next move might be. No doubt he was convinced in his mind that the man would make a pass at me. How wrong he was, for the only move Bill made was to offer me a three-picture deal worth half a million dollars!

Having signed this contract, it looked as if we would have to stay in Hollywood longer than originally antici-pated, and so Dennis resumed his property negotia-tions – this time to buy a house in Beverly Hills. But on reflection – and it is always easy to be wise after the event – this was a silly thing to do. We had the Rank contract in England, our Penthouse, the coffee-bar, plus 'Woodhurst', on which all work had stopped in our absence. Therefore, instead of buying yet another property, we should have gone home after the first film was completed, simply return-ing to Hollywood when any of the contract films had to be done.

What we could not realise, though, was how fickle the Americans were; that despite the fact that we were treated like royalty when we arrived, our popularity would wane as others' had done in that crazy film city, especially if an artiste's film was not good box-office. The British were not too popular in those days, either, and the worst thing any Briton could do was to be seen loafing around with nothing to do.

Films stars were so sensitive, and gossip columnists so powerful, that if there was a big party and one had not been invited, it was considered a terrible failure. Stars stayed at home, rather than be seen in restaurants and so make it quite apparent that they were not in demand – and therefore not important. However, the fashion was changing: to be elusive was becoming much more attractive.

Dennis, bored with nothing to do, livened up at the idea of finding a house, and with his usual aplomb he set about purchasing the most magnificent mansion he could find – an enormous white building complete with swimming-pool, tennis court, guest house, vast grounds, and equipped throughout with elegant carpets, curtains and furnishings. On the dashboard of the brand new white Lincoln Continental car he also bought, there was a button which opened and closed the garage doors – a gadget he never tired of playing with. 'To frighten the servants', he chuckled, 'in case they're sitting around doing nothing'. But what Dennis did not understand was that the sort of flamboyant publicity and luxury living which impressed the British public meant nothing to the rich, spoilt Hollywood community. Buying a fabulous home with all the trimmings achieved nothing for us and was simply a waste of money.

While all this spending was going on, I continued to work on the film and enjoy the social life and adoration we were receiving. Bob Hope was filming next door at Columbia, and he and Dennis struck up a friendship, sending each other jokes, with Dennis often dropping by to visit him. Bob's agent, Louis Shurr, was working as my agent now, and plans were being made for Bob and me to team up in a couple of films based on old Jean Harlow vehicles like *Blonde Bombshell* and *Platinum Blonde*.

The Monroe comparisons continued, of course, and

there was an offer, which Dennis turned down, from Twentieth Century Fox for me to star with her former co-star, Tom Ewell, in a comedy follow-up to *The Seven-Year Itch*.

'Everyone will compare you with her all the more if you do it', he maintained. 'And it can't be as good as that film.' (The following year Jayne Mansfield starred in what was probably the best film she ever made. *The Girl Can't Help It* was the title of the script Dennis had refused for me!)

Peter Reynolds wired that he was coming over to stay with us and try his luck in Hollywood. Hairdresser Raymond and his wife, Jennifer, having read the exciting newspaper stories of my success, decided that they too were coming out for a holiday. Raymond also figured it would enhance his hairdressing empire if he spent some money on publicity and tried to become famous there. The thought that friends were arriving was pleasant, for both Dennis and I had become desperately homesick. Despite all the dozens of hospitable people we met, there was no-one with whom we felt we could ever be as close as we had been with friends at home. It was odd. All my life I had dreamt of going to Hollywood and being a star. It was my ultimate ambition. And now I was there, none of it seemed important.

The first weeks had been exhilarating, seeing sunny, palm-treed avenues, gorgeous homes and all the places and people I'd read about in film magazines. Then quickly everything began to pall, just as others who had found fame there told me it would. All the glamour, luxury and eternal sunshine made me long for the softer charm of England, springtime and even a shower of rain.

One evening I sat alone in the pool-house among the orchids and the orange trees, gazing up at the big, floodlit white mansion. Coloured lights adorned exotic flowers, and the sky-blue swimming-pool, my dream since childhood, stretched before me illuminated in the dark. What happens now? I thought, with almost a touch of panic. This is all I ever wanted; I've achieved a life-long ambition. But where do I go from here? I could not know then that the giddy pinnacle I had climbed was to provide me with a very short-lived moment of triumph. Nor did I know, as I wondered about my loss of ambition, that the arrival of Raymond would toll the death knell of my Hollywood career!

Peter Reynolds arrived first and commenced his tour of agents and producers in an attempt to gain recognition. Raymond and Jennifer flew in a few weeks later, and Raymond promptly hired a top publicity firm to handle his business. Not that Raymond, who had started the 'teasy-weasy' curl for women, was any slouch where publicity was concerned. Before leaving England he had announced to the British press that I was paying him £3,000 to fly across and create a hairstyle! A ridiculous story on the face of it, but in those days the press and public loved it.

A fantastic party was to be held at our house in Raymond's honour. This was the first way to get him off the ground, everyone decided, and it would also be a marvellous opportunity for Dennis and me to invite all the people we had met in Hollywood, so returning their generous hospitality. Raymond was prepared to foot the bill, and plans were put into action.

On the night of the party Raymond's name floated in giant flowers on top of the swimming-pool, a band played at one end and champagne flowed non-stop at the other. Columnists and photographers mingled with stars, who happily posed for pictures – with or without Raymond – and the whole affair was a glittering spectacle. Until an agency photographer chose to take pictures of a different kind!

Dennis and I were talking to my agent and a dress designer from RKO when I noticed a sly-looking man sidle up to them and, with a violent shove, send the two men crashing into Dennis and me. It happened too quickly to shout any warning, and all four of us fell into the pool! At least it was the shallow end for, not being a good swimmer, I might well have drowned in the mêlée that followed. Dennis climbed out of the pool in a fury and, seeing a pair of legs disappearing fast through the crowd, rushed after the man and proceeded to pulverise him into unconsciousness. People screamed, the whole mood of the party changed in seconds, and what had been a pleasant social evening turned into a brawling nightmare. Stars, fearful of receiving bad publicity, rushed across the lawns to their waiting limousines.

The Los Angeles police were summoned, and arrived to hear Dennis, still outraged at the treatment we had suffered, boasting in temper that, as he had once been a boxer, no-one was going to push him and his wife around like that! This was all nonsense – he might have done some amateur boxing at school – but next day the press emblazoned it in headlines that he had used his fists as 'lethal weapons' to assault a good American citizen! The party, too, had been transformed from a sophisticated, genteel gathering to a drunken orgy, hosted by two English publicity-seeking degenerates – that was us. One paper actually headlined their front page: 'GO HOME DIANA, AND TAKE MR DORS WITH YOU!'

No-one would believe that we hadn't deliberately planned the stunt in order to obtain world coverage, which is what we got, not even when it was revealed that the photographer and some of his colleagues had set it up themselves to get an exclusive story. They had originally tried to persuade Zsa Zsa Gabor and others to fall in the pool, promising headline publicity, but when she and everyone else declined they set up their cameras and de-cided to push us over the side instead. Had it all remained at that, the event would have been seen as just another silly incident. But Dennis's violent attack on the instigator made the American press see red.

From being able to do nothing wrong, now we could do nothing right. The gossip columnists condemned us as unsavoury Britishers 'who should know better than to come to our country and behave like hooligans'. One of them even accused me of being a Communist sympathiser because of an article which had appeared under my name in an English magazine. The article praised actress Dawn Adams and rued the fact that, because she had filmed with

Charlie Chaplin, she could no longer get work in America.
Chaplin was bitterly despised, owing to his Communist
beliefs, although twenty years later he was forgiven and
presented with the keys of New York City.

'Up the hammer and sickle, girl, and gather those
Yankee dollars while you may' screeched the *Hollywood
Reporter*, and from then on I was attacked each day.

The RKO heads became very worried about all this
adverse publicity for they had a big financial investment at
stake. And, after a consultation with Bill Dozier, I was
instructed to telephone all the columnists, apologise,
explain that the party incident was not planned, and agree
that Dennis had been hasty and wrong in taking the law
into his own hands. Indignant at the injustice of it all,
I none the less did as I was told, enduring several humili-
ating encounters with the gossip columnists. Mike Con-
nelly, however, would accept nothing, least of all an
apology.

'I was nice to you', he screamed. 'And all the time you
were writing this terrible Communist propaganda behind
my back.'

'But I didn't write it', I tried to explain. 'It was ghosted
for me by a columnist at home.'

'You're a liar!' he yelled, and hung up.

Everything had gone sour. Raymond and Jennifer went
back to England, only too relieved to get away from what
they considered a savage, hostile country. 'Be careful, my
dear', my father had written in a comforting letter. 'They
are a peculiar lot over there.'

RKO would have liked to pull out of their contract at this
point, but it was too late. Plans for my next film were
already under way and could not be halted. Besides which
they could not legally enforce the 'morals clause' in my
contract because of something Dennis had done.

The Unholy Wife, a drama set in the wine-growing area of
northern California, was scheduled to begin shooting on
location in early September, which was when Dennis and I
flew to San Francisco, then on to the Nappa Valley. With us
was Bill Dozier, still reeling from the problems he had

encountered over the 'swimming-pool party' incident. For myself, I was more nervous about working with director John Farrow, who enjoyed a reputation for striking terror into the hearts of those who worked with him. But 'Fearless Farrow', as I nicknamed him, was charming and considerate to me at all times, even employing a guitarist to serenade me between takes and kindly helping out with problems which arose during filming.

He had a special friendship with Louella Parsons, possibly based on his strong Catholic beliefs, a subject on which he had written several books. Louella kept a lighted shrine in her garden, and I sometimes wondered if she and 'Fearless' planned to share the same private staircase to heaven.

Farrow was married to actress Maureen O'Sullivan and they had seven children, including Mia, who later became an actress, Mrs Frank Sinatra and Mrs André Previn. But his Catholic ideals did not prevent him from having a well-known star as his mistress, or scores of other actresses or starlets on the side. There was a joke going round the set that, having spent some time in his hotel room with a lovely blonde stand-in, he rushed her to the nearest Catholic church to confess *her* sins. One day I saw him marching up and down outside the set between three rows of hopeful young starlets, pointing with his walking-stick at the few he selected. Whether they rated a part in the film, or merely a session in his luxurious suite at the studio, remained a mystery to me. But by then I had troubles of my own. I had fallen in love with my co-star, Rod Steiger!

Most people thought ours was an impossible union. 'I know Dors, and I know Steiger, and never the twain shall meet', one columnist had written. Like so many other people, though, he saw only the outward appearances and knew nothing of our personalities. Working with Rod on location, I had been surprisingly impressed by him, not merely as an actor, but in real life. His wonderful sense of comedy quite belied the dramatic roles he had played in films like *On the Waterfront* and *The Harder They Fall*.

My father as a captain in the
First World War.

My mother.

Me, aged two. I hadn't yet learned how to smile for the camera!

Aunty Kit with my father and me (aged three) in Weston-super-Mare.

'Uncle' Gerry.

In my father's rose garden, aged five.

With my father at the start of my teens.

Aged 13, my first pin-up photograph! Taken by the local newspaper photographer.

Aged 15, after signing a film contract with J. Arthur Rank.

Aged 17, my first portrait session.

Playing Charlotte in *Oliver Twist*.

Michael Caborn-Waterfield, with whom I fell in love.

A scene from *The Last Page* with George Brent.

Enter Svengali . . . alias
Dennis Hamilton.

Our wedding at Caxton Hall.

Dennis and me in 1955 at the height of our success.

A scene from *A Kid For Two Farthings* with co-star Joe Robinson.

In *Yield To The Night,* the film of which I am perhaps most proud.

The Variety Club award luncheon when I was named 'Show Business Personality of the Year.' (*L-r:* Ian Carmichael, me, Kenneth More, Valerie French and Nat Cohen.)

The most wonderful week of my life: when *Yield To The Night* was chosen for the Cannes Film Festival

Arriving at the premiere

Leading the flower festival parade

Holding a press reception

Meeting Ginger Rogers at the Aga Khan's villa

Hollywood, and scenes from two of the films I made there.
Top; *I Married A Woman* co-starring George Gobel, with
John Wayne making a guest appearance. *Bottom;* With Tom
Tyron in *The Unholy Wife*.

With Tommy Yeardye.

My fifteenth century farmhouse in Sussex.

Little did I know that this glamour photograph at 17 would be the first of thousands.

My marriage to Dickie Dawson.

With Dickie and
our son Mark when
I was working at
Elstree Studios.

With Mark and Gary in the grounds of my Hollywood home.

Appearing on the Steve Allen show in America.

Rehearsing for my cabaret show in Las Vegas.

In cabaret at Newcastle.

With Darryl Stewart in Australia.

The day I married Alan Lake: 23 November 1968.

Our son Jason's christening with Mark *(left)* and Gary *(right)*.

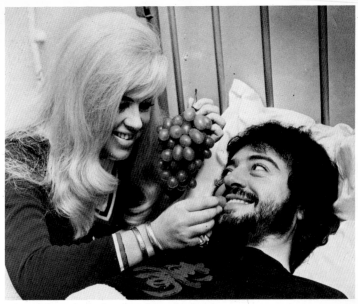

Alan in hospital after breaking his back.

Christmas 1974: at home with Jason.

My three sons

Mark

Gary

Jason

able to do anything to the American photographer now manifested itself in Tommy's direction. Not that Tommy was worried, for he was one man who was capable of taking care of himself where Dennis was concerned. However, not wanting any trouble, and seeing it brewing, I asked Dennis to leave, which he took as a sign that I wanted to be alone with Tommy. He strode off the location angrily.

When we finished shooting, at daybreak, director Ken Hughes said he'd drive me home, for he knew Dennis was furious and had seen him in action on occasions when he was staying at the Penthouse. As we walked into the house, Sholly warned me to ignore things and I soon saw why. There had been an all-night party and several people were still hanging around, looking much the worse for wear. Dennis had a brainstorm the moment he saw us, despite the fact I said nothing to set him off, and I went straight to my bedroom. I developed a fit of the shakes each time he went on one of his rampages and couldn't control them. But nowhere in that house would have been safe that morning, and when he had devastated the drawing-room, leaving the door hanging from its hinges, he set about attacking me.

A miserable week followed, with the film still in progress, Dennis behaving in a strangely remote manner, and Tommy desperately worried about my safety. More and more I became drawn to the gentle Irishman, for to me he represented a strength against Dennis such as I had never known before. Then one evening, to my utter amazement, Dennis told me calmly that he had met someone with whom he thought he had fallen in love and that he was contemplating moving out to live above his club in Windsor. Whether this was true I didn't know. But if it was a ruse to try to win back my affection it failed. I was elated by the news that at last he was actually leaving me!

The next morning, Friday, as I left for the studios, I turned to wish him goodbye as he lay in the ornate gold and silk bed.

'I will not be here when you come home', he said in a sad voice, perhaps half-expecting me to plead with him to reconsider. A wave of nostalgia made me linger a moment, remembering all the good times, but it passed quickly and I left him there. Hardly daring to believe I was finally on my own, I excitedly told Tommy what had transpired. And that evening, on my return, I found Dennis had gone, taking all his belongings, plus many antiques with which to furnish his flat. The house seemed strange without him and his court. Only Sholly was there, but I didn't know she'd been left there purposely as a spy!

Carelessly, and joyous of my freedom – something I had not experienced since the Steiger affair – I organised a celebration party the following night, inviting Tommy and some of his friends. It was the first time Tommy had been to the Penthouse. And on Sunday, four of us – John Hoey, a bubble-gum-machine tycoon, actress Shani Wallis, Tommy and I – went off happily for a drive in the country. It was a glorious spring day, and we behaved in a carefree manner, not realising that the worst siege of all was close at hand.

Upon our return Sholly rushed out into the driveway, obviously distressed.

'Mr Hamilton is here', she stammered.

I could not imagine why he had come back. This time we had separated by mutual agreement; he to live his life, I to live mine. But it appeared that Dennis's ideas on the freedom to live and love were heavily weighted on his side. To admit falling in love with someone else and so leave was fine for him. *I* was expected to live alone in the ivory tower, which was how the Penthouse was beginning to look, continue to earn the money and have no life of my own.

However, at this moment, I had not yet worked out his selfish reasoning, and Sholly was playing her part as he had instructed her.

'It's all right, Mr Hamilton's not in a temper, he just wants you to come in and sign some papers', she wheedled.

Signing papers was a familiar procedure by now, and noticing one of Dennis's henchmen lurking around the front door I assumed she must be telling the truth. Tommy was apprehensive for my safety, but I reasoned that it would be better for him to wait in the car with John and

Shani. There was no point in giving Dennis the opportunity of having a brainstorm at the sight of him.

Like a lamb unaware of slaughter, I climbed the elegant staircase to the house above that great blue swimming-pool, past the huge statue of a man in bronze which did not look unlike Tommy. Hairdresser Raymond had given it to Dennis as a present in the good days before he enticed his wife away. And at the top of the staircase stood Svengali, the man who had dominated me for six years. Nor was he 'all right', as Sholly had informed me. He was in a towering rage, and furthermore he held a shotgun!

There was no way back now, and once again I began to shake. However, I tried to appear calm by walking past him into the great drawing-room, casting a glance through the stained-glass window at Tommy seated in my convertible below.

'I want you to sign this, Dors', seethed Dennis in a tone I knew well. He indicated a piece of paper on the table.

'What is it?' I asked, pretending to be casually interested.

'A list of all the men you've had during our marriage.'

'You must be mad, Dennis.'

'Mad am I?' he fumed. And to my astonishment he reeled off the names of a string of men, some of whom I had met only occasionally, which included Peter Finch the actor. There was no truth in any of them except for Rod Steiger and Tommy Yeardye, but my attempts to remonstrate with him were useless. Another paper was produced, this time containing all the items I was to sign over to him. The coffee-bar, 'Woodhurst', El Dors Club, the Penthouse, two cars, a river launch, camera equipment, Cracker, my boxer dog, and of course all the cash in the safe. The fact that he already had these things in his possession, my name being merely a legal point, did not occur to me at that moment. Indeed, neither list seemed to me so important then as getting safely away from Dennis and that gun. Signing was the easiest and safest thing to do.

Falteringly, for he was hovering over me like a vulture, I quickly scribbled my name on both pieces of paper and nervously started to make for the door. But Dennis was not going to let it go at that. He smashed the stained-glass window with his gun, threatening to shoot Tommy, and then punched me violently on the head.

Quite what happened after that I'm not sure, for I fell to the floor, dazed and with a terrible pain in the side of my head. But I was aware of Tommy rushing in like a hurricane, looking rather like the bronze statue on the stairs and displaying almost superhuman strength. To get into the house he had smashed some glass on the upper front door with his fist, and now he was struggling with Dennis. For the first time in his life Dennis got the worst of it, and when Tommy put him on the floor he sat there sobbing. 'Dors', I heard him saying as Tommy helped me out of the room, 'how could you do this to me? I loved you so much.'

Tommy took me to his parents' little house in London, and also to a doctor who informed me I had a punctured eardrum from Dennis's blow. I refused to entertain any thoughts of taking out charges against Dennis, but without my knowledge and after I'd been given sedation and bedded down, John Hoey called up a gang he knew to go down to the Penthouse and rough Dennis up. He was so angry that a shotgun had been pointed in his direction. Fortunately they did not get in, but it was apparently ugly for a while. Sholly, assuming that *I* was the instigator, was later heard to complain that 'Miss Dors did a really nasty thing to Mr Hamilton by sending those thugs here. There was no need for that!' (Some twenty years afterwards I learnt that the notorious Kray twins had been among that gang; only then they were not so famous.)

This was definitely the end of my marriage to Dennis. There could be no reconciliation; indeed, for the moment neither of us wanted to see the other again! But some things did have to be sorted out, and the first of them was to collect all my clothes. As he was now extremely wary of Tommy, Dennis arranged to be out the day we drove to the Pent-house, but there was no need even to enter the building. Every garment, shoe and handbag I possessed had been thrown into a car, and the only person I saw was a sullen-faced Sholly at the door. I also had to find somewhere to live, for I couldn't continue staying with Tommy's parents for very long – especially with my wardrobe of clothes! For the moment, though, this problem was solved by a film director friend who rented me his small mews house in Belgravia for a month.

During this time, and quite by accident, I met up with Anthony Newley at the studios. He had been through some bad years since I last saw him, including a prison sentence at Brixton for some insurance offence, and his marriage – to his first wife, an actress – was no longer a happy one. It was not to be long before he got divorced. We went out to dinner and I told him everything in my life. His own was not yet at the point at which he attained the great success he would eventually have. There was no question of either of us starting a new relationship, for Tony had become even more complex and I thought I was in love with Tommy.

The Long Haul finally dragged to an end, and Dennis sent me a thousand pounds from the twenty received by him for my services. The situation could not be left as it was, though, for I would soon have to leave the mews house. Papers regarding our properties had to be drawn up, and it was eventually agreed by different lawyers – despite the 'shotgun statements' which I signed 'under duress' (the legal term) – that Dennis was to have everything except the Penthouse. I was to be allowed to live there without further harassment, even though Dennis would be living next door in one of the luxurious flats in 'Woodhurst'. Consequently it was with reservations that I moved back there, despite the fact that I felt perfectly safe physically now that I had Tommy as a bodyguard.

The next few months passed peacefully, helped no doubt by my being in Italy to make a film, *La Ragazza Del Palio*, which Dennis had negotiated before our troubles. My salary was $85,000. Tommy and I flew to Rome, arranging with friends to drive my Cadillac out there so we could see something of the country when I wasn't working.

Rock Hudson was also filming there, and he and Tommy re-acquainted themselves. I knew Rock from my Hollywood days, and could remember the big wedding anniversary party his press agents had thrown. There, floating on top of the swimming-pool in flowers were his name and that of his bride of twelve months, Phyllis. But the whole affair was a syrupy publicity stunt and the couple parted soon after that anniversary celebration.

While we were filming in Rome I arranged for Tommy's parents to join us for a holiday, and from there we went to Florence, a beautiful city filled with statues of god-like men, all of whom Tommy, with his muscle-building ideals, admired a great deal. Then it was on to finish the film in the old city of Sienna, where a famous horse-race, the *Palio*, had been run for a thousand years. It was a violent affair with riders lashing at each other with bull-whips as they fought for the honour and glory of winning, rather than for the prize. Before the race began, the competitors would take their horses into church and pray, which struck us all as being quite hysterical. But what was even funnier was that the American girl I was playing in the film was supposed to ride in the race and win it!

The long, arduous days of filming went by slowly, during which time I became more and more homesick for England. Tommy, who spent most of his time weightlifting and reading, was a tranquil person to have around, and he seemed to me rather like an oak tree I could lean against while I regained my strength after the whirlwind years with Dennis Hamilton. For a while it was all very romantic, particularly dancing beneath the stars at open-air night-clubs, but I was beginning to experience a restlessness I did not understand. Why, with the freedom I had yearned for and a handsome lover who followed my lead, was I growing disenchanted?

Perhaps the answer lay in Bill Dozier's remark about 'having something to talk about when you finally fell out of bed'. Or perhaps Tommy came nearest to being that 'decent sort of chap' my father had once spoken about. Indeed, looking at the men in my life, Tommy was the only one of whom he fully approved, for in Tommy there was no evil and a good deal of common sense.

It was in the middle of all my ennui that George Coburn

arrived unexpectedly on a wild trip. He and an actor chum were passing through Sienna to Rome on a binge. It was good to see him again after many years, for even if he was mad he at least made me laugh. And that was something I had not done too much of with Tommy, despite our romantic love affair smouldering under the Italian sun.

Eventually we returned to England, still owed money for the film and never, despite lengthy legal battles, to get it all. Now that I was back at the Penthouse, a bizarre situation developed. Dennis, living next door in 'Woodhurst', would occasionally phone on some pretext or other and chat cheerfully in an effort to reinstate himself with me. But for the rest of the time, car loads of girls were being driven in and out at all times of the day or night. As if I couldn't see for myself what was going on, mutual friends would tell me how Dennis's life was one long round of wine, women and song! This playboy existence had its dangers, though. More than once I saw one girl being pushed out the French windows to hide her from another who had arrived suddenly, believing she alone was the love of his life. The affair with Jennifer was still going on, the jockey's wife was now living alone in her flat at 'Woodhurst' and being wooed by Dennis when he had the time, and the woman he had left me for, having broken with her husband, was occupying yet another flat there! On top of which there was the ever-present threat of shotgun-toting husbands.

My boxer dog and Siamese cat were next door, too, as was our splendid talking cockatoo, who could be seen perched on the handlebars of the bike Dennis rode around the garden. Naturally Sholly was ensconced as his housekeeper, and parties occurred there all the time. More often than not, friends would pop over to the Penthouse during these to tell me what a fool I was wasting my time with a bore like Tommy.

'How could you possibly split up with Dennis?' asked television producer Dennis Vance, a former inmate of Mr Rank's Charm School in the days when he had been an aspiring actor. 'He's the most marvellous man I've ever known.' George Coburn, home from his Italian adventures, met Dennis for the first time and they became great pals. I was reminded of what Michael's brother, John, had said when I asked him who Dennis Hamilton was. 'He's exactly like George.'

Michael himself visited Tommy and me, along with our circle of friends. He was very successful in some business venture, and we were still extremely fond of each other. 'Whatever happens in our lives', he told me, 'marriages, births, deaths, I will always love you.' In our own way we had quite a social scene buzzing at the Penthouse, and it was almost like a silly game of one-upmanship with 'Woodhurst'.

Tommy knew a girl named Jozy, whom he had introduced to Victor Mature during *The Long Haul*. She was a very attractive blonde and one day, as a joke, we dressed her in a pair of my briefest shorts and sent her through the garden hedge to Dennis. We knew he would take an immediate liking to her, but not even in our wildest dreams could we have guessed the outcome. As she looked a little like me, he announced to the press that he was going to make Jozy into another Diana Dors. He even arranged for photographs to be taken of himself – Svengali style – with her at El Dors, which was now a flourishing business. But Dennis was not the starmaker he truly felt he had become, and failed to fulfil his eager promises.

Apart from attracting playboy publicity and being known as 'Ex-Mr Dors' – the man who made me – Dennis's role in life was now that of property and club owner. He even employed a manager to run El Dors, though he still used the flat there to pursue his affairs. One of these, with the tempestuous daughter of a local policeman, nearly got him into trouble. For while Dennis was making love to her in the flat, her father was raging down below, powerless to get at either of them!

However, another typical example of Hamilton cheek did not pass by without explosive repercussions. One of Dennis's tenants was an ex-stuntman who occupied a smaller flat at the top of 'Woodhurst'. Having obtained it at a low rent, he set about decorating it expensively and considerably improved the flat. But when Dennis saw how good the flat looked, he cheekily announced that he would have to increase the rent. This infuriated the stuntman, who until then had regarded Dennis as a friend, and from then on a terrible feud developed between them, with the stuntman plotting to get his revenge.

One day while Tommy was in London working out at a gymnasium, Dennis invited me over to see how beautiful he had made 'Woodhurst'. Not having been in there since our parting, and with nothing better to do, foolishly I walked across to the big house, where Dennis led me into the opulent drawing-room of his flat. Music played softly in the background, and Dennis was pleasantly charming as he poured wine into two large crystal goblets. Proudly he pointed out various antiques he had newly acquired, including a pair of massive, ornate firedogs by the roaring log fire. A grand piano, which he could not play, stood in the corner and the walls were lined with shelves of leather-backed books. He removed one and gave it to me. It was a collection of poems by his favourite poet, Rupert Brooke.

'I've marked certain pages for you', he said gently, a sadness passing over his face, and I thought how lost he looked in the splendour of his surroundings. Lonely, and somehow weary of it all.

'No-one will ever love you the way I did', he sighed as I prepared to leave that elegant yet unhappy place.

Back at the Penthouse I opened the book of poems to find that, inside the cover, Dennis had written an inscription: 'To my darling wife, I love you more today than yesterday, and less than tomorrow.' There were several indications of pages I should read, and an added message: 'I meant it with all my heart.'

The shortest poem of the three he had marked was the one that most touched me.

> The way of Love was thus,
> He was born, one winter morn,
> With hands delicious.
> And it was well with us.

Love came our quiet way,
Lit pride in us, and died in us,
All in a winter's day.
There is no more to say.

This was the other Dennis Hamilton, someone who had not appeared often in our life together, and I felt both guilty and sad.

Could I go back to him? I had tried before, not very successfully admittedly, but this time it was different. Many months had passed since our separation and I was tired of controlling my own destiny now. Life without Dennis was rather empty after all. But living with Tommy, so quiet by comparison, was relaxed and good. I could not imagine returning to the old Svengali any more, and I knew that, for all the pretty poetry and sweetness, Dennis would revert to the tyrant he had always been. There was no way I could return to that kind of life, and yet I almost wished it were possible.

Naturally I didn't tell Tommy of my visit. He would have been upset and alarmed. But in the days that followed Dennis and I would phone each other for all manner of excuses . . . though in reality just to talk. Usually it was when Tommy was out, and slowly I found myself being lulled into thinking that we should try again. I also received a phone call one day from the mother of his main woman friend, desperately pleading with me to go back to Dennis so that he would leave her daughter alone. She endeavoured to add attraction to the possibility by saying, 'No couple have ever been so good together. He loves you, not all these other women. You were both magic.'

As if all this wasn't enough to disrupt any future Tommy and I might have had, the arrival in England of Rod Steiger, *en route* to America from Spain, created turmoil in my already bewildered mind. He telephoned and asked to meet me in London, but there was no way and rather reluctantly I told him so. However, the knowledge I was flying to New York some days later pleased him and we arranged that he would call me at my hotel there.

Dennis, knowing of my contract to appear on the Perry Como television show, and my subsequent staying on for several weeks, urged me to tell Tommy that he and I were going to attempt a reconciliation, no doubt hoping Tommy might vacate the Penthouse while I was away, allowing Dennis to move back in. There was no way he dared go near Tommy after their last confrontation! But I could not bring myself to be so heartless and told Dennis I'd write to Tommy from America. True, this would have been taking a coward's way out but, as I still had terrible doubts as to what I wanted, it would also give me more time to think clearly.

Trusting £8,000 in cash to Tommy for safe keeping I set off for New York with a heavy heart, wondering as he waved goodbye if this would be the last I saw of him. Well, I consoled myself, at least he could keep some of the money, for since living with me he had done no work at all. Perhaps this was why I had such little respect for him. Certainly I would always be grateful for his protection and love, but here *again* was a man seemingly content to live off my earnings. In fairness, what could he possibly have done to earn the sort of money I made? But Tommy, like others before, foolishly allowed his feelings for me to overrule the sense of insisting on his own independence. In my eyes, that tarnished him.

I had been at the Plaza Hotel for two days, with television rehearsals going along smoothly, when Steiger telephoned. We arranged to have dinner that evening, and he arrived in a large, chauffeur-driven limousine to pick me up. But instead of being taken to a restaurant, we were driven straight to some Greenwich Village apartment belonging to a friend of his. There, without too much preamble, Rod made love to me.

When I first saw him that night, I had tried to rekindle some spark of fire from the previous year, but it was not there. I didn't understand why my heart no longer beat as fast, or why my feelings were not so intense. Perhaps I was too preoccupied wondering what to do about Dennis and Tommy. Or was it just that time had eroded my passion for him? Whatever the reason I knew I didn't look at him the same way. And I was angry, too, that he presumed – in typical male style – that I was desperate to go to bed with him. It was not a good reunion, and when he dropped me back at the Plaza I didn't think I would see him again. Furthermore, it did not matter! 'How much things have changed in so short a time', I thought.

Suddenly the tables had turned, and next day to my amazement Rod appeared with red roses. The idea of him doing this would once have made me overjoyed; now it meant nothing. And the more he attempted to show his feelings, the more distant I became. Nor did it help that my hotel suite was already filled with flowers. For Dennis, in his own romantic way, had made a standing-order with the florist to deliver one red rose a day, each with a small card bearing the words 'I love you'. Another two dozen had arrived that morning as Dennis anticipated my twenty-sixth birthday.

Rod and I had a stormy encounter, but even his proposal of marriage was too late now. I could not stop myself thinking, 'If only this had happened last year', but then I remembered the poetry I thought had been for me alone, and somehow his display of dramatics seemed little but that of a great actor indulging in theatrics. Neither was I impressed by his half-hearted attempt to throw himself off the window-ledge, so there was little sadness in my heart when, vowing never to see me again, he finally left.

We did see each other once more, though; quite accidentally at a Hollywood cocktail party some years afterwards. By then he was married to actress Claire Bloom, and though our eyes met across the room we did not speak. I chose to believe it was because she was there, too, and, as he may have told her of our affair, he was saving any embarrassment to both her and me. Claire, a dignified, sensitive actress, commanded the sort of respect Rod always maintained was essential to the woman who became Mrs Steiger. Even in his most ardent moments of passion, he never really felt that I fitted suitably into that category. But I could smile inwardly as I watched them both, for my mind went back to the days when Dennis and I lived in Chelsea. He often peeped through Claire's window, which was nearly next door to our house, watching Richard Burton's rehearsals for the play in which they were performing.

Having bade Rod Steiger farewell in New York, I went back to televising with Perry Como; *and* trying to sort out the confusion in my head. Eventually I could stand the problem no longer, or the thought of giving Tommy the cruel news that I was going to reconcile with Dennis. I telephoned him and poured out the whole miserable story of what had been happening. I also called Dennis and with difficulty informed him that, regardless of the many feelings I still possessed for him, I could never tolerate our living as man and wife again. Displeased, he kept his remarks abrupt, and the coldness creeping back into his voice made me shudder slightly. All sweetness had gone. I remember thinking, with alarm intermingled with relief, that this was what it would have been like after I had returned to him.

Tommy, for his part, was not going to allow anything else to upset our relationship, and to my surprise he flew to New York, where we spent a week together before returning to England. A grim atmosphere now surrounded 'Woodhurst' and the Penthouse, the two camps standing side by side on the river. Dennis, having completely abandoned any ideas of a life together again, went his own way with girls, parties and more girls, while Tommy and I attempted to carry on socially with friends of our own. We night-clubbed often, and one evening went to the Stork Club in London, where Jozy, the girl Dennis had vowed to build into a star, was working as a cigarette-girl.

'Who's in cabaret tonight?' I enquired.

'A comedian named Dickie Dawson', she replied.

We watched the show, and afterwards Dawson came over to our table. He was a good-looking, cheeky character with a great deal of talent and a forceful ambition. When I casually asked Jozy to bring him to the Penthouse some-time, he immediately answered for her.

'Okay, we'll come this Sunday.'

I was slightly taken aback by this, but as they were coming down I arranged a party, to which I invited, among others, Michael and his brother John. It turned out to be a strange evening, punctuated by loud noises and bangs emanating from Dennis's quarters next door. Tommy and Michael were both concerned, for there had been a series of odd events, even gunfire, over the weeks, but we had laughingly put the sound of gunfire down to outraged husbands who were after Dennis's blood!

We all laughed, too, when John Waterfield complained of feeling unwell that evening, saying he was suffering from rheumatism.

'At your age, John? Ridiculous!' I remarked, nevertheless giving him some pills to kill the pain he felt approaching. He was only twenty-six and had been examined several times by various doctors. What could possibly be wrong with him? None of us knew, as we enjoyed ourselves and Dickie Dawson regaled everyone with jokes and brilliant impersonations of stars, including Rod Steiger, that John was suffering from cancer and would be dead in less than eight months.

The stuntman, still plotting Dennis's downfall over the feud they were having, was also at that party, boring us with his continual threats of what he was going to do. We said we'd believe it when we saw it, and of course nothing happened that night. Indeed, apart from the noises off-stage it was a quiet evening, and Dickie Dawson left muttering that he 'had had more fun at a wake'. He'd obviously not had the kind of evening he anticipated.

It was not until Boxing Day that the stuntman's threat was carried out. Dennis had gone to a party in Sussex, and we were having one at the Penthouse. Everybody was there: film stars such as Roger Moore and Samantha Eggar, producers, directors, writers and comedians; all celebrated Christmas 1957 with close friends like Michael and many not connected with show-business. The stuntman was there, too, but few of us took any notice of his mutterings, or his glances towards the river where a beautiful boat, Dennis's latest acquisition, lay moored in the darkness.

It was the early hours of the morning, most of the guests were disappearing, when suddenly the peace was shattered by an enormous explosion and the surroundings were lit up in a gigantic flash of light. We rushed to the windows, and from there we saw Dennis's boat enveloped in flames.

'He's done it, he's done it!' cried Tommy joyfully. But Michael and I had other feelings as we gazed at the burning boat.

'God, what a shame', he said sadly.

The police and press quickly found their way to the scene and Dennis returned, inconsolable. As it was assumed by everybody on his side of the fence that either Tommy or Michael had been responsible, the war between us was now decidedly open, for no-one – including the detectives investigating – suspected the stuntman. Not even Dennis, who had provided the motive. We couldn't possibly disclose the truth, and from that day we had to endure the most terrible retributions. Bricks were thrown through our windows by Dennis's henchmen, our telephone was tapped, and on one occasion the Penthouse was broken into and everything turned upside down, though very little was taken.

Dennis threatened revenge, stating openly that he had witnesses who saw Tommy set light to his boat! Dennis Shaw, the ugly actor from my wild days in Chelsea, who had now become his friend, was prepared to say, for a small fee, that he was sitting on a bench near the river that night, for no apparent reason, and had observed Tommy climbing aboard with a can of petrol. None of this came to anything, but it did show us how determined Dennis was to even the score.

Life had become too unpleasant to remain in such close proximity to 'Woodhurst', and Tommy proposed we move to a fifteenth century farm in Sussex which he had his eye on. If I bought it, he promised, then everyone would see what he was capable of doing. It was indeed a beautiful place, and the idea of getting away from all the trouble and gangsterism at Maidenhead appealed to me. I had just completed a film, *Tread Softly Stranger*, for which I was paid £20,000 and with this money the farm was purchased for £15,000. I sold the Penthouse to a wealthy businessman for £13,000, and in the spring of 1958 we moved.

It was a far cry from the Penthouse and noisy parties, but I happily basked in the beauty and peace of it all. It was too quiet for my little Irish butler, though, and he didn't stay long. Waiting for Tommy to become the farmer he had assured me he wanted to be took much longer. Apart from the time he painted a barn door, I saw him do little except lift his bar-bells, sunbathe in a garden chair, or ride the horse I gave him as a present.

By now, because of the bad publicity surrounding my professional and personal life, my career had slipped badly. Two poor films in Hollywood, plus the pool fiasco there; my reconciliation with and second break-up from Dennis; appalling notices for *The Long Haul*; the boat explosion and other troubles at Maidenhead which were reported avidly in the press; all these helped to frighten away producers and directors. And so when I was offered *Passport To Shame* at a smaller fee of £8,000, I was grateful to accept. Indeed, it was good just to be back in harness, for life at the farm with Tommy had become uneventful and often dull.

When my role was finished, I had to look around and take stock again. A business friend had the idea of producing a 'Diana Dors Shampoo', to be sold at Woolworth's, and he persuaded me to invest £7,000 in the venture. But I couldn't sit around and wait for that to come to fruition. Then an agent, Joe Collins, father of Joan and Jackie, asked if I would be interested in taking the Diana Dors Show around the remaining variety theatres, and to some cinemas. I took his offer, and it was arranged we'd put our bill in on a percentage basis with the theatres.

Joe said he could fill the entire show with acts he managed, but that we needed a good comedian to do several spots and, having warmed up the audience, introduce me. It was all rather like the old days of touring in variety and cashing in on my screen name. Except for one big difference. In those days I was on the way up; now I was on the way down!

Digby Wolfe, an actor friend from when Michael and I were together, was fast making his mark as a television comedian, and Joe suggested him. I liked the idea, especially knowing Digby so well, but Tommy had a better thought.

'What about that Dickie Dawson?' he volunteered.

I wasn't too keen, nor was Joe, but for once Tommy asserted himself, and when Dickie was found to be available for the tour, Joe signed him.

As I was doing some additional shots for *Passport To Shame*, Dickie came down to the set, and together we wrote a script we could perform on stage. Working with him, I found he was extremely funny, very quick-witted, and I was happy Tommy had insisted on his being in my show.

The tour was due to start at Coventry, and I set off with an entourage that included Jozy, who was to act as my dresser, and another old friend, Jackie Wadham, as chauffeur. Tommy had lost his licence as a result of a stupid incident in London months before when an eager policeman threw himself on the bonnet of our car in a theatrical gesture! Once again this had been blown up by the press, providing yet another piece of bad publicity. 'Why did the bubble burst?' was typical of the headlines used by some columnists, anxious to kick me on my way down the ladder. Before we left I placed £11,000 cash in a safe deposit box at Harrods, giving Tommy a key and authority to open it in case I should need ready money while I was away from home. But as things turned out it was to be the one occasion when I should not have trusted him!

The show was a great success, and Dickie and I often had the audiences giving us standing ovations. He was marvellous to work with, and as the weeks went by I began enjoying his company off-stage, too. I realised I was in love with Dickie when Tommy had flown to Switzerland to collect some money owed me from a previous film.

To recount it all now seems harsh on Tommy, for he was

given a raw deal. But the game of love has no rules, and the simple fact was that Dickie made me laugh. Tommy did not. I made no attempt to hide how I felt; intrigue and deceit were not what I wanted. However, there is no easy way to tell someone you are no longer in love, or that you love someone else, and Tommy was utterly destroyed. I pleaded with him to go back to the farm and not create trouble – we had had enough of that in our time. Eventually, after much emotion had been spent, he returned to Sussex, leaving me to continue a giddy tour of the country with Dickie, wildly in love and with success following success.

As the show neared its end, I telephoned the farm to ask Tommy if he would leave, for I wanted to return home. Angrily he accused me of wasting his time for eighteen months, and flung many contemptuous remarks about Dickie. He also warned me he'd done something I wouldn't like, though I paid as little heed to this as to his other angry statements. It wasn't until Dickie and I were in London one day and I asked at Harrods for my safe deposit box that I discovered what Tommy had referred to menacingly as the ace up his sleeve. He had taken all my money, £11,000, and left me with an empty steel box.

I was stunned. Perhaps I deserved it for falling in love with Dickie. But I had always trusted him implicitly. Frantically I rang his mother and asked her where he was. 'My Tommy is a good boy. He has not taken your money', came her loyal answer as I tried to explain what he'd done. Mutual friends, too, refused to reveal his whereabouts and I realised that, because the cash was secret, there was nothing I could do legally. Indeed, it was going to be difficult convincing anyone exactly how much, if anything, had been there at all.

Yet reporting the matter to the police seemed the only move left to me. Once again I begged Mrs Yeardye to tell me where Tommy was in order to avoid such a measure, but she remained adamant, steadfastly refusing to believe her son was capable of doing anything wrong. And so, after several dreadful days of silence, I reluctantly walked into

Chelsea police station and made a statement. The officer I saw, who was later murdered in a shooting, sympathised over my predicament and said confidently:

'We'll find him and get your money back.'

However, had it not been for a chance meeting with Frank Craddock, the man who bought the Penthouse, I don't believe the problem would ever have been resolved successfully. He had remained friendly with Tommy and me after our move to the farm, even making us a present of a Land Rover in which we used to speed around the eighty acres, knowing we were safely on our own property. Now he told me that his wife had seen Tommy on the beach where he was holidaying in the south of France. He was even staying at the same hotel as she was. Frank, who knew what had happened, immediately informed the French police, and they insisted that Tommy return to England at once to give his account of the matter.

By now the newspapers were full of it, and I realised with dismay that my £11,000 would be of great interest to the taxman. Large photographs recorded Tommy's arrival at London Airport, and there were reports in which he said he had taken the money only to teach me a lesson. He had hidden it in a safe place ready for the time I came to my senses! But for my part all I wanted was my money returned and for the glaring spotlight of publicity to be turned off. I told the police that I did not wish to prefer charges against a man who for more than a year had been so close, smoothing the matter over with them and the press by pretending it was just a lovers quarrel! Then Tommy, having retrieved the money, and I met for a showdown at Frank Craddock's London home.

'You're a fool to fall in love with Dawson', Tommy said bitterly. 'He'll turn out to be like all the rest of the men in your life.'

Obviously he excluded himself, despite the events which had just occurred. But there was no use arguing any more. Tommy and I were finished. I was sad, for he had been wonderful in many ways, and yet even though I knew 'there was no evil in him', as my father had said, selfishly I discarded him for a new romance.

We parted company on a cool note, but some weeks later he rang me at home. I listened in amazement as he itemised sundry objects still in my possession which he felt belonged to him. I agreed about the long-playing records, but as the list grew longer and he began to discuss who should have custody of an ice-bucket we had been given as a house-warming present, I felt the conversation had gone far enough.

'Really, Tommy, we were not actually married', I said. 'There is no obligation on my part to let you have anything.'

'You had eighteen months of my life', he replied curtly. 'The very least you could have done was to give me the *farm*!'

CHAPTER EIGHT

FOR BETTER, FOR WORSE

Little Jack Horner sat in a corner,
Eating a big plum pie!

'Dickie Dawson *had* to marry a star', show-business associates of his told me twenty years later as they remembered the man who was born Colin Emm, in Gosport, Hampshire. But had I heard their stories then, I would not have listened, so besotted was I with someone who made me laugh all the time, impersonated stars like Robert Mitchum, Jerry Lewis and, of course, Rod Steiger, and whose every waking minute was devoted to making me happy. Dickie wrote brilliantly funny material for us to perform together on stage, was filled with ideas to reshape my sagging career, and seemed a perfect match for my personality. He was also fiercely ambitious and ruthlessly determined to become a star.

Colin Emm came from a simple working-class background with no qualifications other than a talent for comedy. But Dickie Dawson, a name suggested by an agent who thought it might sound good for a comedian, told me he was a Canadian Jew whose mother had died of cancer and whose father and brother were living somewhere in America. He never saw them, he said sadly, because there had been a family rift at the time of his mother's death. But an uncle and aunt, who lived in Gosport, had looked after him when he first arrived in England and so he gave his affection to them instead! There was also an elderly Jewish grandmother, hospitalised near Bristol, whom he visited occasionally! At least that is what I was led to believe.

Thrilled as I was with this vibrant new man in my life, I never questioned any of what he told me, content only to think that I had at last found the answer to everything I wanted. I was even able to resume on good terms with Dennis, whom I had not seen since the move to Sussex. He actually telephoned to express his pleasure over my association with Dickie.

'I like that young man', he told me. 'He's very talented. I used to enjoy his act at the Stork Club.'

It was good talking to him again after all the bad times of the past, and I enquired about his health. Rumours had reached me that he was not well, tiring quickly on the tennis court and sometimes experiencing severe heat spasms which necessitated changing the sheets on his bed several times during the night. I couldn't imagine Dennis ever being unwell, or lacking in energy, and he waved away my fears by casually stating that he was going into the London Clinic for a check-up.

'I've probably been overdoing things!' he said cheerfully with his usual old exuberance.

Dickie quite enjoyed living on the farm, for it was truly a lovely place, and its charm had recently been enhanced by the arrival of Betty Lou, a Jersey cow given to me when Dickie and I were appearing in Dublin. But neither of us knew anything about running a property which boasted good land for growing corn, a herd of beef cattle, 400 pigs, several horses, chickens and goats, for to make a profit things had to be done personally. Instead, I was employing a manager and two labourers to do the work, and that meant paying wages as well as spending vast sums for all the necessities a farm demands. Despite the fact that Betty Lou made a pretty picture in her stall, I was seeing no financial return.

Away from our idyllic home, though, stormclouds were gathering in other areas. RKO Studios, in an effort to prevent paying any more money on my contract, pulled the infamous 'morals clause' on the basis of a report in a scandal-raking newspaper, *The New York Enquirer*, that I had danced topless on a table at a house-party in Hyde

Park's Rotten Row. The fact that there are no houses there, merely horses cantering along (hence its name), was overlooked as RKO seized their chance to save a quarter of a million dollars due to me. It did, however, help me to win a libel suit against the *Enquirer*, and eventually the dispute with RKO was settled in 1961. By then so many lawyers were involved that everyone except me made a fortune.

On the British front I had a very interested taxman and an even more angry agent making enquiries about my earnings on *Tread Softly Stranger*, £10,000 of which I had asked for in cash, unknown to anyone. So I needed money badly, and in desperation I agreed to terminate my £25,000 Rank contract and settle for the small sum of £7,000. Rank must have been delighted, especially as they had no future film plans for me.

On the personal side, I developed health problems – an acute stomach pain, which occurred intermittently, causing me to double up in agony and take to bed for days at a time. It reached the point where a doctor had to be summoned in the middle of the night to administer morphine. He diagnosed something called pancreatitis and warned that it could be fatal if I ate or drank certain things during my lifetime. Dickie and I had been in the middle of performing our show in a London theatre when I became ill, and now he cared for me attentively, sometimes showering me with expensive presents. So in love with him, it never bothered me to wonder how he could afford such gifts, for I knew how much he had been making from our show. I simply enjoyed his presence.

Dennis, too, was now seriously ill in hospital, and it seemed that things were going badly for him as well. The previous months had seen him involved with the notorious landlord, Peter Rachman, to whom, owing to a shortage of cash, he had sold 'Woodhurst' and the coffee-bar. Sholly had been dismissed, and died soon afterwards from a brain haemorrhage, apparently being buried in a pauper's grave in Chelsea, near to the block of council flats where her husband lived. Dennis rented out El Dors and reluctantly moved back to a small, luxury mews flat in Belgravia. He had never been a city boy. When he was in hospital and learnt that Dickie and I would need somewhere to stay while doing our show in London, he offered to let us live there.

Having recovered from my illness, I went to see Dennis in the hospital, taking him flowers. He was in a highly emotional state, and kept repeating that the doctors had told him he had only a few years to live.

'That can't be!' I said incredulously. 'What's wrong with you?'

'I have a heart infection', he moaned. 'The bastards are giving me twenty injections a day.'

'Thousands of people have heart complaints', I commiserated. 'My father was given ten years to live in 1918, and he's still going strong. You'll just have to slow down when you come out; take life at a quieter pace.'

'God, you don't understand. Nobody understands!' he cried, burying his face in the pillow.

'He keeps on like this all the time', said Vera, a little blonde actress who had lived with him in the Belgravia house until he had been admitted to hospital. 'I've tried to tell him everything will be all right, but he insists he's going to die.'

'Dennis has always been so healthy, he can't come to terms with being confined in hospital', I whispered to her. 'He's probably feeling sorry for himself and just after sympathy.'

I genuinely felt this to be true, for Dennis made a habit of telephoning all his friends every day, sobbing that he was dying or that the doctors didn't know what they were doing. He was also paranoiac that everyone was after him – which was not surprising considering the number of husbands he had upset – and matters were not helped when his parents, now legally separated, came to visit him at the same time and had a stand-up fight over his bed!

Yet there were also times when the cheeky old Dennis shone through. My lawyer was trying to draw up a divorce petition on my behalf, with Dennis's agreement, so that Dickie and I would be free to marry. But when he wrote to

Dennis asking for a list of his infidelities, he received a reply that he [Dennis] could write all of them down only if the lawyer had a spare week in which to read them!

Dickie and I received an offer to go to South Africa in December for a cabaret season in Johannesburg and Durban. As it was worth £1,000, we happily accepted and flew off to the sun. I'd also received, through an American agent I knew, a contract to appear on the Steve Allen television show in New York for $7,000 early in 1959, news that thrilled Dickie, for his greatest ambition was to go to America. Again it did not occur to me that, if he was a Canadian and his father was living in the States as he had told me, he could have gone there any time before we met!

Although Dickie was still the amusing, witty character I had always known, little upsets were occasionally creeping into our relationship. For one thing he was extremely jealous. On one occasion he destroyed a photograph of Tommy and me with a foal at the farm, a photo especially treasured as it was the first foal I had seen born. There had also been the weekend when Jon Pertwee, now fully recovered from the break-up of his marriage to Jean, visited us and he and I went to view an old cottage Jon contemplated buying. Dickie became extremely jealous, refusing to speak to us for hours.

Jon, when discussing Dickie's behaviour with me, told me in serious tones: 'I knew you two would be attracted to each other when I heard you were working together. But he is not the man for you. Dennis had his faults, but this one is certainly not the answer.' For a while I felt he might possibly be right, but eventually Dickie came out of his mood so, optimistically and in love, I put Jon's advice behind me.

The South African trip went well. We enjoyed the sunshine, scenery and hospitality everywhere, not knowing that in England Dennis had been discharged from the London Clinic – on condition he took things carefully. It was an impossible condition to impose on someone like Dennis. His first act, within hours of release, was to drive straight to the club at Windsor and beat up the manager whom he believed was not paying rent. Not that anything was solved as a result of this action. The man had a lease, Dennis didn't get his money, which left him short of badly needed cash, and he completely upset his health. Within weeks of being let out he was readmitted, this time in much worse condition.

Christmas came and went, and soon it was time for Dickie and me to leave for New York. On our last evening at the farm, Dennis phoned from hospital. As before he was in a distressed state, this time asking sadly why I had burned his boat. 'I had nothing to do with it', I replied, not seeing why I should bear the blame any longer for the wretched incident. 'Someone else was responsible.' His tone changed and, despite how ill he felt, the old Dennis spark momentarily returned as he tried to extract the culprit's name. Wearily, and somehow realising there was no way in his state of health that he could gain retribution, I told him, and I could sense, at the other end of the line, Dennis frustratedly plotting his revenge. Berating himself, too, for ever blaming me.

'I must go, Dennis', I said when he calmed down. 'We leave for America tomorrow, and I have so much packing to do.'

'Goodbye, darling', he almost whispered. 'Remember, I love you.'

'I'll be back in about a month.'

'I will not be seeing you again.'

'Why ever not? Come on, Dennis, pull yourself together. You upset all of us when you talk like that.' I imagined that once again he was deliberately trying to get sympathy.

'I will not be here when you come back', he affirmed quietly.

The conversation disturbed me, and I tried to put it out of my mind by thinking that, in his own typical way, Dennis was attempting to ruin the trip.

'He's been talking like that for months. Just forget it', Dickie said, trying to put my troubled mind at ease.

In New York my success on Steve Allen's show, the biggest in America at that time, proved fantastic. I was instantly contracted to appear on three more throughout the next few months, at a fee of $7,000 each. Dickie was elated and, as we were already in the country, we decided to fly out to California for a holiday. I was a little apprehensive, not having been back to Hollywood for two and a half years, but Dickie was eager to see the film capital and so I overcame my fears.

We stayed with a girlfriend of mine who was expecting a baby by film actor Stephen Boyd, but I was often uneasy there because Dickie did not like her. Indeed, he appeared not to like any former friends of mine, and the pleasure of showing him around LA was marred by the old jealousy always creeping in! Two of the people he did not mind seeing, however, were Liberace, whom we both had met before we knew each other, and Roger Moore, then married to singer Dorothy Squires. Roger was under contract to Warner Brothers and he and Dot lived out there permanently. It was thanks to Lee Liberace, in fact, that we had such a wonderful holiday, for he invited us to journey with him from Hollywood to another beautiful home he had in Palm Springs.

While we were in Palm Springs, there was a telephone call for me from Lionel Crane, a British film writer living in Hollywood. My thoughts naturally flew to Dennis, but, thinking Lionel was after some silly story and used to being tricked by columnists, I told Lee's maid to inform him I was not there, even though he had said it was urgent.

On returning to Hollywood, Dickie and I went to visit Roger and Dot. It was a warm January day, and as we laughed, recalling old times in England, particularly Blackpool 1952 when Dennis and I first met Dot, the phone rang. 'It's Lionel Crane', said Dot, her hand over the receiver. 'He says it's urgent, and wants to know if I've seen you.'

Telling her to keep my whereabouts secret, I hurried to the bedroom and picked up an extension.

'What seems to be the trouble, Lionel?' Dot enquired.

'Dennis Hamilton died in the London Clinic today!' he replied grimly.

I could not believe what I'd heard. The rest of the day was a blur to me; so was the immediate flight home, which in those days took twenty-four hours via Denmark.

On my arrival at the farm, the hordes of waiting pressmen plied me with questions as to how I reacted to the
news. Would we have divorced? Could we have reconciled?
Was I going to marry Dickie now? Would I benefit from
Dennis's will? And then at last alone, as the mists swirled
around the farm on that winter evening, stunned by events
I never thought possible, I reflected on the shared years of
happiness and unhappiness. Dennis had gone. Nothing
could bring him back; that terrifying, vibrant, charming
man who seemed indestructible. Death was so final! Why
had it claimed him at only thirty-four?

How often had we all said of him: 'The Devil looks after
his own; he'll always be all right!' And this was true
throughout Dennis's life. But now the Devil had cruelly
cheated in this game of chance they played together. There
was no turning back the clock, no time for remorse or
recriminations. Just a lifetime to face, with unforgettable
memories.

The newspapers were having a field day, and I
remember thinking, sadly amused, that Dennis would have
revelled in the publicity! Indeed, I found it amazing that a
man of humble birth, with very little education and no
outstanding career, was being written about as if he were
royalty. Announcements of his death were made on the
radio, with the news containing a detailed report. Large
placards told London 'Dennis Hamilton Dies'. Columnists
wrote glowing epitaphs, one writer dedicating half a page to
'this extraordinary man, the kind who comes along every
now and then', comparing him with other notable
characters and mourning the emptiness which would
follow in his wake. The piece did go on to say, however, that
his playboy star had waned in the last months, and having
mentioned most of the women in his life, ended sadly by
stating that the 'girls who frequented his parties had moved
on to other parties'.

Because our time at Bray had been the happiest I knew
with Dennis, I telephoned his new lawyer the next day to
make arrangements for the funeral. I would have liked to

bury him in the little village churchyard there.

'I've done everything', he curtly informed me. 'The funeral will be at the Catholic Church in Spanish Place, London, on 3 February at noon.'

'But Dennis wasn't a Catholic', I said, my mind flashing back to the troubles we had had in America with the Women's Catholic Guild, Louella Parsons and the rest.

'Dennis Hamilton was received as a Roman Catholic three days before he died', came his answer.

I couldn't believe what was happening; it was all so impossible. I rang a friend to ask if this latest news was true.

'That lawyer is a fanatic Catholic', she told me. 'He was determined to convert him. The last time I saw Dennis he was sitting there in bed with a rosary around his neck!'

I tried to compare such a picture with that of the man I knew, and it seemed unreal. Yet if Dennis really did know he was dying, then, for all the lawyer's good intent, it was his own last, desperate attempt to straighten himself with God! Wheeling and dealing to the end, Dennis had tried to buy a fast ticket to heaven by turning Catholic before he met his Maker. Perhaps, I thought with half a smile, it was Dennis and not the Devil who had cheated.

As the lawyer obviously had everything under control, all I could do now was order a cross of flowers in readiness for the funeral in two days time. The simple wording,

'To my darling Dennis, with loving memories that words will never express. My love always. Diana.'

seemed so brief, almost hypocritical, remembering all the troubles we had endured, the fights, the separations. And so, for his private epitaph, which I knew the world would not see, I wrote:

When I am dead
Pull down my house
And leave the memories to crumble in the dust,
For this is all that's left of me
The monument of my accomplishments.

A tombstone for the rain to sprinkle with a watery hymn
And a shell that is a silent silhouette of all my thoughts
    and dreams.
Let the wind wail eerily through the broken walls
A song of things past,
Of joyous things, and tears that gave it sadness,
Of moments which were wonderful and good
And bitter-sweet remembrances.
In time there will be nothing there for anyone to see
Save the thin spider that crawls from under a secret stone
To keep a date with destiny
As we did.
And in the night will come the hooting of an owl
Who being wise may sometimes see
Strange ghostly shapes of all things past
Pale and silent in the cold moonlight
Until the coming of darkness as a cloud passes over the
    moon.

Somehow I felt this summed up his life, the house we
dreamed of and built, even though it had such bad
memories.

How could I have guessed as I wrote this poem that
eighteen years later 'Woodhurst', not the Penthouse, would
be totally destroyed to make way for two large blocks of
luxury flats? The old mansion we bought on a mortgage for
£12,000 – 'consolidating for our future', as Dennis often
said – had become a property worth £3,000,000.

The funeral, which Dickie had decided it was best for me
to attend alone, turned out to be more like a star-studded
premiere, with hundreds of people lining the streets outside
the church. Inside it was packed to capacity, and silently I
walked to the front pew. The atmosphere was heavy with
incense and ornate gold fittings were everywhere. Dennis's
coffin stood in the centre aisle draped in purple, with four
large tallow candles burning at each corner. It was the first
time I had been to a Catholic service, and when the priest
began talking in Latin, which I did not understand, it all
seemed like a scene from a foreign film.

Behind me sat many women, a number of whom had known Dennis intimately; others who had simply read about him. Jennifer Raymond, wearing a heavy black veil, cried nearby. She had visited his coffin to say a private farewell the evening before. When the service ended and I was walking down the aisle, strange women grabbed me, shouting 'All right, Diana, we still love you' and other nonsensical things. One even asked me for an autograph! Outside, too, there was mild hysteria, with men and women crying and Dennis's parents sobbing, calling out my name as if somehow I might be able to bring him back. Michael was there as well, though I didn't know it at the time, standing silently on the opposite side of the road, observing the whole charade. John, his brother, had died the previous year, and now Michael paid a quiet tribute to Dennis, away from the noisy crowd where starlets jostled for position to pose in front of cameras.

I couldn't bear the thought of going to the cemetery; and anyway no-one had told me where it was! I felt like a stranger who had gate-crashed a party, only no-one was laughing the way they usually did at Dennis's parties. Not one of his male friends offered to help me, or find a taxi in which I could get away from the whole bizarre affair.

Dickie was strangely remote when I returned to the farm, but I was too unhappy to care whether his mood was due to jealousy. There was no need for that as far as Dennis was concerned; he was no longer someone who stood in the way of our getting married, which was what Dickie wanted. But, in retrospect, he probably felt at the time that his chances of marrying me were somehow diminished by the grief I felt.

The day after came a further bombshell. Jon Pertwee, in a sombre, strange tone, phoned to ask if I would go to London to talk privately with him.

'What's the matter?' I enquired, a cold shiver passing through my body.

'Did you know the cause of Dennis's death?'

'Why, yes, his heart gave out. He had some sort of infection. More than likely it was due to the exhausting life he led.'

'Please come up here right away', said Jon. 'It is urgent and I can't discuss it on the phone.'

Without hesitation, Dickie and I drove to his house.

'I have a doctor friend at the London Clinic', Jon began as gently as possible. 'He got into conversation with the doctor on Dennis's case and heard the true facts.'

I couldn't imagine what he was leading up to, but obviously it was serious.

'Dennis died of tertiary syphilis!' he said grimly.

'My God, what's that?'

'Syphilis in its last stages! He must have contracted it about seventeen years ago. The germ lay dormant in his system after the first year, but gradually it ate away at his brain, his eyes and his heart until, in the end, it killed him.'

Suddenly all the events of the past years made sense. The brainstorms; the heatwaves that made him throw open windows when everyone else was cold; the blurred vision of which he complained. The syphilis had undoubtedly attacked his heart and blood vessels, leaving them, at the end, like blotting-paper! His outbursts of temper were the result of the brain's gradual disintegration. Now I understood his continual insistence that he was going to die, which we all believed to be merely an over-emotional reaction. Dennis had been told the truth by his doctors, but pride would not allow him to discuss the nature of his disease.

'I think you'd better get yourself a good lawyer', said Jon when the full shock had subsided slightly. 'Find out what the situation is regarding a will. If Dennis was insane at the time of his death, as seems highly probable, you need to know where you stand.'

'I'm not really interested in his money', I replied miserably.

'Nevertheless, why let the vultures take things that you worked to pay for originally?' Jon persisted, and he gave me the address of a firm of solicitors in London.

Dickie agreed with Jon that, under the circumstances, I should seek legal advice, and so reluctantly I went some days later to the firm Jon suggested. Our affairs were in such a ghastly state that I didn't really know what I was doing. Dennis had always handled the business side of my life so successfully, it seemed. Without him, I was already finding myself prey to men with smooth-talked legal phrases and financial deals that were little more to me than a jumble of figures. Now that Dennis's dance with Lucifer had come to an end, I was having to place my affairs in the hands of the Devil's earthly ministers – lawyers and agents.

The taxman, too, was to become another grasping man in my life, and now that Dennis was dead his attentions were growing increasingly intense, thanks to the publicity about our vast fortunes in and out of England! Her Majesty's Inspector of Taxes, like the world, waited to see how many millions Dennis had left in his will.

There were also foreign companies Dennis had formed, with the help of the now-disappeared Jimmy Mellon, monies owed in taxes for films I'd made over the years and a jigsaw of financial tangles concerning me which only a genius would attempt to unravel. All those papers that were pushed into my hand to sign on my return from the film studios could now be used against me in court. For how could I, now a grown woman of twenty-seven, convince a judge that I merely signed business papers on demand, without understanding or knowing what I was doing? And yet that is what happened.

At home, I took time to read about the disease of syphilis in a medical book, and it was like reading Dennis's biography! Brainstorms, emotional neurosis, persecution complexes, delusions of grandeur – the ornate furnishings and attempts to buy a Welsh castle and Fort Belvedere – sexual aberrations, disturbance of conduct that might necessitate bringing in the police, writing large cheques, schizophrenia, and completely demented behaviour. Now at last I knew what had been wrong with the man I married. A man who, when not bedevilled by these symptoms, could be a kind, gentle, artistic and loving person. How had I managed to survive six years with him?

My American television contract with Steve Allen came into force two weeks after Dennis's funeral, and so Dickie and I flew across to New York to fulfil it. By the time we returned to England the full extent of Dennis's will had been published, and to everyone's amazement, except mine, he left just £800 – to his parents. Where had all the rest gone? Again the press besieged me, but what could I tell them? Peter Rachman had 'Woodhurst', I didn't know who owned the coffee-bar or El Dors club. The Belgravia flat and its contents were tied up with one of the many companies Dennis had set up, and Jimmy Mellon was rumoured to have taken a large amount of cash and be living in the south of France on a yacht which had once been Dennis's.

The newspapers made much of the fact that I received nothing. And I could not really tell them that the only thing Dennis had bequeathed me were debts of thousands of pounds to the Inland Revenue for past income tax in the days when I believed he, Jimmy Mellon, and others were attending to everything. Being the only person left to attack, I was the obvious target for the taxman . . . and the bankruptcy courts. All that money I had made over the years, and now this. It seemed so unfair. All I could hope to do was salvage what I still had, and to do so I allowed everything I owned to be placed in a trust, with Dickie, myself and any children we might have as bene-ficiaries.

The question of marriage was now foremost in Dickie's mind, and before we left for America to do the last of the Steve Allen shows he bought a ring, insisting that we wed in New York. I was not keen to rush into marriage so soon after Dennis's death. It seemed wrong! Furthermore, I wanted to have a wedding at home, inviting all my friends and making it a happy celebration when it eventually happened. Dickie, however, was adamant that America was the place to do it, and the sooner the better.

On reflection, as I continually look back while writing about my life, it is difficult to imagine how weak-willed and stupid I was. Everyone makes mistakes, but I made more than my fair share and have no-one to blame other than myself.

Dickie went ahead and made all the plans as I rehearsed the show, and on the night we finished it he whisked me off immediately afterwards to the apartment of my American manager, on smart Riverside Drive. There, before a Jewish judge brought at great expense to perform the ceremony, we were married. The only people there who were actually friends – the rest were all business associates of the manager – turned out to be Jean Marsh and the actor of whom she had talked on Dennis's tape-recorder several years before. He was appearing in a Broadway play and they were living in New York.

A large reception was held at some fashionable night-club. Flashbulbs popped, we cut a beautiful wedding-cake and guests toasted our future happiness in champagne. Most of them were show-business personalities and columnists, but other than Steve Allen I knew hardly anybody! It felt strange being 'Mrs Dawson' suddenly, after the years as 'Mrs Hamilton'. When someone said, 'Your husband is over there looking for you', I thought she meant Dennis. In only eight weeks I had been an estranged wife, widowed, and married again!

Dickie had also changed his name, by deed poll now, to Richard Dawson, and Richard was what he preferred to be called. What I didn't realise, though, was how changed I was going to find this man now that we had exchanged marriage vows. I was given cause to think about it many years later when I was chatting with comedienne Hylda Baker about the broken marriage of a well-known show-business couple. I expressed surprise at how much the husband had changed since the days when we were all friends, but Hylda was blunt in her approach.

'He didn't change', she said. 'He just went back to being who he really was before she picked him up!'

How similar to Richard Dawson, I thought.

Gone was the man who made me laugh all the time. Gone were the impersonations; the hilarious sketches before breakfast. Now I found myself living with a man who could not be spoken to until well past noon, who stopped amusing me alone unless there was an audience or friends to impress. Not that there were many of those, for few of my former friends were acceptable. I became aware of the change in our relationship slowly. It was slight at first, manifesting itself more and more as time went by so that, once again, I was not fully aware of everything until it was too late.

Dickie was now busy writing the script for a television show called *The Diana Dors Show*. Naturally I was the star; he also took part, and two American guests were flown over for it. Singer-actress Shirley Jones had just won an Oscar for her supporting role in *Elmer Gantry*, and she appeared on the show with her husband, handsome Jack Cassidy, father of David who became an international pop star when he grew up. Jack and Shirley later divorced, and he was tragically burnt to death some seventeen years later in a fire at his Hollywood apartment.

The show, on which I impersonated Marlene Dietrich, Eartha Kitt, Clara Bow and Marilyn Monroe, as well as singing, dancing and performing sketches with Dickie, was a great success we were instantly signed to do another. However, something happened that was to put paid to such plans – temporarily at least! I discovered I was pregnant.

Unlike Dennis, whose reaction had been to find me an abortionist, Dickie was thrilled by the prospect of parenthood. Indeed so was I, for at nearly twenty-eight I thought I should have a baby before I grew too old. As a woman friend had told me once: 'There's no perfect time to start a family, but if you keep putting the moment off, eventually it will be too late.' Nevertheless I would still need money, and so my agent, newly acquired by Dickie, arranged a quick succession of cabaret engagements.

Accompanied by Dickie, I appeared at the exclusive Palm Beach Casino in Cannes, at several others in Italy, and did a week of exhausting late-night shows in Madrid, not appearing until two in the morning. As before in the early days of pregnancy I felt very sick and wanted to do nothing but sleep all the time. Some nights I would fall asleep after dinner, only to be woken at midnight, have to put on make-up and get down to the club where I waited endlessly before doing my show.

Dickie and I also decided to sell the farm, for it was a tremendous expense and much too far away from London for convenience. So we looked around, found a pleasant, modern house at Virginia Water in Surrey and sold the farm for £25,000, a vast sum in those days! It certainly meant we would be able to relax when my working days had finished, especially as Dickie's earnings seemed to be limited to occasional cabaret performances.

But, as I discovered, there were other sources of income, pregnant or not. An agent approached me with the idea of selling my life story to the *News of the World* newspaper. A little prematurely at twenty-eight, I felt, but all such thoughts evaporated when he told me he had extracted the phenomenal amount of £35,000 for a twelve-week serialisation! Errol Flynn had sold his story for £36,000, beating me by a thousand. What I did not realise, though, was that my 'life' story was going to turn out to be a cheap, lurid version of life with Dennis, his voyeurism, two-way-mirror parties and so on. Scandal and shockable sensation were what the readers wanted on Sunday morning, and scandal and sensation they were given, however untrue were some of the colourful accounts written to sell more newspapers. But what could I do? The contract was signed; they were paying such a gigantic figure. I tried to pretend I didn't really mind what they wrote, and closed my mind to my father's reaction when the story finally poured out in the press. The effect it would have on my career and my reputation didn't bear thinking about.

The irony of it, of course, is that it was only my reputation that was on the line, but other people were partaking in the fee. The agent, having negotiated such a brilliant deal, took his healthy percentage, and then before publication came another hand for its share – the writer with whom Dennis had done a deal to write my life story, all those years ago in Hollywood. Injunction threats were being waved about like flags at a football match; out came contracts which Dennis had signed and which I knew nothing about. The lawyers tugged their wigs and pontificated over their port before presenting me with an ultimatum: the writer would have to be paid a substantial sum or we could not go ahead with publication in the *News of the World*. So disappeared another chunk of my share.

Once the story began running in the newspaper, all my worst fears were realised and I came under some of the worst attacks I had ever experienced. The Archbishop of Canterbury denounced me as a wayward hussy! Baroness Stocks, a campaigner for decency, stated on radio that the best thing I could do for my unborn child was to have it adopted when it was born! And the world in general, though eager to read the tawdry rubbish dished up each Sunday, condemned me for allowing such a story to be printed. And of course *they* were right. I *had* sold my soul to the Devil – or at least to his advocates – for money. For this was only early 1960. The Christine Keeler scandal that rocked the Government was still three years away. England was not yet the free-thinking, unconventional country of the permissive society and the Swinging Sixties. So my memoirs in the *News of the World* were considered disgraceful. Today, rather like my innocent little pin-up picture book, *Diana Dors in 3D*, they would be laughed at.

Nor did my ordeal end with the completion of *my* story. Two friends from the old days, who had enjoyed Dennis's and my hospitality to the extent of being lent money, now decided that they too were going to get in on the act. With the birth of my baby imminent, another paper emblazoned their story of MR DORS AS WE KNEW HIM. Containing untrue facts about our private lives, it ran for three sordid weeks and was followed by Tommy Yeardye's version of *his* life with me.

The whole episode upset me terribly and was not an ideal preparation for any woman giving birth to her first child. Consequently I was in great emotional turmoil when I arrived, labour pains racking my body, at the London Clinic, where Dennis had died just a year earlier. 'Please don't let them write it!' I screamed before succumbing to the anaesthetic, and then my mind and body gave way to the process of nature. It took twenty-seven hours to give birth to my son, Mark Richard, who was nearly suffocated in the process. But the unbelievable pain I suffered vanished from memory at the sight of my baby. It was an experience I will never forget, and I loved him with all my heart. Dickie gave me a bracelet with the inscription, 'Thank you for Mark Richard', flowers poured in from everywhere and, as all mothers feel after such an event, I was contented and happy. No post-natal blues for me. Just relief that it was all over and, after such a horrendous ordeal, thankful to God that my son was perfectly healthy.

Once more the press made headlines out of it, just as they had when Brigitte Bardot gave birth to her first child three weeks earlier. 'I wasn't aware there was any contest', I told them icily when they excitedly phoned to tell me she had won the race. But now it was 'our' turn, and photographs appeared of 'baby Dors' and his beautiful frilly cradle fit for a fairy-tale princess. I had secretly hoped my baby would be a girl! No matter; I was thrilled with having a son. And in the ecstasy of motherhood, how could I envisage then that babies grow into people, inheriting the traits of their parents?

Within a month of Mark's arrival, Dickie and my agent flew to America to negotiate a contract for me to appear in Las Vegas, at $7,000 a week, and there was also work in a television play in England. I was quickly being made to come to terms with the fact that I was a working mother! But if my agent was proving his ability in show-business circles, his judgment elsewhere was not always so shrewd.

A company were planning to film the novel *Saturday Night and Sunday Morning* with a new, exciting, young actor named Albert Finney, and they wanted me to play the leading female role opposite him. As they had very little money, they could offer only £500. But when I read the script, I was horrified to see that the part called for the woman to attempt an abortion! Disciplined as I had been for years with strict censorship in Mr Rank's film industry, I was embarrassed at the idea of acting such a scene, even though I

longed to make a film that would restore my reputation as
an actress.

What I did not realise then was that this film would
signal the beginning of a new era in British films with
censorship, along with everything else, going haywire. But
it wasn't the problem of my portraying a pregnant woman
trying to have an abortion that influenced my agent's decision for me not to do the film. It was the fact that it paid no
money, and that Albert Finney was an unknown quantity!
So he turned down a role which could have put me back
where I was after *Yield To The Night*, thereby rejuvenating
my professional reputation and helping to overcome the
social abyss into which the newspaper serial had plunged
me. Rachel Roberts accepted the part and won many
awards for her portrayal. Years later, at a Hollywood party,
she graciously thanked me for giving her the chance of a
lifetime!

Money, it seemed, was the keynote as far as my career
was concerned now, and a contract was signed for me to
appear for a month at The Dunes hotel in Las Vegas. That
old Jewish joke, 'Never mind the quality, feel the width',
seemed altogether very appropriate as I found my professional life coming under the dominance of several
shrewd but highly ambitious men.

I was unhappy at the thought of leaving Mark, even
though I had luckily found a most reliable nurse to care for
him. Amy Baker was an incredible woman who had never
married and could do anything and everything
domestically. She was slightly psychic, often seeing things
far into the future, but she also lived in a total fantasy
world – to the extent of regarding Mark as her own! Not
that I realised any of this at the time as plans went ahead for
me to fly to America. I was simply grateful that she loved
my son and would die rather than let anything happen to
him. There had already been one kidnap threat on his life,
but the police caught the offender, a boy of seventeen, and
sent him to prison.

I was sadly ignorant of how to care for an infant; indeed,
I was stupid about all domestic matters then. Whereas

Amy developed an affinity with this tiny baby of mine from the start and took him over completely. With her long black hair hanging down to the waist of her nightgown, she looked strangely witchlike as she crooned to Mark when he cried in the middle of the night.

'I knew from the moment he grabbed hold of my little finger that he was *mine*', she muttered quietly before I reluctantly departed to appear in Las Vegas. Was it just my aching heart at going away, or was it some deeper knowledge that made me feel, even then, that those safe hands in which I was entrusting my son were one day going to steer him away from me?

Our first stop was New York, where Dickie and I enlisted the services of a musical arranger and producer for my début in Vegas. And then, after a week, we all journeyed out to Los Angeles to stay for a few days at Liberace's house in order to rehearse and develop the act before heading for Nevada. It was a beautiful home on Sherman Drive, and had I possessed the crystal ball Amy once informed me her father had smashed, I would have been able to see the baby for whom I pined grown to manhood and living with his first real love in an apartment just opposite Liberace's home.

I opened successfully in Las Vegas, where the temperature was 119 degrees, and where I worked seven nights a week, three shows a night for a month. It was a peculiar existence, and one which I didn't much like. I would sleep all day, awaken and breakfast at 6.00 p.m., be ready to appear on stage two hours later for the dinner show and then hang around the casino or talk to people until the second show at midnight. My final appearance was the two o'clock late-night show, and I would be off-stage by four. However, sleep was impossible immediately, so I usually played a little blackjack or roulette, had a meal in the coffee-shop, watching the sun rise over the desert, and finally retired to bed – the coolest place to be in that inferno – until six in the evening.

After several weeks of this strange life I began to feel really ill, added to which I was very homesick for Mark.

What was the point of going through all that pain and misery for nine months if now I was parted from him? Dickie was enjoying life to the full, gambling, meeting American comedians and stars, as well as gangsters, who fascinated him, but he sensed that I was growing restless and unhappy when I missed a couple of performances through illness. Moreover, The Dunes wished to renew my contract for a further month, at a rise of $10,000 a week, so something had to be done to keep me appeased.

One evening, when I returned to our suite after the dinner show, he announced that our lawyer had arrived to discuss our business affairs, and to begin working with American lawyers on the case against RKO for the money they owed me on the cancelled contract.

'He's in the next suite', said Dickie mysteriously. 'It's been a tiring journey, but I think you can go in and see him now.' As I opened the door of the adjoining apartment, there gurgling in Amy's arms was my son Mark, now four months old. My joy was indescribable, and the knowledge that they were going to stay for the rest of my engagement made me a stronger, happier woman. The lawyer was there too, of course. And during the daytime, as Mark learnt to splash in the pool, I sat with him and Dickie, signing papers and trying to concentrate on legal matters but all the while really watching my beautiful baby. He was something special; everyone agreed. A devastating-looking child with his vivid blue eyes and golden hair.

My show finally ended, and at last I hoped we could return to England. I'd had enough of America and wanted the beauty of my home where, despite the fact I'd put in a marvellous indoor pool and cinema, I had lived for only six months! Dickie had other plans, though. He loved America as much as I disliked it and was in no hurry to leave. So an offer for me to appear twice-nightly in cabaret for $12,000 a week at a club in Lake Tahoe was accepted on my behalf. We had our own chalet overlooking some of the most glorious scenery in the world. Roger Moore and Dot Squires visited us and we had a wonderful time. But it was not home. Nor was our next stop, Hollywood, where Dickie had fixed a two-week engagement at Ciro's nightclub so we took up residence in what had once been Greta Garbo's mansion.

My cabaret at Ciro's caused quite a stir, and suddenly there were a few offers of films, one with Jerry Lewis and the other for Danny Kaye. It all seemed to be happening again for me career-wise, but I truly wanted to return home to England and so did Amy, who really missed the quiet life of our home in Virginia Water. She was constantly grumbling to me about everything American, though never daring to do so in front of Dickie, of whom in an odd way she seemed frightened. What had brought this about I don't really know. However, I was becoming aware of the intensity of his ambition, which became more and more determined as I went from strength to strength professionally. On a personal level I suffered more from his moods. Naturally they were nothing like Dennis's, but at least when Dennis blew up it was all over in minutes. With Dickie it was like a cold war; days of silence would pass between us and were much more damaging to our relationship than any physical violence. Where, I often wondered, was the amusing, witty young man I had met and married? Had he hoped to take America by storm as a comedian, and had the lack of overnight success left him bitter and frustrated? Was he awe-struck by the depth of talent in Hollywood, but afraid to voice his fears to me?

Pam Mason, whom I'd met on my first visit to Hollywood with Dennis, was shrewd in her assessment of people, and she thought highly of Dickie's talent. Dickie adored her, for she was an extremely clever, witty woman with a brilliant mind. She had her own television show, too, and knew every influential person in town. But Pam was too old a hand to know that you don't find success that easily. Dickie might have gone to America expecting to be the next Jack Benny, but he was going to have to wait for five long frustrating years to see his names in lights, and in the meantime someone had to pay the bills, playing places in Chicago, New York, Texas and God knows where. Moreover I was doing it mostly on my own, for Dickie preferred to remain in Los Angeles where the action was.

The decision to stay on in Los Angeles was made not so much by myself as by the threat of bankruptcy in England and the fact that I could earn so much more money in the States. Advised to sell our lovely new house, and receiving an offer of £21,000 for it – a small fortune in 1960 – I agreed to part with it, and Dickie flew back to negotiate the final arrangements and sell off most of its contents. Items I treasured, mementoes of my years with Dennis and many of them valuable, disappeared out of my life forever – and without my knowledge at the time. Others were put into storage and shipped to America to find a place in the lovely house we found on Angelo Drive in Beverly Hills. At $175,000, it was considerably more than I could afford, but with the help of a mortgage and the money from the Virginia Water house it seemed the most sensible thing to do. I couldn't go on indefinitely paying rent for Greta Garbo's mansion.

Dickie, of course, was delighted that we were going to live in the United States. And yet at the same time I began to feel that he almost preferred not to be associated with me. It's hard to remember the actual moment I noticed it, but getting ready one night to go out with Pam, I suddenly realised how little Dickie and I went out together as a couple. Indeed, it began to be a joke between Pam and me that we went out together so much more than Dickie and I ever did that we would become a 'hot item' in the gossip columns. And on those few occasions when Dickie did accompany me anywhere, immediately we entered the room, it seemed, he would leave my side and go off to entertain whomever else was present.

It was almost as though, having married me for who I was, he now resented my status and desperately wanted to become known as a personality in his own right. Where Dennis had revelled in being known as 'Mr Dors', Dickie detested it. There was nothing wrong with this, but he married me knowing that I was the star. Why fight against it now? When I wore plunging necklines and figure-hugging dresses, which in the early days he had liked, he now scorned me for looking like a tart! In short, I could do nothing right, and I began to feel that he almost despised me.

Nor was Dickie the only one who seemed to resent my presence. Mark, now just one year old, worshipped Amy to the extent that he would scream 'get out' if I so much as entered the room where they were. Amy, knowing she was indispensable because I needed her to care for him when I was forced to go away and work, ruled the house as if it were her own, creating unbearable atmospheres if things did not go to her satisfaction. What with her and Dickie's moods, I would sometimes creep into *my* house not daring to see anyone and go straight to my bedroom in case someone somewhere was throwing a tantrum.

Dickie's extravagance was also alarming; not just to me but also to our financial advisers. One day I returned home from working on an Alfred Hitchcock television film to find that the entire terrace had been converted into what looked like a fairground, with slot machines and rifle-ranges, all bought at vast expense. He continually bought Mark toys and gadgets he was much too young to appreciate. It was as if he was trying to make up for all the things he had not had himself in childhood. I also discovered, through an American manager I had acquired, that Dickie lost a sum of money, said to be $10,000, in a new nightclub in Florida which went broke!

My protests about such a waste of money were ignored, and he would retire to his own bedroom for days on end, sleeping the clock round with the aid of enormous quantities of sleeping-pills. (He suffered badly from insomnia.) It was almost as if he was trying to hide himself from the world by finding security among the sheets and blankets.

Inevitably, when a man treats a woman with disdain and contempt – especially when and because she's paying the bills – another man will come along to give her the love and attention she craves. For me, that man was a young Hollywood actor named John Ashley. We met on his television series, *The Racers*. I fell in love, if that's what it can be called, and started having an affair.

Our romance was helped by the fact that Dickie decided
to fly to England to help the lawyers sort out income tax
matters, and we were both scheduled to go to Miami: John
for his television series, and me to guest on a big television
spectacular being filmed there. It was a perfect setting for
lovers, and by the time we returned to Hollywood John was
begging me to divorce Dickie and marry him.

A doctor's son from Oklahoma, John was anxious to
inform his family of his intentions, but before he could do
this it was essential that divorce proceedings begin and
determinedly he dragged me to a lawyer. Sam Brody, who
was later Jayne Mansfield's lover and was killed with her in
a terrible car crash, listened to John's pleas for some kind of
divorce to commence. However, there was not a great deal
to go on. Even in America it was going to prove difficult to
obtain a divorce simply by describing Dickie's complex and
peculiar behaviour towards me.

Moreover, my own feelings about a divorce were very
mixed, for although my infatuation was for John, my
sympathy lay with Dickie's predicament if we divorced. He
would have nothing, or nowhere to live, as a result, and this
preyed on my conscience. Not that John knew anything of
my thoughts. He remained optimistic and was happy that
he had at least persuaded me to do something regarding a
forthcoming marriage. He drove around town in his
Porsche, with a gold bracelet of mine clipped to the exhaust
pipe like an engagement ring; and with Dickie away we
spent idyllic hours at my home, oblivious of the critical eye
of Amy and, as only lovers can, thinking no-one else existed
in the world.

One evening, after dining at our favourite restaurant, we
arrived back at the house hand in hand, entering through
the sliding glass door that led into the enormous drawing-
room. And there sitting on the sofa was Dickie! He had, of
course, extracted the whole story of our affair from Amy
and white-faced with anger told John to get out of *his*
house.

That night was truly the beginning of the end for Dickie
and me. Nothing can ever erase the scars left by such

wounds or mend the broken bonds of trust. Ashamedly I tried to explain the facts of my affair and to tell him it was better that we divorced. Our marriage had hardly been perfect. But his main concern seemed to be what he would do. Where he would go. And I felt responsible for him!

John and I met the next day to discuss matters, but our immediate plans were not helped by the fact that I was contracted to do a three-week cabaret tour of South America. At first he considered accompanying me, but then we both thought that would be foolish. And so, after a week of secret meetings with the situation at home growing more miserable, I sadly bade John goodbye, and, with a heavy heart, set off on my marathon trip.

They were three of the worst weeks of my life. Despite the presence of my American manager, I felt totally alone and despondent, touring around countries like Argentina, Peru, Chile and Uruguay, surrounded by foreigners and unable to contact John by phone or letter. Slowly, though, the wretched tour drew to an end and I flew back to Los Angeles with only one thought in mind. To see him as soon as possible.

But it was Dickie who met me at the airport, carrying little Mark with a red rose held out to greet me. It all presented a pretty, sympathetic picture and made me feel more guilty than ever. No doubt the object of the exercise, for it was a long time since Dickie had welcomed me back from work. However, there was a depressing scene at home when I told him I was going to see John. And later that day, at John's apartment, I learnt that Dickie had met with him during my absence and agreed he would not stand in the path of our future happiness *if* we waited for one year before meeting again. As we talked, Dickie arrived and a terrible scene ensued in which the man I thought I adored completely disintegrated in my eyes and my husband, who was not a violent person, triumphed.

As much as I abhorred the situation, I could not help respecting Dickie's behaviour. As for John? My infatuation for him still prevailed, but I now knew he was not the man for me. This did not mean Dickie was, either, but John and

I decided to break with each other from that moment and I went home to an even lonelier existence than before.

Dickie and I talked at length. He was sympathetic towards me, saying that he understood how affairs like John's and mine happened. Without too much confidence we attempted to mend our marriage and for a short while things went smoothly, with Dickie attempting to be the sweet, amusing man he was when we first met. He even admitted that the cause of our troubles had been his own fault.

A London agent telephoned with an offer for me to do a cabaret there, and the thought of working in London again was so cheering that we immediately agreed. Besides, we had another good reason for accepting. In order to obtain our residents' cards, we had to leave America for a short period. We did not wish to become citizens, but all the time we were living there as aliens we were being heavily taxed.

We decided to leave Mark in Los Angeles with Amy, much to my father's relief. For on a quick visit home some months earlier, Amy had taken my son to stay with his grandfather and Aunty Kit.

'God save me from that impossible woman!' my poor father actually blasphemed. 'She obviously serves her purpose where the baby is concerned but she's no friend of yours.'

Amy's lies and fantasies had nearly driven him mad, and although he did not fully believe the tales she invented about me taking drugs, drink and heaven knows what, it was none the less worrying and disturbing for him. She had related dreadful stories about Dickie, too, but none of these either surprised or bothered my father. His opinion of Dickie was nearly as low as it had been of Dennis and Michael!

During the period when I was appearing in cabaret twice nightly at a new London club, we set about filling in the necessary papers for resident status in America. There seemed to be limitless questions pertaining to one's life, past, present and future, and as all our answers were fully investigated, we had been told it was unwise to lie or invent

them. Yet while perusing Dickie's form somewhat absent-
mindedly, I noted with amazement that as his parents'
names he had written those of the uncle and aunt in
Gosport.

'They're really your parents then?' I asked incredulously. 'Why did you lie to me about them?'

He gave a muttered story of 'not wanting to bother me
with relatives', and went off on some sudden errand in
order to avoid discussing the subject. I questioned him
again many times after this, but it was to be another five or
six months before I met them in person.

In September 1961 I was scheduled to do a film in Spain
and, as Amy also had to leave America to organise a
resident's card, I took her and Mark with me. But the whole
episode was a disaster! After I'd been working non-stop for
two weeks, and having to put up with Amy's continual
grumbling about the Spanish hotel, the project was
abandoned because the production company ran into
financial troubles. Even my hotel bill, which they were
responsible for, was unpaid, and when I wanted to return to
London, the management insisted that Amy and Mark
remain there until the bill was paid. Eventually they
relented, and Amy and Mark joined me in London, leaving
an associate of my agent to sort out the problem. How it was
resolved I never did find out, but the associate was later
seen in London so he must have worked something out!

As another film had been arranged for me to do in
London, I rented a mews house and proceeded to film from
dawn to dusk, coming home at night to more moods and
temperament from Amy. Indeed, I often used to wonder
who was the artiste in our set-up. Even friends of mine were
saying she'd missed her vocation in life.

For a surprise Christmas present, Dickie flew over from
America to join us. He had lived alone at the house in
Beverly Hills for two months, still waiting for his big
chance, and now he arrived with presents for everybody.
He was also to assist me in a cabaret appearance at a
London club. However, I had an even bigger surprise for

him. I was pregnant again and really delighted, for I felt Mark needed a companion.

Dickie, too, was thrilled at the prospect of another child, even though Mark had a special place in his heart. But like me he was alarmed at the influence Amy had over our son. If she so much as walked from a room, Mark would rush out, screaming with fear in case she had gone for good. And once, when Dickie challenged her about it, she threw a fit of sulks for several days, which did not make life any easier. Many people wondered why we put up with this behaviour, but the simple answer was that there was no-one whom we could trust to look after our child better than Amy. She doted on him, buying him presents faster than Dickie could and referring to him as 'her boy'. Of course it was unhealthy, and maybe we should have cut her off from him before it was too late. But we were too inexperienced to comprehend fully how serious the effect on Mark was going to be.

What with filming all day and appearing in cabaret at night, my life was demanding and uncomfortable. Even without being pregnant it was an arduous schedule, leaving little time for my own enjoyment and virtually none for any social activities. Not that I was especially interested in the latter after what had happened the previous Guy Fawkes' night. At a party at the riverside home of a friend, some fool threw a firework into the room, resulting in three people being burnt to death, the house being razed to the ground, and me jumping from a high window into the arms of none other than Tommy Yeardye! It was the first time we had met since our parting, and now he was the hero of the hour, helping me along with many others to hospital for treatment. In times of tragedy – and near-tragedy from my point of view, though mercifully I did not lose the baby – the stupid acts of the past seem unimportant.

While Dickie and I were in London I insisted that the moment had come for me to meet his parents, and one day I sent a car to bring them to town. They were a sweet couple – neither of them Jewish, as he had stated – and we got on marvellously, especially as it was the first time they had seen their grandson. I found the whole thing very embarrassing, for how could I explain the real reason why they hadn't been invited to his christening, or even to the farm when we married. It was good to be able to invite them out to Hollywood, though, when I'd had the new baby, and they readily accepted the invitation. My father and Aunty Kit had been invited on numerous occasions, but my father could not fly because of his weak heart.

Dickie went back to America ahead of us and I stayed on to finish the cabaret contract. Not that I ever held in my hand the money I earned from all those continuous days and nights of exhausting work. And when I asked what was happening to it, the answers from all my different advisers were so complicated and full of financial or legal jargon that I almost wished I'd never raised the matter. Leave it to the men, I thought, and concentrate on your work and your family.

Back in Hollywood, as I awaited the birth of my baby, life for a few months was peaceful. Dickie was fairly pleasant and Amy, perhaps because I was supposed to be treated with care, threw only *half* as many tantrums. Pamela Mason, Liberace, Steve Allen and Terry-Thomas agreed to be godparents, and on 27 June, 1962 at Cedars of Lebanon Hospital, my second son, Gary, was born. His christening at our home in Beverly Hills was a wonderful affair. Mark, now two and a half, was thrilled to have a baby brother, but I was a little concerned how Gary would fare in future years against Mark, who was a strong-willed, rebellious boy far advanced beyond his tender years. I needn't have worried. As time went by little Gary grew into a tiger and beat Mark at everything. He had to, in order to survive!

Within ten weeks of Gary's birth, Dickie, still involuntarily idle, had me back in cabaret again, this time in Chicago. The RKO contract had finally been settled, with a certain amount of money coming from it, but it was not enough to enable me to sit around doing nothing for long. One could not maintain a mansion in Beverly Hills for nothing!

From this engagement another booking was secured in

Las Vegas, this time two weeks in October at The Riviera
hotel. Dickie came up for the opening, together with
Pamela Mason, but then returned home. I could never
understand why, as he had no work there, and alone in
Vegas I reflected on our marriage. The new baby had made
little difference to anything, least of all to Dickie's
behaviour and moods. Perhaps it might help if his parents
came for the holiday I promised them. Take his mind off the
fact that he was in an uncomfortable position professionally, with me always working and having nothing to do
himself.

Mr and Mrs Emm duly arrived, and stayed with us for a
year! Not that I really objected to the length of time, for it
was such a relief to have normal people around the house.
Despite all the jokes about mothers-in-law, I found Josie,
Dickie's mother, a lovely woman, and got along much
better with her than I did with her son! She didn't
understand Dickie very well either; his days of locking
himself away in the bedroom, never sitting down to a meal
with the rest of the family and never socialising to any great
extent. But it was obvious when she spoke of Johnny,
Dickie's older brother, that she saw him much more as a
person to whom she could relate. And being so far away
from home, she missed his cheery manner and ordinary
way of life. Dickie, for some unexplained reason, disliked
him with a deep intensity.

Having lately acquired a manager for himself, Dickie
had made a couple of small appearances on television, one
of them with Jack Benny when English comedian Max
Bygraves was a guest. This was just days before Gary was
born, but even though I was not really up to socialising I
willingly invited Max and his wife to the house for drinks
when Dickie asked me to. I'd met Max years before, and it
was pleasant to entertain and talk with old friends from
home. Throughout the evening Dickie stayed in his room
watching television, not even coming out to say hello.
When they were leaving – I offered to drive them back to
their hotel, despite my condition – they looked through his
open door and saw Dickie sitting there, but all they received

was a nonchalant wave. He made not a move in their
direction!

In April 1963 I was booked to do cabaret at a club
called The International in New York. This kind of work
was about all I seemed to be able to get now, for films and
television were hard to obtain in Hollywood, although I
had made a brief visit to England in the bitterly cold
January of that year to complete a small role in *West Eleven*,
with Dennis's old mentor, Eric Portman. I had seen
Michael, who was doing well, and also visited my father
and Aunty Kit in Swindon, taking photographs of baby
Gary whom they had never seen. My father did not appear
too well, and that desperately cold winter finally got the
better of his health. While I performed in cabaret that April
in New York, I received a call from Dickie's manager – not
Dickie – that a telegram had arrived at Beverly Hills,
stating my father had passed away in his sleep.

Somehow, because I had always expected my father to
die during my youth, the shock of his death was not really
great at all. I did not cry, or feel the way I did when my
mother died. But then we were never close. And, sadly, I do
not think I ever truly loved him, even though I came to
respect many of the things about which we once disagreed.
Aunty Kit tearfully informed me, when I rang, that she had
found him dead in bed that morning, so at least he had not
suffered. There was no necessity, she insisted, that I return
for the funeral, although now I realise it was my duty to
have done so, instead of fulfilling my cabaret contract in
New York simply because we needed money out there in
Hollywood. The house payments had to be kept up,
swimming-pool and grounds maintained, Amy's wages
paid for, the children's needs met, and Dickie's parents
were also being given an allowance each week.

My next job, once I'd spent a few weeks at home, was a
musical, *The Pyjama Game*, in New Jersey. So once again I
said goodbye to my family and also bade farewell to
Dickie's parents, for they had decided a year away from
England was long enough and were preparing to return to
their little house in Gosport. To simple folk like them

Hollywood, with all its sunshine and glamour, still did not beat home.

En route for New York I stopped off in Ohio to guest in a television show, using any spare time I had to study all the songs and dialogue I would have to know for the musical as, once in New Jersey, there would be only two weeks to rehearse. When I arrived in New York I booked into the Plaza and the next day made the first of what were to become a summer of thirty-minute journeys to the Meadowbank Theatre in New Jersey. It was a restaurant-theatre 'in the round', which I didn't like very much, being more used to a conventional stage with backcloths and an audience out in front. But the money paid for this summer-season work was good, and I sent my salary back to Hollywood all through the two-month engagement.

My life had taken on a pattern of work, work and more work. I rarely saw my family, for whom I provided, and when I did I stayed only a few weeks. Amy was in full control, resenting my presence in her otherwise private domain, and Dickie spent much of his time brooding in his bedroom. But the leavings never became easier, and I began to yearn more and more for my two small sons.

It was to be expected, Pamela Mason had once said, that alone and travelling the world I was bound to meet men who paid me compliments and treated me like a woman. The man in New York that sweltering summer was Frankie Jacklone, a handsome Italian-American whose wealthy father had bought him a nightclub with which to make something out of his life. He had been married, but was divorced, and worshipped his little four-year-old son, Dean, whom we often took to play in Central Park. I used to buy him toys, as in a way he substituted for Mark and Gary. At night, after my show, Frankie and I played at all the smart clubs, restaurants and haunts frequented by the jet-set, enjoying life to the full.

There was only one problem. Frankie drank too much and it ruined many evenings. This was the first time I had been involved with a man who drank heavily, for not even Dennis was a big drinker, and it bothered me to see someone who had everything in the world destroying himself with alcohol. I tried to keep up, but I was hopeless at it. Indeed, towards the end of my time in New York I felt it was just as well that I had to go back to the comparative sanity of Hollywood! Frankie wanted to marry me, but I could not envisage living in that city with him for the rest of my life, both of us playing around in café society and drinking ourselves into oblivion. I made a quick departure for the airport one day, leaving him a letter!

My return to Beverly Hills got the same lukewarm reception as always, except for little one-year-old Gary who greeted me with his chubby arms outstretched in delight. But if I thought Frankie was going to be put off with a letter I was mistaken. An Italian is not dismissed lightly when it comes to the game of love, and telephone calls and telegrams arrived daily, begging me to go back to New York. I told him it was impossible, saying that we were all going to Hawaii for a vacation. While there, I promised, I would think things over and make a decision.

Hawaii, naturally, was beautiful; the last and best two weeks we were ever to enjoy together. On our return, Dickie's manager met us at the airport with the sad news that our boxer dog, Caesar, had died in our absence, and this news sent Dickie into a very depressed state!

Frankie wasted no time in my absence. First, he sent two friends to rent a house near mine on Angelo Drive, and they now called me continuously. His next move was to fly out to Hollywood himself and, more to keep things quiet than because I really wanted to see him, I agreed to meet him at his hotel. My old friend Jozy from England, who had married American star Channing Pollock and was living on a ranch, had already warned me that Frankie could cause unforeseen trouble. Far worse than the John Ashley situation, she told me, advising me to invent some kind of story that might send him back to New York, temporarily appeased. What had been a summer flirtation seemed to be turning into a Mafia-style drama!

When we met, I informed Frankie that I had to go to Australia for a cabaret and television tour, which was, indeed true. Tactfully I suggested that, if he loved me so much, he might join me there at a date to be mutually agreed, and this seemed to appeal to him. We had lunch and I left. It was all rather sad, but as he could see my life was very difficult now. I did not control my own destiny the way I had when we were together in New York, for in addition to work obligations I had a husband and family to consider.

With the idea that he would fly to Australia, Frankie left town. I was relieved, of course, for I thought I could prevent him from ever doing so when the time came. Yet I also felt sad that our romance was over. He had been an exciting, devotedly affectionate man. Who did I have now? Dickie was more remote than ever, and as the great majority of women know, a son is no substitute for a lover.

The Australian tour drew nearer, and with the passing days I came to dread it all the more. Nor could I get out of it, for my London agent had signed the contracts. All I could do was miserably contemplate my fate for the coming two months, wondering how I would survive travelling all that way to a country where I knew no-one and which had never appealed to me. At least home, despite the awful atmosphere that prevailed there for much of the time, was home. I knew people, friends like Pamela and Jozy, and most important Mark and Gary were there.

Now I was off again; to experience that horrible feeling of waking in strange beds, jet-lagged and wondering which hotel, or even what country, I was in. Dickie had arranged that an English friend of his, Les Bennetts, a guitar player, should go along to accompany me in my act – which is what I thought Dickie should have been doing – and supposedly to keep me company. I liked Les, who had a great sense of humour. But as someone with whom to spend two months in the Antipodes! That was another story!

One night, shortly before I was due to leave, I lay alone in bed on Angelo Drive, worried and confused about the immediate future and, even worse, the future beyond. What sort of life did Dickie and I have? We were neither companions nor lovers. He lived in his own world of fantasy, putting on an act for people he wished to impress but at home, with me and the children, remaining sullen, brooding and withdrawn. Was this to be the sum total of our lives? He locked away in his room, hiding, until he became a success. Me working all the time to provide the money we needed to live in that Hollywood mansion. I was homesick for England, but I'd been told I couldn't go back and live there because the taxman was after me seriously. I figured that facing him would be better than living in this luxury hell with Amy governing the domestic front and Dickie despising me for everything I did, not only professionally but, since the John Ashley affair, personally.

Yet there were bound to be other Ashleys as time went on, for I was a woman who needed the attention of men, desiring the compliments they paid and the affection they bestowed. Especially as I never received them from the man I married, for better or worse.

If life was bad with him now, what would it be like in twenty years when the children had grown up? Dickie and I, who never conversed anyway, would then be alone. The prospect was unthinkable, and in a cold panic I realised the moment had come to discuss our problems openly and honestly. It was also a fair thing to do from his point of view, for I was not the woman he wanted to have as a wife. I'd felt conscious of that for a long time.

As usual he was lying in his bed, a lonely, forlorn figure. But I knew from past experience that I would be treated with contempt if I tried to speak softly, and so I launched into an artificially strong monologue, explaining my thoughts in the best way I could and stating that I knew in my heart it would be best for him, too, if we ended this farcical marriage. A painful silence followed, though I was relieved I had managed to bring everything out into the open. I had hated the deceit, the intrigue, the moods and atmospheres. Now I waited for him to say something; and all he did was stare at the ceiling, as if I wasn't even in the room.

'Dick', I finally persisted, determined to get some

reaction out of him. 'What do you think of everything I've just said?'

Without looking in my direction he rose from his bed and, walking towards the door, replied, 'You are mentally unstable! It is quite obvious to me that you need a psychiatrist!'

CHAPTER NINE

RUSSIAN ROULETTE

Goosey, Goosey, Gander, where do you wander?
Upstairs, downstairs, in my lady's chamber.

I travelled to Australia with a sinking feeling in my stomach. I was leaving nothing behind, other than my children, and there was nothing in the future, except the emptiness of a country completely new to me. Yet as I endured the exhausting flight of eighteen hours to Sydney, I could not have realised in all my deepest despair that this would be the start of my descent into madness! I was going to experience depths in my professional and personal life over the next five years which would make the past seem almost blissful.

On arrival in Sydney, where we had a three-hour wait before embarking on a six-hour flight to Perth, I was met by Alma Cogan, who was appearing in cabaret there. Dickie had introduced us several years earlier, and it was typical of her to invite Les and me to her apartment for the wait between planes. She had an incredible sense of humour, and I felt a great sense of loss when she died in 1967.

I imagined Perth to be some sort of dusty sheep-shearing town in the back of beyond, and the prospect of being there, combined with the weariness of the seemingly endless flight, filled me with dismay. Certainly the last thing I needed, or expected, was a grand welcoming party with dozens of pressmen, a brass band, soldiers on parade and a police motorcycle escort.

'I know you're exhausted', coaxed Jack Neary, who was arranging my tour, 'but please try to hang on for another hour while we get the publicity shots and interviews out of the way. Then I promise you can go to the hotel and sleep.'

How I got through it I do not know; but I managed to walk up and down the ranks of soldiers like a queen, accept bouquets of flowers, parry difficult questions from the newspapermen, and pose for pictures. I did not dare to think what I looked like in such a jet-lagged state.

Finally I got to the hotel, where I asked for a simple bowl of soup. It was all I desired, other than a soft bed!

'Are you sure that's all you want?' Jack Neary enquired, bustling about in an attempt to make me as welcome as possible. 'I have a special dinner laid on in your honour at a superb restaurant by the Indian Ocean.'

'Let's make it another time, Jack', I pleaded, wishing he would let me go to bed in peace. I didn't even know if it was day or night!

'Whatever you say', he replied cheerfully. 'By the way, I just want to introduce one of my singers. He'll be appearing with you in the show.'

Not another introduction, I thought irritably! Hadn't I done enough hand-shaking and courtesy conversation back at the airport?

'This is Darryl Stewart', Jack announced.

I glared in the direction of an extremely handsome young man. Despite his good looks and pleasant manner, however, I was not in any mood to appreciate him. Instead I brusquely muttered a few words before excusing myself and hurried off to my suite. There I found two dozen red roses! From Frankie, with a poetic message of love.

I must have slept for at least twelve hours. And when I awoke, the old fear of wondering exactly where I was overcame me for a few seconds. Then my tired brain started to function properly and I drew back the curtains to see brilliant sunshine. It was October, and the beginning of an Australian summer.

The following days were spent rehearsing and publicising the Diana Dors Show at Perth's leading theatre. And on the opening night, as I waited for my cue, I was able to look with more interest at Darryl Stewart, who was in the process of ending his act. Something about the scene reminded me of those days, long ago, when I used to watch Dickie from the side of the stage. It thrilled me when he made them laugh, and I was always excited and proud for him! Now Darryl was receiving an ovation, and with his dark, curly hair and smart appearance he looked incredibly attractive.

That night, back at the hotel, Darryl and I dined together, and flippantly speaking it was 'love at first bite'. We laughed, recalling our introduction when a bowl of soup made more impact on me than he did. With the candlelight flickering between us, and music in the background, there was no doubt in either of our minds that the rest of the week in Perth would be spent together. From being utterly depressed and miserable, I was suddenly transformed. Life was idyllic now as we worked and played amidst glorious scenery which I had certainly never associated with Australia. To me it all resembled England; the green grass, roses and elegant homes. But there was a difference. Every day the sun was hot. And with every night, as moonlight bathed the Indian Ocean in silver, Darryl and I became more enchanted with the spell of each other.

There were, however, two problems to spoil our otherwise perfect situation. The first, and most important, was that Darryl had a wife and two small children in Sydney, where I was due to play the following week. Not since Guy Rolfe had I been involved with a married man, and it troubled me. The other problem was Frankie, now bombarding me with telephone calls and cables, telling me he had sold his club in New York and was waiting in Hollywood to fly over as soon as I gave the word. I made an instant decision and called him, lying to him that Dickie was flying out shortly to join me. I was sorry about everything, but selling his nightclub had not been my idea – and I half suspected that it had not been such a successful business anyway.

Once back in Sydney life took a completely different turn, for now I was appearing in cabaret alone and Darryl was working elsewhere. I rented a penthouse suite at the top of a leading hotel, where nightly Les and I held parties. Many American stars were working in cabaret, too, and they, with Australians I came to know, helped enliven many evenings before and after work.

Darryl joined me whenever possible, but I understood his predicament. Now that he was back with his family, we had lost the freedom we so enjoyed in Perth. When I did see him, though, it was wonderful. We were both more in love than ever, and the sensation of a forbidden affair gave everything much greater excitement. Where it would end was forgotten in the rapture of it as we stole nights together or flew to Melbourne or Brisbane when either one of us was working there.

Our happiness was nearing its end, however, for as Christmas approached, and my work in Australia was done, the parting we dreaded had to come. How strange that a country I had not wanted to visit had proved to be so fantastic! I had enjoyed eight weeks of heaven. But my home was in Beverly Hills and, even though I didn't relish going back, I missed my children and wanted to see them.

When the moment arrived, I could not envisage life without seeing Darryl any more. It would be intolerable. Darryl couldn't accept things, either, or so it seemed. He announced that, as a former resident of America, he needed to enter the States within the one-year period necessary to validate his resident's card, having acquired it while once working in Las Vegas. He decided to return to America with Les and me! It was a wild, dangerous idea; insane certainly. But love has no fears, and my happiness was complete now that I knew we could continue our relationship in Los Angeles.

In the giddy excitement of it all, without caring that it was me who'd be paying his fare and everything else until he obtained cabaret work there, I went ahead with arrangements for our flight back through Hawaii for one last glorious holiday. Darryl and Les would remain there over Christmas, and when they arrived in Los Angeles I would rent an apartment for them in a large block that Pamela Mason owned.

We left Australia on the first lap of what proved to be a disastrous venture! Hawaii was idyllic, and as we played on the beach and swam in the deep-blue waters of the Pacific I put aside any apprehensions I may have felt. For the moment I did not want to know what insanity and misery might be waiting for us beyond that beautiful Polynesian island, selfishly not giving a thought to Darryl's wife and family – or, for that matter, my own. Then came the day when I sadly bid Darryl goodbye, for it was time to fly back to Los Angeles and pave the way for him and Les. The thought that their stay in Hawaii was going to be at my expense never bothered me! Money was still something with which I never involved myself. As long as I worked, there were, and always had been, men to handle it for me.

At home in Angelo Drive, Aunty Kit, whom I had invited to stay for a few months, was waiting alongside Dickie, the boys and Amy. But she didn't seem very happy, and I soon discovered that, for the few weeks she'd been there, Amy had made life unbearable. Dickie, of course, hardly spoke at any time.

'I wouldn't have your life here if they paid me a thousand pounds a week!' she stated firmly. 'I miss England, Diana. Please make arrangements for me to go home in January.'

My father had left me the house in Swindon, but stipulated in his will that she could remain there for the rest of her life if she wished.

However, I was so busy making arrangements for Darryl and Les that I couldn't spare much time worrying about Aunty Kit. I had problems of my own to consider. Pam was sympathetic over the situation regarding Darryl, and instantly offered one of her available apartments just near Sunset Boulevard. Slyly I informed Dickie that Les had found a friend in Australia, a singer, who was coming back to try to obtain work. So now all was ready for the day they arrived.

For a short while life proceeded along devious lines, following the familiar pattern of the John Ashley affair: secret meetings, telephone calls and so on. I hated the whole situation, resenting the fact that I was forced to conduct my life in such an underhand, deceitful manner. Nor was it a very satisfactory existence for Darryl, who was now experiencing what I went through when he had not been free in Australia. Such a state of affairs had to explode, and both Darryl and I were stupid to expect it wouldn't.

After a depressing New Year's Eve party at Pam's, hailing in 1964, with Dickie brooding in a corner most of the evening and Darryl hardly daring to glance at me, the explosion came. A letter to Dickie from Darryl's wife, in which she unhappily poured out the whole story of our affair. That would have been bad enough, but there was another twist to the plot. In two more months she was expecting Darryl's child!

Oblivious of the fateful letter, Darryl and I were driving along Sunset Boulevard when I observed Dickie following directly behind us in his car. Not knowing quite what to do, we journeyed a considerable distance before finally stopping outside Darryl's apartment building. Immediately Dickie leapt out of his car and confronted us both, shouting that he knew all about our affair and telling me to leave home.

No-one likes to be caught red-handed. I was disgusted with myself over the misery I had caused and was totally unprepared to believe that Darryl was capable of abandoning his wife, knowing her to be pregnant! There was nothing to do but leave him at his apartment and rush, as always, to Pam for advice.

'You can stay here', she said. 'I'll take you to see my lawyer and get him to sort everything out.'

How typical of Pam that was. Matters had to be dealt with from a business aspect before the emotional side of life was even considered. The lawyer she advised me to see, Marvin Mitchelson, was later to become one of the wealthiest, most successful lawyers in America, but then he was at the beginning of his career.

'Who does the house belong to?' he asked.

'It's mine', I told him, believing this to be the case as I was the one who paid the deposit and met the mortgage payments.

'How much money do you have in your joint bank account?'

'I think there's about $1,500 there.'

Both Mitchelson and Pam winced somewhat at this, for by Hollywood standards they were expecting hundreds of thousands! Anyway, I was instructed to withdraw the sum while he went ahead with all necessary divorce proceedings against Dickie. I was to remain at Pam's house.

'But what about the children?' I asked with concern. 'How will they exist if I have the only available money?' Now that the anger and confusion were subsiding, guilt and responsibility were beginning to well up within me instead.

'Let Dickie go and get a job', said Pam.

'You know that's impossible!'

'He mustn't be allowed to stay in your house dictating the terms. Once Marvin has the divorce papers ready he'll have to move out. Then you can return and look after the children financially, as you've always done', she emphasised.

'But where will he go? How will he live? You know he can't get any work in Hollywood. I was a fool to bring Darryl here', I sobbed dejectedly. 'It was asking for trouble.'

'No-one can help falling in love', she persisted. 'What the hell did Dickie expect would happen, letting you tour around the world on your own? Mark my words. Unless you do something now, one day you'll find the door bolted and barred against you, with Dickie calling the tune.'

'No, I honestly don't think he would ever do anything like that, Pam. He's just very hurt at the moment, and rightly so.'

Pam could see I was weakening. And even though I drew the pathetic sum of money from our joint bank account, and agreed to Mitchelson preparing divorce proceedings, she knew it was inevitable that I would soften eventually.

Dickie, stunned by these events, changed his tactics, writing tender notes of apology for everything and inviting me to my own home for discussions. There were tearful scenes and pleas, saying he would not bother Darryl and

me any more if I withdrew the divorce proceedings and
allowed him to remain in the house. In the madness which I
had created, anything seemed plausible at this stage. But
nothing had really changed, in the sense that I was still
expected to be the family provider. Nor would I be truly
free to follow my heart, whether it was Darryl or any other
man with whom I happened to be in love.

Despite Pam shaking her head and warning me that one
day I would regret it, I called a halt to Mitchelson's
activities by paying his already large bill. Darryl, meanwhile, had been keeping a very low profile, and when I next
saw him I learnt that Dickie had visited him recently,
vividly describing my affair with John Ashley and warning
him that the day would come when I would throw him
aside for someone else.

He was hurt because of the things Dickie had told him,
but I was hurt too. For despite still loving him, I couldn't
trust Darryl any more, knowing that he had left his
pregnant wife behind and at the same time hidden the truth
from me. It left me with an empty, gnawing feeling, and it
was obvious that our love affair had reached a critical point
where neither of us could foresee or plan any kind of future
together.

There was, however, little time to sit and ponder. Work,
as always, prevailed; indeed was very necessary because
the money I had earned in Australia was still not forthcoming from London. My American manager offered me a
play for a month. *Miranda* was the story of a mermaid, and I
had performed in it many years before when I was living
with Michael. Then it was a small East End theatre and ten
pounds a week. Now it was Chicago and my salary was a
great deal more.

Part of the deal for any guest-star appearing in this large
theatre-restaurant was a luxury penthouse at the top of the
building, and so Darryl decided he would follow me to
Chicago after we opened. This meant I was alone during
rehearsals, and missing him, but once he arrived we had
several fairly happy weeks, living very much as we had in
Perth. It was, of course, only a temporary respite, for we

both knew our association had to end.

Yet, in spite of everything, we refused to accept it. Darryl had to return to Sydney for the imminent birth of the baby, we agreed that. But later, we planned, he could join me in England where I was due to make a film called *Allez France*. An Anglo-French low-budget film, it would do my career no good but it was as good a reason as any to get away from Hollywood and earn some money. Most important, it would give me the chance to be with Darryl for the summer and once again, in our typically insane way, we could forget life and just be selfishly, deliriously happy!

The day came too quickly when we had to part at Chicago airport. Like all farewells it was highly emotional, and many were the protestations of undying love, with promises and hopes for the future. After another week of terrible emptiness at the theatre, I flew back to the same old scene in Hollywood. Dickie silent and bitter; Amy temperamental and grumbling. The boys, aged two and four now, welcomed me as if I was a fairy queen, eager to see what presents I had brought. But soon they were back to the only real mother they knew, Amy, who wielded her power over them and flaunted it at every opportunity.

Darryl wrote sometimes as many as three letters a day, professing his love for me and describing everything in Australia. He had not moved back into his home, but was staying elsewhere, and so I in turn was able to write dozens of letters to him. It was one of these that prompted my next disaster. In my stupidity, and not imagining Dickie cared about the situation any more, I wrote an acceptance of marriage – *when* we were both free – in reply to a proposal from Darryl. Dickie intercepted this letter, read it and made what were, I suppose, justifiable threats as to what he would do if I tried to divorce him at any time.

Before I commenced the new film, I had been signed to do a six-week tour of nightclubs in England. With gambling now legal, there were many more clubs over there and cabaret work was plentiful for star names. It was an exhausting but successful set of engagements. Darryl continued to ply me with daily letters and would occasionally

telephone wherever I happened to be. His wife had had
their baby, a girl, and despite his denials that they were
reconciled, or his protestations of love down long-distance
telephone lines, I couldn't help feeling that they were living
together again. What, I wondered, had he told her about
the future?

Although it was a lonely life for me working in all the
Northern cities, when I was in London I sometimes stayed
with Michael at his home in Chelsea; or went down to the
beautiful manor house he now owned in Dorset. We had
always remained close, just as he once said we would. He
was then engaged to an exquisitely lovely model, known as
'Boots', and they were planning to marry that summer.
How wonderful, I thought, if Darryl could be in England
for the wedding. Briefly I returned to America to see my
sons, taking with me several thousand pounds I had earnt
on the cabaret tour to deposit in the bank for Dickie and the
family to live on. While I was there, Pam Mason told me
Dickie had been romancing her daughter, Portland. She
also said that he had been describing me as 'just a "good-
time Charlie" only interested in having fun' and that I was
sending money home because I felt guilty.

I thought this was very unfair, considering I did nothing
but work to pay the bills. Of course I had done many of the
things of which he accused me. But at times in my life there
seemed to be nothing I could do to prevent my own inter-
mittent insanity.

Feeling something like a robot, once more I bade farewell
to my children and flew back to England. The pattern was
so familiar now; all of us at the airport, having been driven
there by Dickie's manager, and the boys saying their sad
goodbyes. The only compensation this time was the
thought of seeing Darryl in London after what would have
been nearly three months. No matter how much I hated
leaving Mark and Gary, at least Darryl and I would be able
to enjoy a wonderful summer together. Afterwards the
future could take care of itself.

However, if I ever thought there had been madness over
my Australian journey, it was an understatement for this

trip was to turn out to be the worst period of my life. I would descend to the darkness of a bottomless pit from which madness might be regarded as an excuse!

My immediate work before the film was a television play, and while doing it I took out a six-month lease on a perfect little cottage in Chelsea where Darryl and I could live. I also saw Dickie's parents, who came to visit one day, and for the first time I met his brother Johnny, a cheerful fellow and quite unlike Dickie in his ways. His parents indicated that it would be nice to return to America to see their grandchildren, and as I liked the idea of two such lovely people being with the boys again, I offered to send them for another holiday there. Arrangements were made and they flew off to Hollywood.

Now that I was living at the cottage, the stage was set for my big reunion with Darryl. Only one thing was required before the show could start. The leading lady was waiting, but the leading man had not yet appeared on stage to play his role. And from the tone of his next letter it did not look as if he was going to!

'My darling, I cannot come to England just now', he wrote. 'But I promise that one day I will make it.' I stared at the pages in disbelief. After all I had manoeuvred and organised for our idyllic summer together. I was filled with anger and selfishly, with no thought for his predicament or that of his wife and three children, I wrote a scathing letter. I was not prepared, I informed him, to carry on having an affair with a telephone or a writing-pad any longer. Either he arrived this time, or not at all. That would spur him into action, I thought confidently. No more deceiving his wife while he wrote passionate letters of undying loyalty and love to me. Now he'd be honest with her and fly to England immediately. How wrong could I be? I was not to hear from Darryl again for fifteen years!

The same evening that I wrote demanding his arrival, I decided to give a party, perhaps to prove to myself that I cared not whether he came or stayed in the Antipodes for good! And once more fate played her hand, steering my future course through a 'would be' pop-singer with the unlikely name of Troy Dante! A dark-eyed young man looking rather morose amid the music and noisy atmosphere of people drinking, talking and having fun, he was wearing the standard gear for those pop-singers emerging mushroom-like after the advent of the Beatles. But after a few attempts at conversation and finding him appearing to be quite lacking in personality I moved on to talk to some of my other guests, among them Michael and singer Shirley Bassey.

How misleading first judgments can be. Suddenly, as if struck by lightning, Troy leapt off the sofa where he had spent most of the evening and launched into some of the funniest chatter I had heard for a long time. He described in the most comical way his inability to sing very well, or even to speak English grammatically. Then he related hilarious tales of disastrous pop concerts and 'near miss' records, which with *luck* could have provided him with a hit! His idol, he claimed, was Anthony Newley, and his speech and general demeanour were very similar to Tony's. However, I assumed he had probably tried to imitate him a good deal, and myself thought that he bore a far greater resemblance to Welsh actor Stanley Baker. Troy, too, was Welsh, as I learnt later, having come from Swansea. He had lived in London for most of his life, though, which accounted for his partly Cockney accent and the cheeky humour which, now displayed to the full, was amusing not just me but most of my guests.

It is strange how a spark ignites between two people. If I were to analyse my own emotions at the time, it would be true to say I was in a very vulnerable state because of the letter I had written to Darryl that morning. And Troy *had* found my Achilles' heel, making me laugh all the time. I didn't stop to think what his reasons might be for making an all-out play for me. In a vain, feminine way I chose to believe he found me attractive.

In short, Troy arrived at my house one night for a party and stayed a great deal longer! But after an exhilarating start, the course of true love did not run smoothly. On our second evening out together we had a quarrel. What it was about did not matter. We were to have thousands more like them during our association, during which I discovered a dimension to my personality that I never knew existed. It was almost as if I were looking into a mirror and seeing the dark side for the first time. Troy brought out the worst in me, and there was no doubt that I did the same for him.

Within a week of our meeting I had to go to Paris, where *Allez France* was to be filmed, and throwing caution to the wind I gave Troy the key to my house. At least someone would be using it, and I had to admit I did miss him while I was abroad. Absence certainly did make my heart grow fonder and, when I returned to Chelsea after filming, ours was a truly romantic reunion. Furthermore, there was also Michael's wedding to look forward to, especially believing that Troy would accompany me there. But when the time came there seemed to be some mysterious reason why he couldn't come to Dorset with me, and as at that point I did not wish to find out exactly what it was, I left the matter alone. I arrived at Michael's London house to be told the wedding was off. 'Boots' had changed her mind.

There seemed no reason to stay in London for the weekend, so Michael and I went alone to his beautiful country manor, where we attempted to eat everything that had been prepared for the wedding breakfast. As the weekend went by, with Michael bravely trying to conceal his feelings, there was a pleasant surprise for me. Troy phoned to say he could get down after all.

It was a glorious summer evening when he arrived, and we strolled hand in hand around one of Michael's large meadows. But the expression on Troy's face told me there was something on his mind, and when I asked him to tell me what was wrong, he confessed that he was married.

'Oh God, no! Not this again!' I exclaimed with a sinking feeling. 'I've just been through all that and it made me vow never to look at another married man.'

Genuinely, at that moment I did not want to carry on with our relationship. But once more, touched perhaps with summer madness, I permitted my heart to rule my head, and Troy moved into the Chelsea cottage. An extraordinary few months followed, during which time Troy accompanied me on a tour of nightclubs throughout Italy, and life was very romantic. But when I started occasional weeks of cabaret in dreary Northern towns, it was a different story. That was not Troy's scene at all.

The Swinging Sixties were well and truly under way now, and besotted by this amusing, plausible man who could make me laugh or cry depending whether or not we had had our daily fight, I pretended to the press that I was going to manage his pop group. This obtained a great deal of publicity for Troy, and he was absolutely delighted by it all, for he was extremely ambitious. Ambition is one thing, though. As Pamela Mason had once remarked to me, working hard to achieve it is quite another matter.

It was just as well that my agent could keep me employed in working-men's clubs, for I was beginning to go downhill badly. No film companies wanted me, and what with the the upkeep of the house and family in Beverly Hills and my own expenses – which now included Troy – I had very little to spare. Not that it stopped us having parties every night, and if life was grim professionally, socially it was great! Blissfully unaware of Troy's continued liaison with his wife, Barbara, and enraptured by the incredible, hypnotic effect he had on my emotions, I sailed along on a cloud, allowing love and the pursuit of pleasure to overcome my doubts about his weakness for gambling, or the despair I sometimes felt regarding my own career.

In the excitement of it all I even began drinking quite considerably. Not to an enormous extent, but things were reaching the stage where Troy and I needed a bottle of whisky each evening to start the ball rolling! Life once again seemed to be full of amazing people, actors and pop-singers, and among them was an amusing character nick-named Leapy Lee. He became something of a court-jester at our parties. Consequently it was hardly surprising that I loathed having to go away and perform in cabaret for a week in order to make some more much-needed money. Especially when the clubs I was forced to appear in were not nightclubs, such as those I had known in Las Vegas and other places, but austere buildings with fluorescent lighting, formica tables and audiences of men heckling me over their pints of beer. I was now prostituting my talent; peddling a screen name that had once been big; enduring shouts of 'Get 'em off' or 'Show us your tits'. It seemed to be the only way left to earn a living.

As my personal happiness revolved solely around Troy, I had no desire to leave England for long and so I tried to obtain a booking in pantomime for that Christmas. A theatre in Bromley, Kent, was producing *The Sleeping Beauty* and I signed as principal boy, also getting them to give Troy a small part as a strolling minstrel. Before rehearsals commenced, I flew back to America to see the children whom I missed so badly. I'd have loved to have them in England with me, but I honestly felt it was better for them to grow up in the warmth and peace of Southern California than to expose them to a life of hotel rooms, cold towns and a mother who had now, seemingly, failed professionally too.

When I returned to England, having experienced the usual heartbreaking, tearful farewells at Los Angeles airport, Troy and I moved from the cottage to a flat in the King's Road, Chelsea, and life went on as always. Parties, quarrels, laughter and tears! Troy gambling while I worked to pay his stake-money, our rent and all the bills in America. Then one evening, to my amazement, his wife appeared on the scene to reveal that he had indeed been two-timing us both. She tolerated things at first, for she believed I was helping him with his career. Now she wanted him back. There were arguments, suicide threats, tantrums; and all to no effect, for my common sense did not yet prevail where Troy was concerned. Like a cancer he had grown over me and I was still powerless to do anything about it. Had I been able to think clearly, I would not have believed him when he insisted everything was now truly finished between him and Barbara. Instead, I wanted us to continue our mad life together. At a later date I even took him to Los Angeles, where I ensconced him in a hotel on Sunset Boulevard while I stayed with my family, and then across the country to a club in North Carolina where I toiled in cabaret for two weeks, never receiving payment because the owner went broke!

From America we travelled to such faraway places as Turkey and, later on, South Africa. Germany was another port of call, touring around American Army bases and standing in makeshift clubs on barrack sites while half-drunk soldiers threw beer cans on the soaked floor as I endeavoured to perform an act which had once been received so well in Las Vegas.

My London agent exploited what was left of my commercial name to the best of his ability. But he was moving up in the world professionally by handling Elizabeth Taylor, Richard Burton and stars of that calibre. Diana Dors, touring around, trading on an old sex-symbol screen image, was fast becoming small time for him. However, an agent in America did come up with an offer to do a show at the same theatre in New Jersey where I had performed *The Pyjama Game*. This time it was to be a two-month production of *One Touch of Venus*, and as there was nothing forthcoming in England, I took Troy off to America again.

On this trip I foolishly asked Leapy Lee to accompany us so that Troy would not feel lonely when we spent a few weeks in Hollywood and I stayed with Mark and Gary. How disastrous that decision proved to be. Regardless of *my* stupidity in taking either of them, Leapy could not control Troy who spent every penny, allotted to him for the American visit, at the racetrack. As a result, when we flew to New York, Leapy remained behind with a girl he'd met, not knowing how he would get home because we could no longer afford to pay his fare!

Over the next six weeks I laboured at the theatre while Troy remained virtually imprisoned in the hotel. There was nowhere for him to go and he had no money with which to gamble. Apart from our expenses I was, as always, sending my salary back to Hollywood, believing Dickie to be worried about finances out there. But I was in for a big shock! As I prepared to leave for England, I telephoned the children to say goodbye and was innocently informed by Mark, with great excitement, that 'Daddy's bought an ocean-going boat'. Shock number two came when my financial adviser in London told me an E-type Jaguar was being transported to America, for my family, because Dickie wanted a new car!

At this point Troy obviously considered he had had enough! So, too, should I, but as Dickie had said to Pam Mason, I now really was a 'good-time Charlie' when not working. Whatever happened to the money I made, whether it went to appease Dickie – because of my association with Troy – or to pay for my lover, mattered not to me. Just as long as I could find happiness. Happiness! That was a bitter laugh. All the time I was away from my sons I would never find peace of mind. And that, plus my desperation at the tattered remnants of my career, meant I could never truly enjoy the good times, the laughter or the loving with Troy.

A dramatic telephone call from Barbara's mother, saying she was ill, sent him rushing to their home. He then informed me that he was going back to live with her and that our affair was finished! The unhappiness I felt was not helped by a two-week cabaret engagement in Newcastle, but Leapy, thankfully back from America, was always around to keep me company.

'Do yourself a favour', he advised me several times as he drove me up to Newcastle. 'Forget him. He's never been any good to you. Go back to America.'

However, when a woman is as much in love with a man as I was with Troy, no amount of advice or common sense will suffice. Leapy's words fell on deaf ears, except that the more he said them, the more of a sick challenge it became to get Troy back!

Had I but known it, getting Troy back was going to be easy. And like everything else in our association, the circumstances were completely bizarre. I received a dramatic telephone call from him, vowing undying love for me and stating that he could stand living with Barbara no longer. After only a week! He was heading for Newcastle on the next train, it appeared, but there was a slight problem. He was bringing his wife with him, and dropping her at Doncaster so that he and I could first have a private talk about the future, which had to include her.

It appeared I was now as brainwashed as she, for I happily agreed to this plan, just to be with him again. We had a weird reunion, during which he explained that, as she could not exist without him, perhaps the three of us might live together. Besotted I might have been, but there was no way I would agree to this idea. However, the following day Troy rang Barbara at her Doncaster hotel and told her to join us for further talks. Now, with Troy and me staying in one place and his wife in another, eight miles away by the sea, we met for talks that went on nearly to the end of the week. Leapy, quite rightfully having lost patience with me, returned to London in disgust!

The insanity had now reached its peak, and though I was as guilty as anyone I somehow stuck to my guns. Eventually it was decided that they really were going to separate for ever, and on my arrival back in London I met Troy, who stated that he would at last get a real job of work. We would rent a house he knew was available near Ascot, there would be no more gambling, Barbara had bowed out of the picture completely and he loved me beyond belief.

Troy secured an office job with an agent but it didn't last. The parties, the loving and the fun did go on, however, even though work and money were not always easily obtained. My agent had announced that he no longer wished to handle my affairs, and so I had to rely on the odd week in cabaret coming from someone else. I was working in a Blackpool nightclub when I received a desperate letter from Dickie, saying that all he had in the bank was $275 and could I send some money immediately. In panic at the thought that my children might have nothing to eat, I somehow arranged an overdraft of £1,500 at a local bank, not having the slightest idea how I would pay it back.

This happily was the last occasion I ever had to send money to him under such circumstances, for soon afterwards Dickie landed a television series. It was to become extremely successful in America, and so at long last he started his climb up the ladder of fame. For me it was back to pantomime, *Jack and the Beanstalk*, in Bournemouth. But the salary was good and I accepted the offer with relief, even managing to persuade the producer that Troy was capable of playing something in it.

Having made a hit in his new television series, and as I was renting a house in Bournemouth for the pantomime season, Dickie allowed the children to come over that Christmas. It was the first time four-year-old Gary had been to England, and despite Amy's usual tittle-tattle about Dickie's activities in Hollywood, plus general complaints all round, we spent a delightful time together. Then came the time for them to return to America and I felt sick and lonely. I never knew when I'd see them again, especially the way things were looking for me in England. The income tax demands, going right back to my life with Dennis, had become more than just dark thunder-clouds on a distant horizon. Bankruptcy was imminent, and I could no longer afford to visit America to see the children. At no time did Dickie, with his new-found fame and finances, offer to help, as I had always aided him.

Each week, in addition to all the other expenses I paid, a large rent had to be met for the furnished house Troy and I were occupying, but when I wasn't away somewhere in the North performing in cabaret to earn the money needed to run it, life was great socially. We threw the house open to everybody, and as it was near Wentworth golf course, stars who played there would always come over after they'd finished their game. Sean Connery, Bruce Forsyth, Ronnie Carroll, Ty Hardin, and Stanley Baker were among those who joined in the fun provided.

On other occasions, when we held real parties, there might be a hundred people gathered there. P. J. Proby, John Gregson, Tom Jones, Bobby Moore, Richard Harris, Bobby Darin, Richard Johnson, Billy Walker; all mingled with starlets and models. Once even Joan Crawford deigned to appear, as I had appeared briefly in a film with

her. Other friends from days gone by were guests: George
Coburn, who had changed his name to Hamilton, after
Dennis whom he adored, and Bobby McKew, Michael's
partner in the Jack Warner fiasco. Michael, however, I
sadly saw little of, for he did not like Troy. Leapy Lee was
always on hand to provide laughs. Actors Harry Fowler,
Andrew Ray, Peter Reynolds and singers Jess Conrad and
Kenny Lynch contributed to make good evenings. But the
happiness was short-lived and we knew it. Rather like
soldiers preparing to go into battle, we grabbed our chance
of enjoying life before everything came to an end!

Ridiculous as it seemed, with my career at such a low
ebb, I decided that at thirty-five years old, I wanted a home
of my own in England. Working in California and living
there with my sons was, I could see now, out of the
question. One day I found a lovely house in Sunningdale,
just up the road from our rented house. My only problem
was money, and I asked my lawyer about the best way of
raising it.

'You're out of your mind', he said, looking at me in
amazement and providing me with anything but the advice
I wanted. 'With the Inland Revenue threatening bankruptcy, you must not own anything, whatever happens!'

'But what about the money I put in trust so long ago?' I
argued. 'Mark and Gary are the beneficiaries, and it would
be a home for them if they ever come here to live.'

He remained adamant that he would not consider
allowing me to see a penny of the trust.

'I'm tired of renting houses', I persisted. 'Why shouldn't I
have a home? Haven't I earned the right to a roof over my
head?'

We argued back and forth. I was determined that my
money, which Dickie had once wanted to transfer to
America, would now buy a home in a country I loved and
where I wanted to stay.

Dickie's reaction, when he was told what I wanted to do,
was entirely predictable. Why did I want a place that had
five bedrooms and a tennis court? This, coming from a man
living in a Beverly Hills mansion complete with swimming-

pool which was still mine, seemed more than an imper-
tinence.

The war raged on, during the course of which I added to
my list of advisers a tax consultant to guide me on the
forthcoming bankruptcy.

'I don't quite understand your problem', said the man,
grave-faced. 'Is it absolutely necessary that your husband
and two sons live in a palace in Beverly Hills? Why not sell
the house there and simply pay your tax bill?'

'But where would they live?' I answered him, panicking
at the thought of selling up in Hollywood and causing
everyone there worry and stress. 'Even if I bought the house
I've just found, Dickie would have nowhere to go. His life,
his work, is in America.'

Suddenly, in the middle of it all, Dickie phoned with a
solution. Both he and I had been warned that the Inland
Revenue could reach across to America and take my house
in Beverly Hills, with all its contents, in lieu of the money
they were owed. He suggested that, as we'd been separated
for so many years, I might allow him to divorce me without
defending the case. Sweetly he explained that we would
probably divorce one day anyway, but if we did it
immediately and I permitted the American courts to give
him the house – and of course the children – no-one could
legally waive the order.

On the face of it, I considered his plan to be a good one.
But the part about the children worried me and I expressed
my concern.

'You know I'd never do anything to hurt or jeopardise
them', Dickie said soothingly. 'And this house is yours
whenever you come to see us.'

After the conversation I reflected on the situation. Really
I had no alternative. It was either the taxman taking
everything away from them, or allowing things to be done
in this manner, thereby saving everything for them at least.
For my part, all I had in the world would be given away.
Despite Dickie's reassurance that things would be all right,
I insisted that he must give me an undertaking to put the
house into a trust for the boys, so that if he married again

they would not be left out in the cold. As for my own wish to buy a home in Sunningdale? The directors of the trust at last relented and purchased the property for me.

Fired with the success of his own idea, Dickie actually flew over to London and we met in our lawyer's office to sign papers and seal arrangements. Yet even though I was giving him everything for which I had worked so hard, Dickie's attitude towards me remained cold. When the necessary business had been completed, he spoke no more and went to stay with my former agent.

I stood alone outside the lawyer's office, the London traffic rushing past, thinking about what I had just signed away; and a momentary shiver ran through me as, for no reason at all, I suddenly remembered all those pieces of paper Dennis had put before me to sign so many years before. But I was so excited at the prospect of having a home of my own in England again that all doubts or misgivings were quickly swept away. There was the big move to Sunningdale to plan for, and I rushed around happily buying furniture. With all my belongings now in America, I had to start from scratch. As luck would have it, I signed to make a film, *Hammerhead*, with Vince Edwards, on location in Portugal, and with the money from that I was able to stock Orchard Manor with most of the fittings required.

Life went on as usual until Christmas, when I had to leave Troy while I undertook a cabaret engagement in Las Vegas. It was at a downtown hotel and rather seedy, but at least it was money. More important, it gave me the opportunity to visit the children. I was now able to tell them that I had a lovely home for them to come and stay in whenever they liked. But as they were so young, neither of the boys seemed to care much whether they came or not; and of course Amy was certainly not keen on the idea.

Gary began to cry as I prepared to return to England, however. 'Are you going away again?' he asked sadly, for my life to him appeared to be one long round of airports and farewells.

In the plane I wept over what he had said and the look on

his little face when I last saw him stayed in my mind all the way back. If only they could come and live with me permanently; but then Dickie would be alone. And he now had a more secure income than I did to provide for the boys. It was back to Troy and cabaret work, when I could get it. Even my fees for doing that were declining rapidly!

Life during 1968 proceeded along the same course as the previous years. Work, parties, friends staying for weekends, trying to find work to keep us going, and coping with Troy's gambling. He seemed to have become unsettled by his life and new surroundings, and our relationship wasn't helped by some of his friends hinting that it was time he left me and got on with his career. Why should he accompany me on cabaret tours just because I paid the bills, they sneered. Why shouldn't he go out more with the chaps and play around with other women as they did?

But I had more than Troy on my mind by this stage. My bankruptcy proceedings had started, and several days a week I journeyed alone to London, there to sit for long, harrowing hours in the tax consultant's office, going over my whole life and affairs in readiness for the court case. It was one time I really did want a man by my side, and in my hours of need there was no-one.

There was one consoling feature in the bleak picture. That summer I arranged for Mark and Gary to be brought over by Amy for a holiday. They loved the house and gardens, and we had such a wonderful time that I desperately wanted them to stay for good. But, I kept thinking, they were all Dickie had in the world; it would be selfish and unfair to keep them from him. Perhaps, I thought optimistically, they could live in England for part of the year, and stupidly I mentioned the idea to Amy. Even putting up with *her* would be bearable if I had my sons. She promised to discuss it with Dickie when they returned, but I should have known better than to trust the woman. As soon as she was back in America she launched into a tale of how I had tried to keep them permanently! Only through her cleverness and loyalty to Dickie had he got them back at all. This naturally sent Dickie into a rage and he vowed never to let them visit

258 *Dors by Diana*

me again. No amount of pleading on my part would persuade him otherwise, and now that he had legal custody he could dictate the terms.

Meanwhile, as the bankruptcy case neared its big date in court, I received two telephone calls. One was from the Australian agent I'd worked for all those years before, inviting me to go out there for another cabaret season. The other was from the local bank manager, and his news was not so good. The small amount I had placed there, which of course was in Troy's name because, being nearly bankrupt, I was not permitted to have an account, had all gone. We were virtually broke.

At thirty-six, after working all my life, I did not have a penny! I was forced to borrow £100 immediately from a club owner friend for whom I was going to make a personal appearance. As far as my life with Troy was concerned, this was the last straw. I realised I could never leave him in charge of Orchard Manor as he did not want to go to Australia with me. Nor did it appear that we could live together like normal people, which is all I really wanted from life.

Before this, I'd hoped that things could have been good for us personally, if not professionally. Dickie and I were divorced now, a judge somewhere in California having ended our marriage without me even having to be there. It was a strange, empty feeling, after a liaison which had started with such great love and hope. The children knew nothing about it, nor did the press, and so for the moment all was quiet. We had not heard from Troy's wife, Barbara, for several years.

Now I realised the time had come to take a grip on my life, and I decided not to go to Australia. As if fate were approving my change of attitude, I was offered a guest-star role in a new television series entitled *The Inquisitors*. And when the producer came to my home to discuss it, I enquired who the stars were.

'Two very good actors', he replied. 'Tony Selby and Alan Lake.'

I remembered seeing Alan Lake in a television play some

months before; probably because he portrayed a character remarkably like Troy. He was extremely good, and I had even mentioned the play to Troy, who as usual was at a greyhound meeting when it was shown. It was just the sort of part I felt he could have played to perfection had he only chosen to concentrate on acting. Instead, it seemed, he preferred to play the role in real life!

The night before we began rehearsals for *The Inquisitors*, I had a strange dream in which I fell in love with Alan Lake! Perhaps this influenced me the next morning, for as our eyes met something happened between us which one only reads about in romantic novels. He was exactly the sort of man I'd been searching for all my life. His handsome looks were of gypsy stock; black curly hair and dark brown eyes. He wore a small, gold ring in his ear, was talented and intelligent. Here, at last, was someone with whom I had everything in common; an actor who loved his work and whose sense of humour was the same as mine.

We had lunch together, and that evening I confided to a friend that I thought I'd met the man of my dreams, literally!

'But he's sure to be married', I said pessimistically. Having been through two miserable affairs with married men, I was not about to embark on another, no matter how much he attracted me. The following day I plucked up courage to ask him. To my amazement I found that, at twenty-seven, he didn't even live with anyone.

'But there must be some woman about to throw herself off a bridge because of you?' I persisted, hardly able to believe that this romance, for that is what it was definitely going to be, might run along smooth, easy lines.

'There's no-one', he answered quietly.

That day passed, and on the next evening after work we went out to dinner. Alan gave me an amethyst ring which his uncle had bequeathed him many years before.

'I promised him I'd give this to the woman I wished to marry', he said. 'And that's what I want to do, for I'm in love with you.'

'We've known each other only a few days', I countered.

'I feel as if I've known you all my life. I've never been in love with anyone else.'

I then told him all about Troy, but confessed that I, too, was in love with him, and eventually we parted for the weekend.

Things truly had taken a crazy turn. Here I was in love with a man I had only just met, wearing his ring and knowing he loved and wanted me as much as I did him. Moreover, it was a bad time to tell Troy I had fallen in love with somebody else. Leapy Lee had suddenly hit the pop charts with a record made as a result of an all-night poker game Troy had organised some months previously at our house. One of the card-players had been Tom Jones's manager, Gordon Mills. The song, *Little Arrows*, had soared to success, and now Leapy had money and fame, everything that Troy always wanted himself.

Despite the unfortunate timing, though, I was determined not to deceive Troy. I was going to be honest. As I expected, he took it badly, but he quickly resigned himself to the inevitable because, regardless of Alan, our affair had really drawn to an end. Now, I explained, he would be able to do all the things he felt unable to accomplish while living with me.

On Monday morning, as I left for the television studios, Troy bade me farewell, saying he would take his things and leave. He said he needed the little Mini we owned, and relieved that he was bowing out of my life I did not object to this. I could always buy another car from the money I was earning from the show. Before he left, however, he emptied our slot-machine which friends had kept filled with coins. Somehow the picture of him driving off in a second-hand Mini, with his pockets bulging with sixpences, sadly seemed to sum up our four years together.

CHAPTER TEN

TIGER BY THE TAIL

Here comes a candle to light you to bed,
And here comes a chopper to chop off your head.

The first few weeks spent with Alan were rather like being transported on a magic carpet to paradise! It was as though I had been asleep or in some kind of insane trance for years. To say all those years were bad is probably an exaggeration but, despite the laughter and fun, I had sunk, both professionally and personally, to depths which I would never have dreamed possible.

Now fresh life was ebbing back into my body and a new sparkle effused through my mind. I was in love with a brilliant, incredibly handsome actor who wrote beautiful poetry and had a wonderful sense of humour. The whole delightful aspect of it all seemed too good to be true, and paranoiacally I began worrying what might go wrong.

'You had such a dreadful time with Troy', said a friend. 'Now it's your turn for happiness, just relax and enjoy yourself!'

I readily accepted this advice, deciding it must be right. Why shouldn't I believe that the ripe old age of thirty-seven was not too late to find someone like Alan who, even if he was nine years younger than me, loved me so ecstatically? And if the situation did seem straight from a romantic novelette, I knew from experience that truth was indeed stranger than fiction.

The television series we worked on went well. Acting together was as natural as breathing. In short, starry-eyed and enraptured, we were perfect for each other. And as if

the affair hadn't been breathlessly fast enough, Alan stated
that he wanted to marry me as soon as possible. I was
divorced and there was no reason not to, he insisted. For my
part, caught in the whirlwind passion of love, I forgot all the
bitter experiences of the past, which should have made me
wary of trying marriage for a third time. Instead, I decided
that this must be my last chance of finding happiness, so I
had to hold on tight for fear it slip away.

At great speed, with my divorce papers secured to ensure
legalities and having known each other only seven weeks,
we married at Caxton Hall on 23 November, 1968. The
wedding took place in the same room in which Dennis and I
had gone through our bizarre ceremony seventeen years
before! But this time it was a vastly different affair. The
bride wore white lace, the groom black velvet, and we were
surrounded by family, friends and dozens of press photographers. Afterwards we proceeded to a glittering reception
at a London club. Champagne flowed, flowers were
presented, and later, on the Simon Dee show, Alan
eloquently parried sharp questions as to why he married
me at all, winning everyone's approval when he joked,
'Obviously I haven't married her for her *money*!'

The subject of my bankruptcy was already well known,
for I had undergone a horrendous experience in court when
I had tried to explain some of the situations which occurred
with Dennis, but neither the judge nor the prosecutors
believed me.

I had written to Dickie, telling him of the forthcoming
marriage because I would have liked my sons to be there,
but he never bothered to reply. I also felt it important that
the truth should be revealed to the boys about our divorce,
now that they were growing older.

Gary, watching television one evening, was shocked to
see a report of my wedding on some news item, and rushed
to his father in bewilderment to ask what it meant.

'Nothing, just a load of publicity!' came the abrupt
answer. How much better a gentle explanation of the situation and the circumstances would have been.

With Alan starring in the series on which we met, there

was no chance of going away for a honeymoon. But it didn't really matter. We were so deliriously happy at home. Here I was in the house I loved with a man whose grandfather, an illegitimate son of the mad Duke of Sutherland, had married a gypsy girl named Saranne. Perhaps there is something to hereditary influences, for Alan had inherited her strange powers of vividly foreseeing the future. Furthermore he had an explosive temper, his enormous dark eyes flashing dramatically if anything was wrong. Yet at heart, although an artistic, temperamental actor, he was sensitive, kind and truthful.

I often wondered why there had never been a regular woman in his life, but it was out of curiosity, not jealousy. Perhaps women couldn't keep up with him, I calculated, for his over-abundance of energy truly was exhausting. His high-spirited attitude to everything usually left both men and women worn out long before he finished quoting poetry and Shakespeare or telling amusing anecdotes far into the night. There was another aspect to him, too, as I discovered very early in our relationship. Underneath all the bravado, Alan was actually an extremely shy man. And by speaking to women in a rather shocking manner, as he often did, he was using such outrageous behaviour to protect himself in case they hurt him.

There *had* been one girl with whom, while a young actor in rep., he fell in love. Tragically she died of cancer, and from then on he devoted his full interest and time to acting, treating all females with a certain contempt. This, contrarily but inevitably, made him more interesting to the opposite sex!

A strange thing happened on the first night he visited my home. A medallion, given him by his dead love and which he had worn for years, suddenly disappeared and was never found again. With his gypsy superstition, Alan took this to mean she had finally released him – in favour of me. Though I had always been interested in the occult, I laughed at this. But gradually I came to see many things which occurred around this extraordinary man, whom his grandmother Saranne had foreseen would die at thirty-three and was nearly proved right! Certainly among his gifts was that of incredible healing powers, for I observed many cases of people cured when he concentrated on their ailments.

Being with a man who fascinated and enchanted me saw our early marriage sail along on a sea of blissful happiness. And as if the speed with which everything had happened wasn't already enough, I discovered that we were expecting a baby. Alan was elated, but I experienced doubts as to what the advent of a child might do to our new-found wonder. I remembered the misery I had had with Dickie, and was *still* having, regarding the children. Added to which there was the consideration that I might be just a little too old at thirty-seven to cope with it all.

Certainly an addition to our family, although wonderful, would curtail the good times we were having, and I dearly wanted to continue these for a short while with my perfect husband. Alan, in his innocent delight, could not possibly know the domestic problems that went with babies and nannies. God forbid I should find another like Amy! Even if she did care extremely well for my two sons in Hollywood, she had created so much trouble between Dickie and me, right from the beginning.

Yet a nanny would be important. As we were by no means rich I would still have to work after the birth, taking whatever I could get in the way of cabaret. Alan, unlike every other man in my life, worked all the time, but he was not yet in the star bracket. The kind of money he proudly made, and showered upon me at every opportunity, was not enough to cover the expenses of a country house and lifestyle such as we had.

Having accustomed myself to the fact that we would not be able to prolong our honeymoon existence, owing to the expected baby, I decided to relax and enjoy my pregnancy this time, pushing aside all thoughts and misgivings about the future. As before I went through the early, wretched months of sickness and biological change, but gradually this subsided. And while Alan worked in Manchester on a new television series, I tried to get used to being a lazy expectant mother. I missed him very much and rejoiced when he came home at weekends.

My whole life had changed in such a short time. Not that it could ever be dull with a vibrant, tempestuous personality like Alan around. But things were *so* different. I had a man, a husband, who worked hard and paid the bills instead of living off *my* earnings. Moreover, he worshipped the ground on which I walked and hated the idea of people referring to me as anything but 'Mrs Lake'. I was contented but in no way could I be bored. Living with Alan, as with Dennis, meant I had to remain permanently at his high level.

I often wondered how long this idyllic association would last. It almost didn't seem right that I could go on being in love with, and loved by, a man who was my ideal. But last it did. And when our baby son, Jason, was born, and Alan opened in a starring role at a London theatre two weeks later, receiving fantastic notices for his performance, our cup of happiness seemed to be overflowing! He was truly a magnificent actor, and whether on stage or screen possessed a charisma that surrounds only a selected few. So when that play closed, it was not long before he was being pursued with an offer of another, this time at the celebrated Royal Court theatre in Chelsea.

Happy at home, enjoying playing the role of wife and mother for the first time in my life, I would have been perfectly content to stay that way. But the producer and author asked our mutual agent if I would read the script, too. Frankly, neither of us liked it at all, feeling it to be a very involved, artistic piece; confusing and not particularly commercial. But they were amazingly persistent, even to the extent of coming to the house to implore us to accept the roles offered.

It is a well-known fact that actors are the worst judges of what is good for their careers. And so, despite not being keen to do this play, we finally allowed ourselves to be argued into it. Going back to work, of course, necessitated hiring a nurse for Jason, but eventually I found a young girl efficiently trained to care for babies and we commenced

rehearsals. Not, I must add, without a number of misgivings as to what we'd let ourselves in for!

With Christmas 1969 approaching, and as we were
having Jason christened, I wrote to Dickie's manager – for
it was useless trying to contact *him* – insisting that Mark
and Gary be brought over for the event. Earlier that
summer, while pregnant, I had paid the fares, as I always
did, so that both boys could visit us. I particularly wanted
them to meet Alan. But at the last minute, Lenny, the
manager, telephoned to say they were all going to Hawaii
instead, leaving me in tears. Alan had been disappointed,
too, for he was anxious to meet his stepsons. Then, there
was nothing we could do; but this time I demanded their
presence and eventually received a reply that *when* I sent
the tickets they would come. With Amy in tow, of course!

Despite any feelings I had about her, I made the necessary arrangements, warned Jason's young nurse not to
listen to any of Amy's lurid tales, and excitedly awaited
their arrival. I had not seen them for nearly two years!

To say that the boys loved Alan from the very start would
be an understatement. They worshipped him! When we
weren't rehearsing he took them riding in Windsor Great
Park and to their delight played endless games. Gary
voiced his opinion, in the way that children do, when he
said: 'I wish Alan was our father. Dad never plays games
with us like this.'

The christening was wonderful, and so too was
Christmas that year. But once the festivities were over the
time came all too quickly for the boys to return to America
for school. We had a tearful farewell at the airport, with
Alan as upset as me to see them go for they had won his
heart. True, he still had Jason; but at four months a baby is
not as interesting to a man as in later years.

When Dickie met his boys at Los Angeles they were still
miserable about leaving Alan behind and pleaded to be
allowed to return immediately. This obviously hurt him
deeply. Amy did not help by telling him that I had tried to
turn their affections to keep them with me permanently,
and that Alan had filled their heads with fantasies and

nonsense designed to make them prefer his company to that of their own father. As a result, a fierce argument ensued on the telephone between Dickie and me, and he swore it was the last time they would ever be permitted to visit me. Nothing I said had any effect on his decision, even though I explained that, had I wanted to keep them with me as Amy intimated, I would have done so.

'Why did I send them back to you if that was my intention?' I asked. But it was all to no avail. He even insisted on making Mark come to the telephone and sob that he never wanted to see me again.

How the man I once loved and supported for so long could behave this cruelly was beyond me. But I was power-less to do anything at the end of a long-distance telephone line. Amy had not confined her activities to spreading poison with Dickie, either. Jason's young nurse also seemed affected by her presence, and I began to notice a difference in her attitude. Still, there was little I could do about it because we were on the point of opening. I could only hope for the best and get on with my work.

Three Months Gone opened at the Royal Court in January 1970 and was an overnight success. For the third time in my life, Sir Laurence Olivier was in the audience applauding.

'You and Alan will probably become the next Oliviers', he said with praise afterwards in my dressing-room.

It was the first attempt I had made at a character role and I grabbed it with both hands. I knew on that opening night that all the critics were waiting for me, their pens dipped in vitriol, ready to scribble acid reviews! But with the confidence I had displayed all my life, even at the start of my career, I rushed on that stage determined to prove them wrong. It had been fifteen years since *Yield To The Night*, with nothing but cabaret in working-men's clubs, bankruptcy, and professional degradation since then. Now I would show the world. Diana Dors may have been down, but she was most definitely not out!

The sweet smell of success! Suddenly, from being a has-been, a yesteryear sex-symbol and a show-business joke who had once starred in Hollywood, I was the toast of the town. Critics were aghast that, after all this time, Diana Dors could really act' – something I had known all along. And what better experience could an actress have had than the hell I'd been through in recent years?

Life is always balanced by scales. When good moments occur, bad ones usually weigh them down. At the height of happiness over my success in show-business again, with London buzzing and offers of films, television and theatre pouring in, I was not permitted to bask in the glory of glowing notices. Jason's nurse handed in her notice, leaving me to cope with a baby while doing a play each night of the week, plus two matinees. Thankfully friends rallied round until I found another capable girl, who stayed with us for a year.

Alan and I were now on top of the world. He had received marvellous notices, too, and we rejoiced professionally and personally. When news came that the play would transfer to the Duchess theatre in the West End for a long, financially successful run, our lives were actually complete.

Good fortune had followed us from the minute we met. Rather as Dennis and I had been, we were magic for each other. But though never a pessimist, in fact quite the opposite, I kept feeling it was too fabulous to last. Apart from the unhappiness of not seeing Mark and Gary, everything else had been incredible. Our meeting, falling in love so late in life, marrying and having baby Jason. Now a new, respected acting career alongside a successful actor husband; it was like a dream come true.

The dream had to end, though, for all dreams do. As we worked hard that summer in the play, and I continued to implore Dickie to allow the children over again, I noticed that Alan seemed to be drinking a great deal. Oblivious of any drinks which he may have indulged in during our early days together, and blissfully in love, I knew little of the problems that plagued those people who cannnot do without alcohol. I had often seen friends intoxicated, and was well accustomed to men in my cabaret audiences behaving in a drunkenly boring manner. But to live with a man who needed alcohol desperately was a completely different thing.

There had been only one serious occasion, when I was pregnant, yet it should have forewarned me about my husband's illness. However, because I did not understand such matters, I passed it off as the actor prevailing over sense or logic. We had been arguing, and in a fit of passion through a drunken haze Alan took an overdose of pills. Terrified, I called a doctor, who arranged for his departure on a stretcher to hospital. There they pumped the wretched poison from his stomach and he was allowed to return home next day, rather contrite but quite unconcerned as to my condition or feelings.

This, although I didn't know it, was the warning, which might have accounted for my growing doubts as to whether or not our happy existence could last. But at the time I reasoned that we had merely had a fight that got out of hand, rather as most married couples have. I never suspected alcoholism, the early stages of which were affecting my husband. For even then Alan was something of a Jekyll and Hyde. When he was sober I knew only an intelligent, kind and wonderful man; amusing and certainly never dull. But after he'd been drinking he became repetitive, boring and occasionally quite alarming. With his dramatic personality and looks, the louder he got the more terrifying he appeared to everyone.

How could I know that, while never once ruining his performance nor causing trouble professionally, his need for drink had become insatiable. Towards the end of the play's run he took to visiting the pub next door during intervals in order to throw down a few drinks before carrying on. At this stage I imagined he was just a heavy drinker, as many of his fellow young actors from RADA were. Indeed, I had never seen men soak up so much alcohol and put it down to the fact that they were of a different age-group from myself; younger, angry and in need of the stimulation drinking gave them.

Finally, with the help of my former agent and manager, whom Dickie knew well, it was agreed that the boys would be allowed to come over that summer, especially as the play was nearing its end and I could devote time to giving them a good holiday. Alan also spoke to Dickie on the phone, assuring him that he had never tried to steal their affections, and to my surprise Dickie admitted he had been jealous of his sons' reaction towards Alan. The only flaw in the plan was that he insisted Amy had to come too. If she didn't, he was afraid she would hand in her notice, and as he was working full-time on his television series he could not manage without her.

Happily I looked forward to the boys' arrival, thinking of and planning ways of entertaining and amusing them during their stay. Little did I realise then the tragedy that was about to befall and which would affect all our lives.

After my marriage to Alan, I remained friendly with a number of people I'd met while Troy was living with me and one of these was Leapy Lee. By now a successful pop-singer, Leapy had bought a large house near mine and he and Alan developed a good rapport. They shared a similar sense of humour, and both liked to drink together at our local pub.

Leapy had been touring Australia during the summer, and one Sunday not long after his return I invited him and his wife to lunch. As usual Alan and Leapy went for drinks at the hostelry, which was then under temporary management while the regular landlord, whom Alan knew well, was away on holiday. They returned for lunch somewhat the worse for drink, as many men are after a Sunday lunchtime session, and proceeded to carry on drinking throughout the afternoon. That evening they announced they were going back to the pub, and as both Leapy's wife and I had had enough of their raucous behaviour, we were relieved to see them go!

The world now knows what later ensued, for press reports were rife. Suffice it to say that an argument began between the two of them and the stand-in landlord, resulting in Leapy foolishly emptying the contents of his beer-glass over the man's head! Two thugs, anxious for a spot of bother, rushed from another bar and a general mêlée broke out. The incensed landlord hit Leapy with a beer-pump handle, causing a gaping wound in his head that required stitches, whereupon Leapy seized a penknife that was lying on the bar and lashed out in defence. Alan at this time was on the floor being kicked by several other drunks who'd joined the fight. Much damage was done all round and they both arrived home bleeding profusely!

Some ten minutes later the police came and took them away, subsequently charging Leapy with stabbing and Alan with being an accessory. Released on their own bail they returned home, neither really remembering much of what had happened.

Thank heaven my father had not lived to see this, I thought. But eminently worse was the realisation that my sons were due to arrive amidst the publicity which now blazed from every newspaper. I only hoped it wouldn't be reported in America, so provoking Dickie into stopping them from coming, and my prayer was answered. They did arrive as planned, happily oblivious of the trouble, and for their benefit we tried desperately to play it down. This was not always easy, though, because during the boys' stay Alan had to appear before a magistrate, who directed that the case be sent to a higher court.

When the play closed we spent the rest of the time with the boys, enjoying ourselves despite the horrible shadow hanging over us. For physical reasons, let alone emotional ones, I was glad of the rest, for as a result of my new-found success I had also done a few films during the play's run. I managed to get along with Amy, although it was difficult, and at times I seriously contemplated doing what she had accused me of – keeping the boys for good! But always at the back of my mind was how grossly unfair it would be to Dickie. There was no reason why I should feel this way, he had shown me little kindness or consideration, but my heart ruled my head yet again. I reasoned that I had Alan and Jason. If I took away the children he loved, much as I longed to have them with me forever, it would be cruel and callous.

Once again they did not want to go back to America

when the moment arrived, but we consoled them with the news that we would soon be going over to visit them. We were in much need of a holiday, having worked so hard all year, and when Alan was given permission to leave the country on bail we set off.

It was Alan's first trip to America and we had a fantastic time. Dickie was even quite civil when we visited what had once been my house – a weird experience for me – and it appeared that, with his fame, success and wealth, he had at last come to terms with life. Consequently we were able to spend several happy weeks with the boys, who were thrilled to have Alan there and took great delight in showing him around places like Disneyland and Malibu Beach. The miserable spectre of his forthcoming court-case faded a little, but just before our dreaded departure something else happened to wipe away the happy, carefree days that had passed. Though I wasn't to know it at the time, it was going to sever for many long, sad years the relationship I had with my sons.

Dickie, quite naturally, was dating many girls, some of whom we met while swimming at the house with Mark and Gary. But Amy, fearful that he might marry again and that she would be ousted from her position, continually grumbled about them, degrading all of them in front of the boys. To her, they were mostly 'floosies'; dirty, common creatures unfit to be allowed in the house.

One evening while we were there, Dickie introduced his latest date before taking her to dinner and asked Mark to kiss the lady goodnight. Mark was furious and rushed to the rest of us, wiping his face angrily and uttering remarks about the unfortunate female's hygiene. This worried me immensely, for it suddenly made me realise what Amy was actually doing in her efforts to turn the children against any woman who might jeopardise her job.

That night, back at our hotel, I discussed my worries with Alan, and the following morning I phoned Dickie's manager, who dealt with all his affairs. I knew from experience it was no use trying to speak with Dickie on such matters. Having expressed my concern about what I could

see was happening, I also added that it was unfair to Dickie
if he ever did find a woman he wanted to marry. But, and
this was even more important, Amy's attitudes and behaviour could easily make Mark, who had always been so
influenced by her, hate all women. I didn't want that for my
son.

'I shouldn't be too upset', he drawled. 'Dickie will see
that such a thing doesn't happen.'

'Dickie's not there half the time to see anything', I
insisted, and finally won his assurance that he would speak
to Amy carefully.

Later that morning when we arrived at the house, Mark
behaved most strangely, going off on his own and ignoring
Alan and me. After a while I went in search of him, and
found instead a thunderous Amy. Lenny, the manager, had
telephoned and ticked her off soundly for putting ideas in
the boys' minds, and she was furious with me because she
thought I wanted her to lose her job. Already, it seemed,
she had used her influence to turn Mark against me. I could
only hope that Gary was still too young to be affected, but I
knew, listening to the lukewarm goodbyes from my sons as
we departed, that any damage Amy had done in the past
would be nothing to what she might do in the future. I would
be 6,000 miles away and helpless to do anything about it!

I returned to England with a heavy heart, and was met
with the news that Jason's nurse was pregnant and leaving
our employ. It was the last thing I needed, for Alan and I
were due to star in a new television series, *Queenie's Castle*,
for Yorkshire Television. I desperately needed someone to
care for Jason while I was working, and I was both relieved
and grateful when Alan's mother stepped into the breach
and took him to her home in Staffordshire for a few weeks
until I could find someone else. But after my most recent
experience with Amy, I was even more nervous about
interviewing strangers with a view to giving them sole charge
of my child.

Added to this aggravation there was Alan's court-case,
which was being pushed along rapidly so that he could start
work in Leeds on the series. His lawyers, hoping that any

sentence passed would be suspended because he had never
been in trouble before, were advising him to plead guilty to
speed up proceedings. Alan, naturally, was reluctant to
plead guilty to something he had not done, but he reasoned
that the advice must be sound and that, under the circumstances, pleading guilty would be the quickest way of
dealing with the matter.

On the day of Alan's court appearance, with Yorkshire
Television waiting anxiously for us, we had a car standing
by to whisk us both to Leeds to begin filming the next
morning. The judge, however, thought otherwise. He took
a dim view of Leapy and sentenced him to three years'
imprisonment. Leapy, white-faced, clutched at the sides of
the dock as Alan awaited his fate. In his case, the judge
decided, as he was merely an accessory, *he* would go to
prison for eighteen months! Neither of the sentences was
suspended, as we had been led to believe, and down to the
cells they went.

I couldn't believe what was happening. Yet again I had
placed my confidence in lawyers and once again my life had
been shattered! At first they wouldn't even let me see Alan,
but eventually we were given a fast three minutes to try to
plan our present and our future.

We both attempted to be brave, but it was like a terrible
nightmare! I left him in that God-forsaken hole, and was
driven to Yorkshire where, in the tradition of show-
business, the show *had* to go on. In Leeds market the next
day, where we were filming, everyone shouted, stared and
greeted me with the same artificial cheerfulness I had
received at Dennis's funeral. Despite the brave front I put
on, though, I felt utterly destroyed! How I got through my
performance I don't know, except that from somewhere I
drew on reserve strength and did it. In addition I had to see
and comfort Alan's parents, who were heartbroken, and all
the time I was telling myself that I had to retain my grip on
life for Alan's and Jason's sakes. Nothing would be gained if
I fell to pieces!

As often as possible I saw Alan through a glass window in
Oxford prison, reassuring him that everything was being

done about his appeal and that all was well at home. Our courage saw us both through those harrowing weeks, and only once did Alan break down – at the thought of Christmas without his family.

Thankfully I managed to find an excellent nurse for Jason, and that was one thing I no longer had to worry about. Single, old-fashioned and incredibly fussy, she was nevertheless wonderful with him. Alan's parents came to stay for a while and we all visited him at the new prison to which he had been sent on the cold, remote island of Portland, near Weymouth. It took me three hours to drive there and another three to come back, but that was to be the pattern of our marriage for the next year!

In spite of glowing testimonials from Lord Olivier and others, Alan's appeal was turned down. Now his fate was sealed, and the original fears I had about our happiness were confirmed! Our love, marriage and success, which had all started out so wonderfully, had been reduced to a three-hour meeting each month, sitting at a formica-topped table in a miserable prison visiting-room with other convicts' wives.

Still not realising the seriousness of Alan's alcohol problem, on every visit I would take a small flask of orange juice mixed with vodka to help lift his spirits a little in that ghastly place. Of course the warders didn't know about it, and I assumed it was doing him no harm. However, for the rest of that long year in jail he was forcibly dried out, and as a result he looked marvellously fit and handsome. Sadly it was all wasted in there!

Determinedly I carried on with my life and work. My aim was to make as much money as possible and look forward to my husband coming home. I carried a piece of paper with the calendar year written on it, ticking off each day and wishing my life away. Still, I could be grateful that my career had been revitalised, otherwise Jason and I might have been walking the streets.

My first big assignment was a film with Raquel Welch in Spain, from where I phoned Mark and Gary, hoping that they'd like to visit their mother some time during the year. I felt so alone. But the replies were abrupt and disinterested.

'No!' said Mark, quite definitely. 'We're probably going to Hawaii. And anyway, it's cold in England. There's nothing to do there.'

It was more than apparent that Amy had been weaving her spell. And even when I bade them both a sad goodbye, saying 'I love you', no love came back!

From that night on, having sobbed myself to sleep, I threw everything I had into my work. Cabaret was plentiful, and I drove all over England in the following months. There was another film, on location in Germany, and many offers of television shows. In between, each month, I visited Alan, sitting at the formica table, holding hands by a tea urn and planning our wonderful future.

'How will all this affect your career?' was a question he continually asked. Naturally he wondered, too, if I might meet someone else. Had I been out with other men? But he needn't have worried. I loved him deeply, and all I could think of was his release on 16 October. Then we would be together again.

I now realised I'd never loved any man in my life the way I loved him. It was not just a case of being in love, but loving with all my heart and soul, unselfishly, loyally and proudly. I wasn't so blind not to see he'd been a fool to threaten our happiness in such a way, but mercifully I did not know the full tragic events that lay ahead!

As his 'coming-out' date drew nearer, I excitedly planned a big welcome-home party, inviting a hundred friends, and bought him a gift, a beautiful seventeen-hand mare called Sapphire. An uncle in Wales arranged her transportation to a nearby stable, and the idea was to surprise Alan on the night of the party by leading her through the garden, across the floodlit lawn. Sapphire would then be standing there as his special guest!

Amidst tears and emotion, Alan was finally released. The sight of him at home again was almost too good to be true, and on the night of the party Sapphire thrilled him beyond words. It was pouring with rain, but she stood bowing her head at him in regal recognition of her new master!

'Oh God, Diana, you're too much!' sobbed Rachel Roberts, overcome by the scene. Other friends also wept, for they knew how happy we both were that our terrible ordeal had at last ended.

Alan was immediately signed to work with me on a television play, which was almost a two-handed affair. And despite private fears as to whether he would be able to act again, he gave a brilliant performance. However, the year inside prison had left a deep scar, and it was many months before he could even sleep properly. There was also the problem of drink. The fact that he'd been 'dry' for so long meant that his resistance to alcohol was much lower. Yet it never occurred to me, as we began to rebuild our lives, that we were heading for major problems each time he drank. I was so happy and confident after so long a separation that each moment together was precious in itself.

Alan didn't drive, and never wished to, but he did go riding nearly every day. One fateful morning in early 1972 I received a telephone call that he'd had an accident in Windsor Great Park. Could I get there at once? It seemed Sapphire had shied at something and, out of control, had raced towards a large oak tree with overhanging branches. Unable to stop her, Alan pushed her head and his own down so that neither would be decapitated, as had happened to an unfortunate girl a year earlier. By doing so he took the full force of the branch across his back!

In ignorance, the people with whom he was riding walked him to the edge of the park and put him in a Land Rover which bumped him all the way to the stables. By the time an ambulance got him to hospital he was nearly dead and indeed he was put in a small room reserved for those who were dying.

Miraculously he did not die, but the doctors did tell him he would have to prepare himself for life in a wheelchair. He had broken his back and shoulder in five places! Yet in just six weeks, having been brought home to lie in bed there,

Alan stood for the first time and his doctors were astounded. Sheer will power made him determined to walk again and overcome the terrible pain.

There was, however, another effect of the accident. His resistance to alcohol had diminished even more. In the early hospital weeks, afraid of becoming addicted to morphine, he had friends bring him in bottles of whisky or brandy with which to kill the agonising pain.

That year, as Alan gradually grew stronger but obviously could not work, I made three films. And slowly, inactivity, frustration and drinking made him resent the fact that I was, temporarily at least, the breadwinner. There were times when, rising for an early call at the film studio, I was frightened to make a noise in case I disturbed him and he began feeling jealous of me professionally. I knew from the experience of many friends that this often happened when two artistes were married.

Once, we managed to have a quick, five-day holiday in the south of France, taking Jason and his new, young nurse with us. But it was marred by Alan's drinking, which was now producing hallucinations about who he'd been in a previous life! A trip later that year to Canada, where I was invited to do a television show and Alan accompanied me, was equally horrendous. Right from the beginning he was drunk, and after a weekend in New York before we returned to England he was in such a terrible state that I had to beg the airline pilots and staff to let him on the plane.

It was now dawning on me that he might be what the Americans call a lush; a drunkard or a very heavy drinker! But I remained ignorant of the real facts about alcoholism and, because of his prison ordeal and his broken back, I excused him all the time.

As our lives went on, with dreadful things occurring both at home and in public, I tried my best to help him. I suggested he cut down, didn't mix drinks or stayed on beer with an occasional glass of wine with meals. How sadly wrong I was proved to be! Each terrible scene brought me face to face with 'Mr Hyde'; not the wonderful man I had married. Little by little, all the love and respect I felt for him were being drained away. There was, of course, the aftermath, when he swore he'd never touch another drop and was deeply sorry for what he'd done. But however much I threatened, warning what might happen when Jason grew older and saw his father in that state, he paid no heed. Unable to control his craving for drink, he selfishly continued as only an alcoholic can.

Not that our life was all misery, especially when Alan began working regularly again. He starred in a film called *The Swordsman*, which gave him the opportunity to display his fantastic fencing ability. I, meanwhile, made another series of *Queenie's Castle*, and then another for Yorkshire called *All Our Saturdays*. But if Alan himself wasn't working, I could always expect to find him drunk when I returned home late at night after a gruelling day in the studios. This, naturally enough, led to bitter arguments, though usually not until the next day. I had long learnt that it was an exhausting waste of energy to argue or attempt to reason with him when he was intoxicated. He genuinely didn't remember anything that had happened and was mortified if I told him what he'd said and done.

In 1973 I did a couple of films, and then went to work in cabaret for a week in Wakefield. It was there that disaster struck again, only this time it was *my* turn, tripping on a high step one evening and breaking my leg. Alan rushed to the hospital where I'd been taken and made arrangements to transfer me nearer home for the operation I needed to undergo in order to have a pin placed in my leg. For three months I lay helpless, an unusual situation for me, and towards the end of that period I received an offer to go to Sweden for a film. I could even play the character in a wheelchair if I still wasn't walking properly, the producers said.

This was just the morale boost I needed, and so I agreed unhesitatingly Alan accompanied me there, but even though I was incapacitated and totally dependent on him, he couldn't help getting drunk. On one occasion, in a terrible frenzy, he attempted to strangle me, thinking I was someone else. This was quite contrary to his nature for he was not a violent man, drunk or sober – and certainly never where I was concerned.

Outside my immediate family there were other sadnesses, too. Aunty Kit died of cancer, which left me the painful decision to sell the little house in Swindon. Somehow it had always been my home, but obviously I couldn't live there and the simplest thing was to let it go.

Dickie's mother was also seriously ill after a stroke. She and Dickie's father had returned to England some years before, but they never heard from their son, only from Lenny, his manager, who wrote a regular letter each week as part of his job. This made me even more determined to keep in touch with them, and one day when we were near Gosport, where they still lived in their little house, Alan and I went to visit, taking flowers. They were delighted to see us, but I was appalled at the sight of Grandma. Once such an active woman, she was now paralysed and aged beyond recognition.

Her one fear was that she would die without seeing Dickie again, and I assured her this wouldn't happen. That night I telephoned America from my home, and as well as telling Dickie about his mother I was hoping I could persuade the boys to come and see me now that it was summer. They weren't there when I called, or so Dickie said, and so I concentrated on describing his mother's health and fears.

'Please try and get over', I begged him. 'And bring the boys, too.'

But he brushed off my pleas, saying he was busy with rehearsals and couldn't make it.

Grandma was right. She died later that year and never did see her youngest son again. It was left to me to call him and break the news as gently as possible. Dickie didn't come to her funeral; nor did he send a wreath. Instead, a week later, Lenny sent an American gimmick called a sympathy pot!

For some time now both Alan and I had been developing an interest in Catholicism, there being a Catholic church next door to our home. He was first persuaded to go there by our young nurse after a very bad drinking bout. During this he had been hallucinating, screaming that he was a soldier called Jimmy lying in the muddy trenches of France during the First World War. When Alan was as bad as this it almost seemed as if he was possessed by the Devil, for a different voice came from within! It made me wonder sometimes if exorcism might be the answer!

However, the peace and tranquillity we found in that church were unlike anything we had experienced in our lives, and so we resolved to try to become Roman Catholics. Quite simply, the religion made sense to us. Alan, with his beautiful singing voice, was a great favourite with the Italian priests next door and they thought very highly of him. But for me it wasn't going to be so easy because I had been divorced. Nevertheless, for a year I studied the faith, and I was interviewed by various high Catholic Diocesan councils to determine whether or not I could become a Catholic.

Eventually, in the spring of 1974, both Alan and I were received into the Church, with Lionel Jeffries and his wife, two dear friends, acting as our godparents. When we had gone through all the ceremonies the priest, a wonderful man named Father Simon, suggested we might wish to take our marriage vows again, as originally we had had only a registry office wedding. We agreed, and halfway through the service I broke down and cried. Somehow the words stuck in my throat when it came to 'death us do part'. In a simple way, Father Simon wiped away my tears with my hair, in the way Christ had once done for Mary Magdalene.

That summer I was accorded one of the supreme accolades in the theatre. A chance to star opposite Keith Michell at Chichester in a production of *Oedipus*. Alan was thrilled for me but I knew, as an actor himself, he also felt a twinge of regret that he too hadn't been asked to join the company that season. Indeed, he would have made a marvellous Oedipus, and it was tragic that his wild reputation seemed to be going against him in his career.

Rehearsals commenced, the play eventually opened and at home life continued as usual. The nurse cared for Jason, now four, and Alan worked intermittently. When forced into idleness through no available work, and having no interests or hobbies, he drank and dwelt on the injustice that I was acting in classical theatre for which he had been trained. Frankly, he was far more suited to it than I! Many nights, having exhausted myself in the role of Jocasta, I returned home to find myself having to cope with the tyrant Oedipus again, only now privately. I was even forced to call a doctor to help me deal with him, for alcohol had unleashed a monster, uncontrollable and frightening!

When the Chichester production ended, I did a television drama and then looked forward to spending more time with Jason through the autumn. However, tragedy had not struck yet as it had every year, and there were times when I almost looked over my shoulder to see if it was creeping up on us. But October passed safely, if not always peacefully, and then it was November, nearing our wedding anniversary and Alan's birthday. I did not celebrate either of them at home. One evening, complaining of a terrible headache, I was struck down with meningitis and rushed to hospital in a coma. The doctors told Alan not to expect me to live through the night!

I woke up in a London hospital with everyone telling me I'd been close to death and with my room full of flowers. How or where I contracted the disease had everyone baffled, but for the moment there was relief that I had pulled through without suffering the consequences – deafness, blindness, paralysis – that afflict many who survive this illness. Miraculously I had come through unscathed, and I thanked God for saving me.

I was supposed to take life carefully for a long time afterwards, but luckily I have a strong, healthy constitution. I soon recuperated, despite the constant worry of Alan's drinking, which was now getting worse and worse. Foolishly perhaps, I agreed to tour with him in a play, *Murder Mistaken.* But it was a wonderful role for the male lead, and I thought it would be good for us to work together on stage again.

The tour was disastrous from beginning to end. Alan

drank all night and every night after the show. So much for my thinking, as I had on reading it, that the demanding role would sap his boundless energy. On the contrary, his adrenalin became even more charged. And then, to make matters worse, I found that I was pregnant! Not a happy discovery at this point of our lives.

Doctors warned me not to have the baby. I had just come through a serious illness; I was forty-four years old, a dangerous time! But how could I, as a Catholic, go to mass, receive Holy Communion and pretend to be a Christian if I committed murder? I had done that twice before in my life and still felt ashamed and guilty! For several weeks I wavered between the advice of my doctors and the dictates of my conscience. My conscience won the day. Alan's mother was not pleased with the news.

'You'll have to mend your ways for a start', she told him in her blunt Northern manner. Whether he could, though – let alone would – was out of the question. Alcohol had such a hold on him that he was helpless even to draw on his incredible will power as he had when he broke his back.

The play toured to a grinding halt and I settled down at home to expectant motherhood, hoping and praying I was doing the right thing. I cared for Jason without a nurse, which was lovely, and awaited the blessed event which I felt fate had decreed.

One evening during my eighth month, sitting in the drawing-room with Alan, I suddenly experienced a feeling as if the cold hand of death had passed through me. I burst into tears and Alan ran for blankets to cover and warm my shaking body.

'Perhaps I caught cold yesterday in the wet grass', I suggested, for Jason and I had opened a country fête together.

Some days later, when I went for my usual check-up, the doctor expressed concern, because he could not hear the baby's heartbeat. Further examinations were carried out, and gravely he warned me that it was possible the child had died. This was devastating news, and yet I was forced to carry on through the next few days while we waited for the results of the examination. Two days later he rang to say they were still not sure.

'We dare not terminate', he said. 'If it is alive, we would never forgive ourselves.'

Not knowing whether or not I was walking around with a dead child inside my body was a terrible experience. And yet with hope and prayer, I tried to make the best of it. Alan was as marvellous as always when tragedy or illness occurred, and we both waited anxiously to see what would happen.

He was out with Jason and some friends when I felt labour pains, and I called my local doctor for advice. An ambulance was arranged to take me straight to London, but before it came Jason and his father returned. With strange insight, perhaps inherited from his gypsy great-grandmother, Jason asked, 'Are you going to lose the baby, Mummy?' He was only six!

When I entered hospital I knew the birth was imminent. But my own doctor was nowhere to be found and so a nurse, Alan and a young intern delivered my still-born baby son. There was no time to give me drugs; it was the first time I had experienced natural childbirth, and what a cruel twist that it should be so tragic! I never saw the baby, but Alan broke down and wept hysterically in the corridor, for he looked exactly like Jason.

Exhausted and yet relieved it was all over, I now had to concern myself with Alan. For what with his grief and excessive alcohol consumed earlier in the day he was causing havoc among the hospital staff. When my doctor arrived he begged me to call a friend to take him home, which I did. With my usual healthy approach to life I reasoned there was no need for me to lie in hospital mourning for weeks on end. The baby had been baptised by a priest, to be buried in a cemetery somewhere in London; I could do no more for him. So I discharged myself and went home.

Optimistically I hoped our tragedy for *that* year had been accounted for, but sorrow was to visit us twice more before the twelve months passed. Jason's best friend at school, another Jason, was run over by a car and killed. And Alan's greatest friend died of cancer at thirty-four.

The day of the funeral saw me appearing later on an afternoon television show, fulfilling a long-standing contract. That night I was due to appear in cabaret near Salisbury, and not daring to leave Alan, overcome with grief and fortified with alcohol, in the house alone, I took him with me. The management pleaded with me to get him out and never bring him near the place again!

After many more scenes and traumas, which were now beginning to affect Jason, for he was older than his years and understood what was happening, Alan and I admitted that he must be an alcoholic and he agreed to enter a special hospital for treatment. Several weeks later he came out cured and once again our life was joyful, peaceful and heavenly. It seemed as if I was living with a man from another planet. Not even his parents could believe the change.

Three and a half months went by, and they were the happiest we had had together. But then one hot summer day he relapsed, as alcoholics can, and drank a bottle of vodka! With this breakdown, plus the discovery that Alan's mother had cancer, it looked as if we had hit our tragedy for 1976.

Work, drunkenness, arguments, remorse, misery; some-how life went on! I even managed to write my first book. But eventually, after many ghastly scenes, I took Jason and went to friends in Brighton. I could stand no more! However, a few days later, a friend staying at our house phoned to tell me that Alan was desperately ill and needing medical treatment. We hurried home to find him dehydrated and near death, and once more he was admitted to the same hospital. He remained there for nearly a month, undergoing all kinds of frightful tests to effect a cure. This time, he said, he was determined to do it! But when he came out, the pressures and frustrations were too much for him and ultimately he started drinking again in secret.

Cars smashed; appearances in court on drunk and dis-orderly charges; nights spent in open ditches. Life became public humiliation for both of us wherever we went until, in the end, I refused to be seen with him. Socially, we had no life at all. My friends gradually withdrew from our lives, for I couldn't invite them to the house without some drunken fiasco occurring. Moreover, they were losing patience with me, no-one being able to understand why I put up with it.

For that matter, I didn't know either. I was suffering from a kind of malady myself, in so much as I had become completely conditioned to life with an alcoholic. It had taken many years and hundreds of terrifying experiences for me to come to terms with the fact, and I shuddered when I remembered the days of innocently giving him vodka in prison! Now I was reduced to hiding alcohol; or looking for it if he'd done so.

How tragic that someone who seemed an ideal, perfect man in every way was, after all, the victim of illness and a failure at marriage!

'When people see you on television, looking so glamorous, they think you lead such a marvellous life', remarked a girlfriend of mine who had many times witnessed Alan being ejected from restaurants or creating other dreadful scenes. And back came those words of a teacher at Mr Rank's Charm School.

'If everything else fails, you still have your work.'

Thank God I have had the strength to cope with my responsibilities. I was also fortunate that I did not need the stimulant of drink or drugs to get me through life's problems, stresses and strains. But regardless of the misery I endured with Alan, which really was similar to holding a tiger by the tail, I do not scorn alcoholics or drug addicts. They are casualties of this world, and it's up to those of us who are more fortunate to help and understand their illness.

Alan was born a shy boy, inflicted with strange hereditary traits! He had a brilliant talent and should have enjoyed a superb acting career. But in this lies his tragedy. If he had followed an ordinary way of life he would have been a much happier man. Instead he blazed a wild trail, covering up his inhibitions and fears with a bravado that only drink could give him.

A newspaper writer once remarked, 'The lights are going out all over Alan Lake!' It was unnecessary cynicism, for Alan had already composed his own epitaph in one of the many beautiful poems he wrote.

'Time's running out of places now . . .
And all the hard-earned smiles have turned to frowns,
I have chased my life trapeze-like without a net,
Suddenly, it's bring on the clowns.'

CHAPTER ELEVEN

MY SON, MY SON

*Ladybird, ladybird,
fly away home,
Your house is on fire,
your children are gone.*

Throughout the turbulent years with Alan, and taking into account all that happened to us, my greatest sorrow was never seeing my two sons in Hollywood, Mark and Gary. For since that final disastrous occasion when, through Lenny the manager's mishandling of a delicate situation, Amy thought I'd attempted to have her fired, her influence on my boys had reached its peak. This, combined with the distance between us and Dickie's indifference over the matter, created a complete deadlock in our relationship.

From friends in Beverly Hills I sometimes heard terrible statements Amy had made about me. And if she accused me of such things to others, what poison was she indoctrinating my sons with every day?

Birthday cards, Christmas presents, all were deliberately thrown away, never to be received by the children. 'There you are! Your mother can't even be bothered to send you something on your birthday. Thank goodness you've got me. *She* doesn't love either of you!' were the sort of things they heard regularly. Small wonder when I telephoned, begging those little boys to come and see me in England, that they behaved with such coldness!

Sometimes, if Dickie was around when I called, he'd

enquire what I'd said to them, and having had the conversation dutifully repeated, his remarks were usually derogatory.

'She's crazy! Whacko in the head!'

Naturally I didn't know about this at the time, but a column in a Hollywood film magazine, which I'd seen on my last visit, should have warned me what was going on. It portrayed Dickie, now Richard Dawson, as a sad husband, jilted by an unfaithful wife who ran off with some unnamed man and left him to bring up two little boys on his own. 'What a heartless, dreadful woman she must be. How could anyone have left such a wonderful father to struggle and raise those beautiful children?' That was the tone of the article, and it was no doubt people's opinion of me in Hollywood. There were, of course, photographs of Dickie looking hurt but brave, playing with Mark and Gary, and it was headlined in typical film-publicity jargon, 'The time Richard Dawson became a real-life hero'. His television series was called *Hogan's Heroes*, hence the play on words.

Not that it mattered what anyone thought in that town; I'd never been popular there since the swimming-pool incident with Dennis. But it upset me to think that these untrue facts might one day be believed by my sons. How could I have explained to children, aged six and four at the time, the problems of income tax, bankruptcy, working all around the world, and sending money to keep everyone in a Beverly Hills mansion?

Occasionally, over the following years, I also heard reports of a sad Richard Dawson discussing on one television show or another how much he missed his ex-wife, how there would never be anyone to replace her in his sons' lives, and how, as they were all he had left to love, he was indeed a fortunate man. In magazines, articles appeared reporting such things as photographs of us in our happy days together being kept on display at his Beverly Hills home and that he sent me flowers each year on my birthday. In these ways it was inferred that I was evidently a thoroughly hard-bitten woman.

It was all a bitter pill for me to swallow. The fact that he did not insist at any time on the boys writing or telephoning, or that he made disparaging remarks about me to them, was not known to the American press and public. To them he was a brilliantly funny comedian upon whom they had bestowed the title 'King Richard' as he became their number one television host, with an Emmy award and earnings of millions of dollars! Professionally I was delighted for him, and his success meant that Mark and Gary would benefit, too. But inwardly I seethed with anger each time I read the publicity surrounding him.

From 1970 to 1974 a cold war raged between us. In fairness to the boys they honestly believed I did not love or care about them. Alan's imprisonment was held up as a terrible example to the children and naturally it did not help my case as a bankrupt woman, whose husband was an ex-convict, if I ever attempted to insist they came to stay with me.

'Even a murderess is entitled to see her children at some point', I wrote to Lenny in desperation. But my pleas were always met with excuses of trips to Hawaii, or sometimes just ignored!

When I did phone Mark and Gary our conversations were stilted and abrupt. My questions were always answered with a brief 'Yes' or 'No'. The emptiness and unhappiness I experienced after such calls were indescribable.

In early 1974, three and a half years after I had last seen my sons, a magazine asked me if I would care to give an interview about them. Not only did I readily agree to do so, but I myself actually wrote my account of everything that had happened. No writer, I felt, could ever convey on my behalf the sadness of such a situation. Truthfully and honestly, for there was no need to elaborate, I wrote several thousand words on the subject, and these were subsequently printed in two weekly editions of the journal.

It mattered not to me that Dickie might see what I'd written, for *he* would know everything was true, regardless of what the American public might think. And as the magazine appeared only in England, it couldn't ruin the image he had created in America. I did not reckon, however, with Amy's relatives, who must have sent her copies. Alan was back in hospital at the time, having needed to be put in traction to overcome back trouble resulting from his accident, and so I was alone, apart from little Jason, when I received a letter from Mark, then aged fourteen. It was a letter which no mother should *ever* have from a son.

On monogrammed notepaper with a photograph of himself printed in a circle, he berated me for writing such an article about his father and Amy! The letter was laced with swear words and accusations that everything I had said was untrue.

'You dare to imply Amy has put on weight', he wrote. 'Just look at *yourself* in the mirror.' (I had mentioned that Amy looked tired and plumper when they arrived on their last trip.)

After stating that he did not love me any more, he demanded that I should apologise to both his father and Amy publicly.

'If you do not', he threatened, 'I will disown you as my mother.'

My distress was indescribable!

Having read it to Alan in hospital, and also to several friends in the hope they might be able to advise me what to do, I lay awake far into the night examining his thoughts and motives for writing such a letter. Had he done it entirely on his own? Was an outraged Amy behind it? Or had Dickie helped him compose the wretched piece? Some of the statements did sound like Dickie; but then the reference to Amy's weight was hardly something that would upset *him*.

I could not decide what to do. At one stage I tried to write to explain the magazine articles, and their truthfulness, but it was an impossible task. I had a son who, at a very difficult age, was under the influence of forces impossible to combat from such a distance. There was only one course left open to me, and that was to fly to California for a show-down.

It came about, quite by chance, that a Canadian tele-

vision company wanted me to go to Toronto for a debate
interview. I set off on the journey with misgivings and fears,
uncertain now I was on my way whether my plan for a
surprise visit to Hollywood was the right one. From
Toronto I phoned Pamela Mason and explained the
situation to her, asking as usual for her support and help.
Without hesitation she invited me to stay at her home, and
on arrival in Los Angeles I went straight there. We discussed the whole problem and, taking the coward's way
out, I asked her if she'd accompany me to the house on
Angelo Drive. Sensibly Pam advised me to go alone. After
events in the past, when she'd assisted me, Dickie would
certainly not appreciate her interference again in our
affairs. There was no alternative for me but to face the
wrath of Dickie and Amy completely on my own.

My sole strength lay in the fact that everything I'd
written in the magazine articles was absolutely true. They
knew it, but I would somehow have to convince my sons,
without anyone there to back me up. None of my friends
from the past was there to verify what had happened over
the years. I must be prepared to fight alone.

On the plane from Canada I had mulled over the strange
twists of destiny that had led me into this situation. A little
girl from Swindon, who wore a black disc on one side of her
glasses to correct an eye defect, once dreamt of going to
Hollywood and becoming a film star. That same girl,
grown to womanhood, was now going there, where her sons
lived in a luxury mansion complete with the swimming-
pool she had always wished for. But it was not some scene
from a film. This time, having been separated from them for
over three years, she was going to try to prove that, as a
mother, she loved her children and was not guilty of all the
terrible things they believed.

Praying to God for help, for He was the only one I could
rely on, I drove up that long, winding road towards my old
home. There was a sinking feeling in my stomach. What
was going to happen?

In just a few minutes now, it would all be over! Yet for all
my apprehension I was convinced that my plan to surprise

everyone was a good one, for it gave neither Amy nor Dickie a chance to rehearse their answers.

As I parked my car and walked in through the big gates of the drive, I almost expected machine-gun fire to commence. But with the bearing of a soldier, I marched head held high to the front door and rang the bell. It was opened by my beloved eleven-year-old son, Gary. 'Mom!' he shouted, his face a study of elated surprise. We hugged and kissed, clinging together for fear someone was about to wrench us apart, and I hastily looked for Amy, who was never far away from either of the boys. But there was no sign of her anywhere. 'Where's Mark?' I asked as lightly as possible. Gary was no problem; it was my oldest son who'd written that letter.

Gary led me to his brother's room, which faced the driveway on the ground floor. So Mark must have seen me walk in. He sat on his king-size bed, talking to a friend, and behaved as if I lived just around the corner, giving no reaction at all except a casual 'Hi!' The fact that it had been three years since we met seemed of no importance to him. Perhaps, I reasoned quickly, the shock of seeing me so soon after he'd written such a terrible letter was too much for him, and he didn't know how to handle the situation.

'I received your letter', I said, coming straight to the point.

But at that moment a Yellow cab appeared at the gates and Mark, ignoring my comment, began shouting at the driver to wait. I realised my arrival had only just been in time. A few minutes later the three of them would have been on their way to see a wrestling match in downtown Los Angeles.

I remember thinking how dreadful it would have been if I'd had to face Dickie and Amy *without* the boys there to witness the big show-down, and quietly I thanked God for getting my timing right!

As Mark rushed from the room – I imagined to get help, in the shape of his father or Amy – Gary, who appeared genuinely pleased to see me, asked curiously: 'What letter? I don't know anything about a letter.'

'It was something Mark sent me, darling. I've come over because of what he said.'

'Well, it's great to have you', he beamed warmly. And at that moment Dickie entered, smiling in the charming way which, so many years ago, made me fall in love with him.

From his welcoming attitude, I calculated on the spur of the moment that the letter must have been Amy's doing. Perhaps Dickie didn't even know about it. In which case, where *was* Amy? I couldn't begin my tirade without her. But it was too late anyway. The taxicab was hooting again, and after a brisk, polite few words the boys said they really had to go.

I had no desire to stay alone with Dickie, for when I did say what I'd flown 6,000 miles for, I wanted the entire company present. And seeing that there was no chance of this happening for the moment, I offered to drive the boys down town myself, thinking it would at least give us a little extra time to get reacquainted. They readily accepted, and we chatted happily throughout the journey. No further mention was made of the wretched letter. As I dropped them off we arranged that, after the wrestling, they'd come to see me at Pamela's house, and this they did.

To be with them after so long was quite strange, and conversation was not easy. But I was determined to find out something of what had been going on and, trying to sound as casual as possible, I enquired after Amy. I'd assumed she'd rushed for cover when I arrived so abruptly earlier in the day. The answer I received completely took the wind out of my sails!

'She's ill in hospital', they both replied seriously.

Friends had hinted a year before that Amy was suffering from cancer, but I'd never been able to determine whether or not these reports were true. Now I was learning that she had been in and out of hospital for some time. This, of course, was something of a puzzler. How could *she* have directed Mark's letter from her sick-bed? Was it Dickie after all? Or was it the act of a fourteen-year-old boy crying for help?

Whoever had been at the root of it, my course was now

extremely hazardous. With the poor woman probably dying, I could hardly begin revealing truths about her deceit and general behaviour over the years; not to a couple of boys who genuinely adored her. Apart from the fact that it would be heartless, it would not help me re-establish myself in their esteem. The only way of doing that was to be sweet at all times, showing them I was not the monster she had created, even if it meant once again swallowing my real feelings about the injustice of everything. As always, saying nothing would be easy, especially as I was there only for a three-day weekend before returning to England for the Chichester production of *Oedipus*.

Taking the situation in my stride, I grabbed at every opportunity to bring myself down to the interest-level of two enthusiastic youngsters. It was difficult, for I felt ridiculous trailing along behind them wherever they wanted to go. On many occasions I looked very much out of place, and for the first time I experienced the gap in our generations. But I was determined to play the game by their rules, thereby proving I really was a human being, a mother who loved them even though I had missed so much of their childhood. One day, when they were adults, I could explain the facts and I hoped they would understand.

Dickie behaved in his usual, remote manner whenever I went to the house, but I was used to his behaviour and it never bothered me. Moreover, as he usually kept out of the way, and without the harassment of Amy being there, I could enjoy wandering around what was once my home. The place now had a totally peaceful atmosphere and I loved it.

That weekend flew by so quickly, and eventually the dreaded moment came for me to leave them again. It was the story of our lives —a wonderful time together and then the inevitable parting. During those few days I had taken dozens of photographs which I knew I would gaze at endlessly in the months to come. For who knew when we'd meet again? The matter of the letter had remained un-mentioned, for Mark seemed silently ashamed he had written it. And as the situation was so strained, with Amy dying, I thought it better to ignore the matter.

On our last evening, I gave Mark a little crucifix attached to a rosary-bead necklace that Father Simon had given me when Alan and I were received into the Catholic Church. I knew he wasn't religious, and had never been instructed in anything because Dickie was against all that, but I hoped he might find comfort, and the memory of my love, whenever he looked at it.

At the doorway, as I kissed them both and we all became rather tearful, I glanced around the room. How strange that I should be bidding farewell to my sons in a house that once was mine; among the statues, paintings and furnishings that originally belonged to Dennis and me. Each article told its own story, recalling the different times when Dennis had bought certain things. But it was only in my memory that such reminders were stored. They were of no importance to anyone else!

Earlier I had hopefully intimated that they might like to visit us in England that summer, but to my enormous disappointment the invitation received no enthusiasm. However, on my return to Pamela's house, there was a surprise call from Gary.

'I've been thinking about what you suggested, Mom', he said carefully. 'And I've decided I would like to come over to see you all this summer.'

My heart leapt with joy.

'What about Mark?' I asked.

'Well, he doesn't want to come.'

'Then Mark must do as he wishes. It's his decision', I replied, a trifle sadly. But the thought of at least one of them agreeing to visit was a triumph for me, particularly as I'd had such a short while in which to gain their affection.

The following morning, before I left for the airport, Gary called again, this time from his school. At first I feared he'd had second thoughts, but to my delight he was even more enthusiastic about the idea. I told him he could call me in England at any time, that I would send his ticket, and that we would make more arrangements in a month or so.

'I'm really looking forward to it', he assured me. 'And tell

Alan we can play lots of tennis.' Gary played so well that he
was already well on the way to becoming a professional if he
chose to. I drove to the airport with renewed faith, hoping it
was the start of wonderful things for all of us.

Back home I excitedly told Alan of Gary's forthcoming
arrival.

'Dickie will never let it happen', he said, shaking his head
sadly. 'I hope he does come, but it'll be very surprising.'

Some weeks later, during rehearsals of *Oedipus*, I received
a letter from Gary informing me that Amy had passed away
early in June. I could not be a hypocrite and say I was sorry,
although of course I did not wish death upon her. But I did
experience an overwhelming sense of relief that, at long
last, the main stumbling-block between my sons and me
was gone. Perhaps now we could begin to develop a
relationship without interference. Dickie was so busy with
his career that there was surely no reason for him to prevent
our future association.

I sent Gary a greetings-card and money for his twelfth
birthday on 27 June, as I had always done. *This* time he
received it and immediately wrote a thank-you note.
However, his letter made my heart sink, for no mention was
made of the proposed visit to England and his own exciting
news dashed all my high hopes.

'Dad's given me a new tennis racquet and is paying for
me to have professional lessons here all summer as a
birthday present.'

The implication was obvious to me.

I wrote and told him how pleased I was, asking gently if
he might still come, but with the advent of their annual
holiday in Hawaii – and typical of a young boy – he didn't
reply.

Later that year I nearly died of meningitis, but as I lay in
hospital surrounded by flowers, cards, and telegrams from
all over the world, no word came from the ones from whom
I dearly wished to hear. Messages poured in from stars in
Hollywood who had read about my brush with death in the
LA newspapers. But Mark and Gary, it appeared, were not
aware of my illness. Indeed, as I discovered many years

later, Dickie didn't tell them until some time after the
event.

But the following year, when I lost the baby, I did receive
a wonderfully unexpected call from my sons. It had taken
them several hours to get the number, which had been lost,
but both were most concerned over my tragedy. Maybe
now they're growing up, I thought, things will be easier for
all of us. At least they cared enough about me to telephone.

In the winter of that year Alan and I decided to take a
trip to America. We had the time, the money and
furthermore we would take Jason, too, thereby making it a
real family holiday. Mark and Gary hadn't seen their little
brother for six years and he didn't know them at all.

We made arrangements and set off with high hopes.
There, waiting for us at Los Angeles airport, stood two
grown-up boys, or so it appeared, for at sixteen and
fourteen both looked very sophisticated. All our high hopes
were realised, too, as we spent a wonderful month's
vacation with everyone rekindling the love and warmth
experienced on previous visits. Alan, as before, got on
splendidly with the boys, and we were able to take them to
Las Vegas one weekend.

Dickie had now really established himself as a television
star and had living with him a beautiful blonde named Jody,
who seemd to have completely changed him as a person. He
was charming and pleasant, even occasionally inviting us
to dinner, which he cooked himself. Jody was a sweet girl
and I was delighted he had found her, for she certainly
appeared to have mellowed him. Success, too, was an
important factor in this change, for he now had money and
power, two things he always craved.

All too soon the holiday came to an end and we had to
part yet again. It was so very wrong, this business of living
thousands of miles away from each other, and the boys
hinted at how nice it would be if we went to live in
California. They, however, were still not interested in
coming to England. Despite my desire to do so, I hadn't
said anything about the past for I still felt the time was not

right. And with everyone being so pleasant, it would be wrong to spoil everything by rocking the boat. One day, especially now the boys were growing interested in girls, it could all be explained. When they fell in love themselves, and married, they would understand the problems that beset men and women.

Another two years passed. I had long since given up expecting to hear regularly from Mark and Gary. They had better things to do with their time than write letters to me. But at last there was nothing blocking the way of cards, letters or gifts I sent them, and the latter were usually acknowledged. I did, though, receive a postcard from Jody, from somewhere in the Caribbean where she was working, so I gathered that she and Dickie must have parted. In the days when I knew her, Jody worked for Dickie part-time, answering his fan mail!

I remember thinking then that if I'd been the sort of woman who was content to bask in his glory, answer fan mail and have no career, we might have had a better marriage. Circumstances, however, were such that without my career Dickie would not have had one at all in America. Anyway, I was not the type to sit back quietly, allowing a man to take the lead. The only man to make me do that was Dennis.

In the summer of 1977 I began thinking it was time we saw the boys again. As they usually went to Hawaii in August, when Dickie had his vacation from television, I thought it would be a super idea to take Alan and Jason there, too, as they'd never been. Mark and Gary seemed pleased when I told them we'd booked tickets, but a few days later Lenny rang to say that he felt our journey was pointless

'It's silly for you to arrive just as they're off to Hawaii', he said.

'But I thought we'd go over while they're there. I told the boys we were booked.'

Sounding uncomfortable, with yet another unpleasant task to perform, he went on.

'Frankly, the boys would rather be there on their own!

You know how teenagers are. Why not visit them in
Hollywood later on?'

'We can't come later. Jason has to be back in school. It's
just not convenient.'

'Well, that's the way it is. If you want to be here when
they're away, that's your business!' he said abruptly and
hung up.

Hurt and shattered that my sons hadn't shown me the
courtesy to call personally to explain why they preferred to
have a holiday without us, I nevertheless resisted the
temptation to write to them. That had been done before,
with disastrous results. This time I would sit back and wait
to receive a card from Hawaii. Nothing ever came!

Instead, still upset over the rebuff about our holiday, I
received a letter from Lenny, enclosed with which was a
legal document pertaining to the house in Hollywood. 'If
you'll sign this, releasing the property to Richard', he
wrote, 'it'll save us having to go into tax files and records'.

By signing on the dotted line I would irrevocably release
the house to Richard Dawson. I thought it seemed odd;
how could I give away something that was no longer mine?
Hadn't I signed away all rights to the house during the
divorce proceedings? Dickie had been afraid that the
Inland Revenue would be able to take the house away from
me because of my bankruptcy, but his fears were calmed
when I agreed to the divorce.

A friend suggested I consult American lawyers about this
matter, which I promptly did. However, I discovered that
it had been unnecessary for me to sign away the rights on
my house and agree to having no claim over anything,
including the children. The American lawyers told me that
in no way could the Inland Revenue, or anyone else, touch
my home in America!

The final blow came when they explained that, if I
wanted to take my case to court in Los Angeles, it would
cost me in the region of a million dollars and I certainly
could not afford that. I was not wealthy by any means
because a so-called adviser who was supposed to be looking
after my financial affairs one day disappeared, leaving a

large, unexplained debit to my bank account and a mountain of unpaid bills.

It all seemed so desperately unfair, but I could do nothing at this stage of my life except berate myself for having been so gullible and stupid in my youth.

I was also anxious to hear from my sons. Finally, I could stand the silence no longer and telephoned them. Gary was genuinely mystified why I was upset at not having heard from them. Mark, on the other hand, assumed a sarcastic tone when I enquired why he never bothered to send even a card, especially as we'd been booked to go over and join them and were deeply disappointed they didn't want us to.

'How come *you* didn't bother to sign the paper Lenny sent?' he demanded.

'That, at the moment, is none of your business, Mark', I replied angrily, resenting his manner.

As our conversation continued, I gathered that Lenny had more or less rushed to them when their plane arrived from Hawaii, brandishing the letter received from my American lawyers wanting to know why he required me to sign a release document. I was even upbraided for daring to seek legal advice in the first place.

No good was to come of starting an argument with my eldest son over something he didn't know the first thing about. So I tried gently to explain that there were many things I longed to discuss with them; situations which had occurred over the years and facts they knew nothing about. Without wanting to paint their father as a liar, I begged them not to listen to what anyone said in the future, but to wait until the day I could personally clarify everything that had happened in their lifetime. And I assured them that all I ever wished for was their security. Above all I loved them deeply.

'How come, if you thought so much of us, you never sent anything at birthdays or Christmas?'

'Oh, Mark, there's so much you don't know yet. But I promise that, when I come over, I'll not lie about anything.'

This seemed to appease him, though I knew it was just a

matter of minutes before Dickie would be badgering him to
hear what I said. Still, I had had my suspicions confirmed
about all those birthday cards and Christmas presents sent
over the many years.

As always there was the emptiness, and a feeling of total
helplessness, when I put the telephone down. But I'd resigned myself to all that now. I was determined to go to
America as soon as possible, for the time definitely had
come to discuss everything with my sons. They had grown
up, and it was only fair to let them know exactly what had
happened over the years. Not only fair to them, but to me.
More silent months followed, however, as lawyers attempted to unravel matters and my life, both domestic and
workwise, continued. I called the house a few times but
only once managed to get through. The phone was
answered by an icy, growling Dickie, furious, I assumed,
because I had not signed the document relating to the
house. *I* still couldn't understand why he needed it at all!
The American lawyers, having completed their searches,
informed me there was no way the place could still legally
be mine, and repeated their warning that if I wanted to try
to make a claim, it would be costly and lengthy. There was
no guarantee that I would win it either, despite the fact that
the house was now worth at least $1,000,000 – $8000,000
more than I originally paid for it!

In early 1978 there was a sudden, unexpected break-
through in relations with my sons. Mark telephoned to tell
me he was wildly in love with a girl named Margery and
that they were living in an apartment off Sunset Boulevard.
It was, coincidently, opposite Liberace's old house where I
had stayed all those years ago, rehearsing my Las Vegas
act. Mark, sounding happy and elated, gave me his new
telephone number and asked me to call at any time. I
sensed that he was relieved to be free and on his own, and
the fact that he was now truly in love, even though only
eighteen, meant he would understand when I explained the
past to him.

In April, as Alan was working on a television play, I
decided the moment was right to take Jason to Los Angeles,

see the lawyers and finally make everything known to the boys. We were met at the airport by Mark and Margery, a beautiful girl, and then taken to our hotel to sleep off the journey. The following day I awoke to torrential rain and a call from Mark, with a disturbing message.

'We'll come and pick you up', he said. 'But I've got some bad news for you. I've had word from the Fortress' [his name for Dickie's house]. 'You're not to go near there.'

'How can he stop me?'

'Well, no-one can just walk in, Mom. He's installed electric gates now!'

Once again the wind had been taken out of my sails. My idea of a show-down with the boys present, a truthful, honest get-together with everyone asking and answering questions, was out of the question if I couldn't even get inside the house. Pamela Mason's prediction of long ago had come true. 'One day you'll find the door bolted and barred against you!' All my faith that Dickie would never do such a thing had finally been swept away.

'But why is he behaving like this, Mark? I want to talk. It's important that we discuss everything and clear the air', I persisted.

'He says there's *nothing* to talk about. You know what he's like. Anyway', he added in an effort to be cheerful, 'we'll come and get you now'.

I appreciated that Mark was in love, happy, and pleased to have me in town. And I could see that the situation was extremely awkward for both him and Gary, whom I had still to see. If their mother wasn't to be allowed into the house, and their father refused to talk, then apart from seeing my sons my journey would be fruitless.

Two miserable days went by. It rained constantly and Gary, at school during the day, was 'out of bounds' to me in the evenings, being at the house. My lawyers explained I had no right to climb over the wretched electric gates demanding a show-down, and so my only pleasure was derived from the hours with Mark and his girlfriend.

Although it was not how I had wanted to approach the matter, but feeling it was better than sitting around saying nothing, I began little by little to describe events of the past to Mark who, being so in love, listened rationally and was considerate about my problems. Naturally, as Dickie was not present, Mark couldn't ask him whether some of the stories I told were true, which was what I originally wanted to happen. But he seemed to believe and accept what I said, and eventually told me not to worry so much. He loved me and that was all that mattered.

That was consoling, but none the less I was frustrated that things were not going as I had planned them. Furthermore I had still not set eyes on Gary. One pouring wet day I resolved to drive to the house and wait for his arrival home from school. We would then walk in together. There was nothing Dickie could do if I insisted Gary let me enter, and maybe a confrontation could be forced. With hindsight it was a stupid idea, for Gary could have suffered as a result. Dickie might not have believed him innocent of the plan. But that happily did not transpire.

Mark had taken Jason to Disneyland and so, trem-blingly, I drove up the long road and parked outside my old house to wait for Gary. An hour went by, and still he did not come. The rain streamed down the windows of my car like flowing tears. I sat there listening to the radio and reflecting on the whole ridiculously sad scene.

Here I was, at forty-five, waiting outside a million-dollar house from which I was now barred and the gates of which I had seriously contemplated climbing over. Memories flooded back. Finding and buying that house, Mark's childhood birthday parties, friends who visited, eleven-year-old David Cassidy swimming in the pool. Gary's christening with Liberace, Pamela Mason and Terry-Thomas as godparents; the fun, the fights, the home-comings and the farewells. Grandma, Aunty Kit and others who had passed on; they all seemed like ghosts now as I remembered a thousand bygone days.

Dickie's large black Cadillac stood in the driveway, so I knew he was there. Should I march up to the bell and boldly ring it? Perhaps make a joke of the fact that his ex-wife was sitting outside in the rain, afraid to enter the house that had once belonged to her? But that was what the trouble was about. Why should I joke about such serious matters? So I sat there for another hour, waiting in vain for Gary to arrive. I learnt later that he had stayed late at school for a drama audition, and in the circumstances it was probably just as well. Nothing would have been gained by attempting a show-down with Dickie.

Driving back to Mark's apartment, disappointed at not seeing Gary, I reflected with half-amusement on the bitterness of my situation and what a fool I'd been all my life. It suddenly occurred to me that Tommy Yeardye was living here in his Beverly Hills luxury mansion, having made a fortune in the beauty business. And Dickie, now a big television star, lived nearby in his mansion, also having made a fortune! What a long way both had come since the days we toured together in the Diana Dors Show. And here was I, trundling along in a Hertz rental car, feeling genuinely pleased for both of them. Where, I wondered, had I gone wrong myself?

Of course I'd had a fantastic life and career. But somehow Dame Fortune had not smiled on me as readily as she appeared to have on Tommy and Dickie. Everything I achieved had always been through hard work, and yet so many times the fruits of my labours had been taken by devious means.

The following evening I telephoned Gary and we arranged for all of us to go out to dinner, agreeing to call by and collect him from outside the electric gates behind which Dickie had barricaded himself. As Mark, Jason, Margery and I drove up on that warm Californian night, I beheld a slim, beautiful young man dressed casually in white. To my amazement, it was Gary! He had altered so much in two years that it was almost impossible to believe that this handsome apparition actually was my cute little son. All through the meal I couldn't keep my eyes off him. The transformation was incredible. He had such sophistication. And after dinner he played for me on the piano songs he had composed himself, and impressed me with his brilliant impersonations of actors.

Obviously he was highly talented, for he had already won several awards at school for drama. In him I glimpsed the young Dickie of long ago; charming, amusing and ambitious! Mark was proud of him, too, and it appeared that he also wanted a career as a singer, rather like his idol, Mick Jagger. At that time, however, he was working on the production side of Dickie's winning show, *Family Feud*.

I remained in Hollywood only a week, for life, despite my sons' presence, was miserable, being cooped up in a hotel during the rainy season with nowhere to go other than Mark's apartment. Because of Dickie's stubborn refusal to speak to me, I couldn't sort out the business matters I wished to settle, and a meeting with Lenny did nothing but complicate the issue. In front of the boys I set out to explain the truth of what had happened over the years, with Lenny, naturally, taking Dickie's side. Most of my protests about the unfairness of everything, especially the house, were shot down or evaded with legal jargon against which I hadn't the knowledge to argue. There was nothing left but to return home with Jason to the sanity of England.

Later that year I heard that Mark and Margery had parted, which truly distressed me for they had been so happy. When I spoke to Mark, commiserating with him at great length, he tried hard to be brave, which was heartbreaking. I knew how miserable he must be, and for days afterwards I shed tears every time I thought of the pain he was suffering.

'If you're going to cry every time one of your sons has a broken love-affair', Alan joked, attempting to lift my spirits, 'I'd better take out shares in Kleenex!'

After Christmas, the last we were to spend with Alan's dear mother who died in the coming year of cancer, we decided to visit America again. Alan had not seen the boys for three years, and so we arranged to stay for a month, renting a lovely house in Beverly Hills. Mark again met us at the airport, and I couldn't help thinking that he looked much happier than he'd sounded when I last spoke to him.

'How are things, darling?' I asked gently, for it was only a couple of months since the break-up with Margery.

'I think I'm in love again', he announced, beaming.

Alan had been right! There was no need for me to walk around crying at the thought of my sons having love problems. Obviously I was becoming too old to remember how quickly the young recover from such traumas!

The object of Mark's new love was a beautiful woman named Kathy, who was the associate-producer on Dickie's show. She was eleven years older than Mark, but what did age matter? I was nine years older than Alan, and it was quite obvious that the two of them were as much in love as he and Margery had been, although the affair was very much in its early stages and perhaps not so carefree.

Gary was holidaying in Hawaii at that time, but he returned a week later and once again we started to pick up the threads and affections from where we'd last left them. After we'd been there for several weeks, Gary to my delight expressed his desire to return to England with us to study music, for which he now displayed great talent. He had Dickie's permission, and so we rushed around excitedly making plans. I was ecstatic. At last *one* of my sons was coming home to live with me.

Mark, however, did not take the news well, though why I did not know. I'd invited him often enough. From always having a close bond between them, both boys appeared almost at loggerheads at times and it frequently distressed me. Still, I put it down to brotherly squabbles, never having had brothers or sisters myself and so not being in a position to understand the sort of problems that happen. Dickie had not spoken to his brother since I knew him, and now it looked as if history was about to repeat itself.

On our last evening in America I gave a dinner party, to which I naturally invited Mark and Kathy. Somewhat to my surprise she did not come, and all night long Mark behaved badly, at times openly insulting his brother and demeaning him in every way. I pleaded with him to stop, but nothing I said prevailed and his manner grew quite ugly. What had happened, I wondered, to the once-beautiful little boy who displayed such sensitivity? This was even a completely different Mark from the days with

Margery only a year before. It was sad, but I feared that Mark was beginning to follow in his father's footsteps in more than one area.

We left for England the next day with an excited Gary, who settled down to love it as much as I had always done. His music career blossomed. Although Dickie had never bothered to see to it that either of my sons contacted me over the years, I made sure that Gary kept in touch with him by telephone or letter.

We had not been back in England more than two weeks when Mark called to say that he and Kathy were getting married on 4 March, just after his nineteenth birthday.

'Are you sure you know what you're doing?' I heard myself asking stupidly. Mark had never lived outside the cocooned world of Beverly Hills. He was a very handsome boy and I felt he should have enjoyed life and the world before settling down to marriage. But then who was I to talk? I'd married Dennis at nineteen!

It was sad to miss my son's wedding, and I almost wished they'd decided to marry when we were still out there. Still, these things never go by the rules. Months passed before I saw the wedding pictures, and once again long silences grew between us unless I sent letters with news of Gary's progress or Mark scribbled a short note about the latest events in his pop-singing career. Obviously I didn't expect a young married couple always to find time to write. But as time went on and they moved home without informing me of their new address, I began to feel rather annoyed that I was being treated with such indifference. I never even had a thank-you note for birthday wires, or a phone call at Christmas.

Finally I wrote what I considered to be a gentle letter of rebuke, enquiring if Kathy treated her own mother in the same way. I closed by saying that if I still heard nothing, I could only assume they didn't wish to be in touch with any of us again.

To pass off Mark's reply, thinking he was merely envious of Gary's happiness in England, would be naïve. For my pleas as to what was wrong were answered with bitter comments about the fact that his brother had been handed life on a plate without doing anything for it. He went on to say that even *I* did not know what it was like to work as hard as he was having to in order to attain recognition and success. You are already a star, he wrote.

'Kathy and I never send cards or thank-you letters to anybody', he concluded, 'so do not expect them. Just forget the Jewish overtones, Mom. Remember you are a Catholic.'

Oh Mark, my son, that little crucifix I gave you so long ago was just a symbol of how much I loved you, and with it I prayed that God would keep you in His tender care. Whatever you do in life, and whatever you think of me, these thoughts will always be in my heart.

CHAPTER TWELVE

LOOKING-GLASS, LOOKING-GLASS, ON THE WALL

Who was the fairest of them all?

As I near the end of this autobiography, poised at almost half a century in my life-span, I am able to pause and reflect on all that has happened. It has been a strange journey for me, delving into the past and remembering in detail events throughout the last fifty years. Some have caused great pain and sadness; have even made me shudder. But mainly there were wonderful memories to recapture, for I have had a good life, successful and exciting. Though God knows I have made more than my fair share of mistakes.

In the analysis I was forced to make concerning my character, interesting facts have emerged. Looking back, I saw a fiercely ambitious young girl, spurred on by Hollywood films watched breathlessly from the darkness of the cinema stalls during childhood. My mother's own dreams of being a star were woven into the network of my personality before birth, and then encouraged in my formative years by those regular visits to the cinema. And so, without being a typical 'stage mother', she guided me towards the kind of life she dreamed of for me, a life of fame and luxury. Not an ordinary existence such as she was forced to live!

Luckily she also imbued me with all the confidence that she herself lacked. I once found a letter, addressed to a 'Miss Elizabeth Chapman', hidden away at the back of a drawer. It was from a theatrical company in London who were preparing a musical for the West End. 'Please be at the Cambridge Theatre on 9th April', it read. 'If singer, bring music; if dancer, bring shoes.'

There must have been an advertisement in the newspaper that producers were auditioning girls for a show, and on impulse she had written for information, not using her real name but devising a combination of two aunts, Elizabeth Dors and Sarah Dors, who married a man named Chapman. Quite why *she* didn't choose the name Dors, as she cleverly selected for me so many years later, is one of those mysteries that will remain unexplained.

It was obvious that, on receiving an answer to her enquiry, she lost courage, even though she was a trained singer. I imagine she read it from time to time and indulged in fantasies of what might have happened if that audition had been followed through. Those fantasies, and the magic which Hollywood films pretended was 'life', shaped my beginnings!

The man with whom I first lived, namely my father, continually broke the spell of that magic with his down-to-earth practicality, which I detested. Nevertheless, he was an honest man whose outlook on life was sensible. He wanted the best for me, but his ideas were not my ideas. Nor had I inherited his good qualities; if, that is, he really was my father. Perhaps my behavioural pattern would have been better had I understood the reasons for my lack of feeling for him – had I known the answer to the riddle of 'Uncle' Gerry. I could never see the wisdom of my father's intentions where I was concerned, and yet if he *was* my true parent, why did I so loathe his principles, always finding them impossible to accept?

Perhaps if I had done as he wished, married that 'decent sort of chap' and settled down to an uneventful life, I might have found happiness along the way. Instead, I determinedly rebelled against everything he wanted, allowing myself to be attracted to the type of man who was a far cry from the good husband who could have given me security and comfort. My father had certainly been right when years later he said ruefully: 'The trouble with Diana is that she has an appalling taste in men.'

As a young actress I ambitiously steered my course in the direction I knew I had to go. All roads led to Hollywood, and nothing would stop me getting there. Inevitably along the way I fell in love. But my first two 'crushes' at LAMDA, George and Geoffrey, were mere sideline flirtations compared with the real emotional upheaval caused by Guy Rolfe. If I displayed selfishness towards anyone on my early climb to the top, then it was nothing to the cruel, self-centred manner with which he treated me. Because of him I still cannot bear waiting for a telephone call, enduring the suspense of wondering whether someone really is going to phone. Guy was the first man to break my heart. Such misery comes to all of us, and we should gain from the experience. But do we ever learn?

Reflecting on various males since Guy who have broken my heart, it would appear that I certainly never learnt very much from my experiences. My stupidity, naïvety and general aptitude for being gullible when dealing with men seem too incredibly silly to believe. If all these things had not actually happened to *me*, then I would dismiss such stories as quite impossible.

Forgetting my early brushes with sex, like the stable episode when I was nearly raped by Great-Uncle Arthur, or even little Eric Barrett punching me in the eye on my first day at school, I plunged into that mysterious world at sixteen, with Gil, the sun-bronzed iceberg from Norway.

In love again, out of love again, displaying the ebullience of youth, I then embarked on what I thought at seventeen to be a serious, 'in-depth' romance with Tony Newley. And all the while as I pursued fun, life, but above all a career, it mattered not that my mother sat alone at home. The long hours of loneliness she endured as a result of ambition for me left her out in the cold. Whether she regretted those dreams, I did not know. Selfishly, I never gave her one thought.

And then there was Michael! Of all the men I knew, he was the boy with whom I fell in love and grew to love deeply. Over the years we have remained dear friends, if friendship *can* evolve after the emotional turmoil of love has taken its toll. Yet Michael and I might not have enjoyed this good relationship had we married, for there were many occasions when, owing to our temperaments, we clashed badly. But now, after more than thirty years, we have a great affection and respect for each other.

Michael is now in the process of writing a novel based on his true-life adventures as 'Dandy' Kim Waterfield. Like everything he does, no doubt it will be highly successful, and possibly have more style than a Harold Robbins.

As for Dennis, the strangest force in my life and but for whom Michael and I might have married? If only he were alive today! How many times I have wished that as I stumbled through the wilderness. And yet when I was with him it never occurred to me how much I needed his help. Would *our* relationship still be a friendly one now? In retrospect, I think not.

Marriage with Dennis, the most exhilarating, dominant personality I have known, was turbulent in the extreme. Therefore it would not have been possible to remain such good friends with him, however easy it is in the aftermath of a wrecked marriage to remember only pleasant, wonderful times. The mind blots out all hideous thoughts, deeds and mistakes, and it is essential to remember that life was not always good with Dennis. Successful, yes. Amusing, certainly. But never blissful.

I was not at peace with him, and too young to appreciate what he did for both of us. However, despite the unhappiness he caused me, and the tears he made me shed, I felt nothing but sadness when he died. The emptiness, the remorse, the yearning to be given another chance to rebuild something that was gone forever were almost impossible to bear. Dennis was a man I will never be able to forget. He will always be with me!

What of the rest? The 'deluge' as Rod Steiger once so aptly described it. Rod, for his part, still appears to rely heavily on a psychiatrist, despite having won an Oscar and given many brilliant performances. He later parted from Claire Bloom, and before he married his third wife he insisted she sign a contract releasing him from any financial commitment if divorce proceedings ever became necessary. Some years later he then decided he was not able to lead a wedded existence with any woman and promptly left her! If the third Mrs Steiger was as confused by this man's behaviour as I was when *we* fell in love, she has my sympathy. No man has ever managed to create such a holocaust within my brain as Rod achieved.

My man of bronze, Tommy Yeardye, stuntman and muscleman *extraordinaire*, having first climbed aboard the property bandwagon amidst colourful publicity, thanks to his association with me, cleverly went into the beauty business and became managing-director for Vidal Sassoon's salons throughout the world. His black curls turned attractively silver and, married to an ex-model – they have His and Her Rolls Royces parked outside their luxurious Beverly Hills mansion – Tommy has now been appointed world-wide ambassador to Pamela Mason's wool empire which she inherited from her millionaire father.

It is odd, really, that a woman who has been my friend for so long should have chosen, without introduction from me, the man who broke down my door in a valiant attempt to save me from Dennis and who once demanded that I should give him the farm so that he could display what he was capable of doing in life.

Tommy's and Pamela's near neighbour, Richard Dawson, is also living in a luxurious Beverly Hills mansion, the difference being that it was mine before I was misled into signing it and so much else away. Today Richard, not Dickie as I knew him, is one of the biggest television personalities in America. Successful, rich, powerful, he has everything he ever desired. But what does this man from Gosport, Hampshire, really think of himself up there on that sun-drenched Hollywood hill? Sadly he never seemed to meet the right woman. Perhaps he didn't want to? His lack of social communication has turned him into a near-recluse, and so it is easy, now the boys are gone, to feel sympathy for him in his apparent loneliness. But 'Richard' has always done what he wanted to do, and maybe he found the ultimate answer in his own company. As he sits there alone in that large house, watching himself on video cassettes, I wonder if he truly feels it was all worth the price he had to pay?

John Ashley forgot his dreams of stardom and went back to Oklahoma whence he came. Like so many young Hollywood hopefuls, he discovered there was more to being an actor in movies than having a handsome appearance and speeding around town in a Porsche. Frankie Jacklone, who never dreamt of stardom, remained in New York searching for his indefinable dreams.

Over in Australia, Darryl Stewart, who might have been an international singing star, tours around the country performing his act, still married to the same woman he left all those years ago. The baby who necessitated his 'temporary' departure from my life made him a grandfather when she was sixteen. I received a letter from Darryl in 1979, after I had made an Australian tour in connection with the publication of my second book. Reading it sent the years flying back to those sunny days in Perth and Sydney, but it was too late to recapture anything for us but memories.

And Troy? Probably the only man I knew who never did anything with life and the opportunities that came his way. He and the long-suffering Barbara, who took him back when our four and a half years together were played out, still soldier on somewhere.

Now, as I look back on the whole assortment of men who became involved in my business affairs, they make me shudder as much as some of my ex-lovers. What a grizzly picture these devil's advocates present. The grim-faced judges, prosecuting barristers, accountants, lawyers, managers and several crooked agents are men whose actions in my life have been nothing short of evil. Not the least of these was Dennis's friend Jimmy Mellon, who was the only one to know the secrets of Dennis's last finances. He took his yacht and slipped away to the south of France with his cases full of cash. He was later to die from cirrhosis of the liver.

Then, too, there were the 'gypsies, tramps and thieves'!

Not only villains, but actors, con-men and a general assortment of entertaining characters who played out their roles in my journey through life. Some have passed on completely, to wherever any of us go from this world. Patrick Beresford, John Waterfield, George Coburn, Peter Reynolds, Bonar Colleano and Denis Shaw.

They, like Dennis Hamilton, rest in graves without significantly important headstones to mark their impact on this earth. Indeed, it is to my shame that Dennis, who in life loved such beautiful things, has nothing but an empty glass jar to point out austerely the plot where he rests.

And so to those I love who are still living.

My husband Alan's fight against alcoholism raged long and hard, and during that battle we both reached the brink of hell – not once, but many times. Often it seemed there was nothing left for us except tragic despair. Certain stories do have happy endings, though. Now that he has finally emerged triumphant from the dark pit of insanity where he stumbled blindly for so long, our lives, like twin oaks, have intertwined and taken root. The future may only be as good as we make it; but because we will always have love for each other, the future, whatever it holds, must prove better than the past. I pray to God that Alan remains the wonderful man he has become now that he is at last cured.

My three sons really are 'the fairest of them all' as I gaze back into the looking-glass of life. Happiness is the greatest wish I have for them, in whichever way it can be achieved. They are, of course, quite different from one another. Mark is aggressive and headstrong, but I hope he will mellow in the years to come. As the storms of life buffet him, he will realise that love and truth are the most important things in this world.

Gary is easy going and lovable. Eventually, when he has enjoyed his youth, I trust he will find the right woman who understands his sensitivity and gives him the love he needs.

Jason is serious and imaginative, and my prayers for him are that everything comes up to his demands and expectations. If he, too, finds love, then his path through life should not be too hard to tread.

My fourth child; the son I never knew. Perhaps he was the fairest; certainly the happiest, for he experienced no pain or suffering as we who are left must. He waits for us in everlasting peace, and with God's good grace we will meet one blessed day.

Writing this book, reflecting on my mistakes and analysing motives and deeds, has been very difficult. It is not an easy task to cram one's life into a few hundred pages, but I have attempted to be totally honest all the way and am indeed sorry if the truth, hard as it always is to accept, has caused distress to anybody other than myself.

Doubtless, many men described herein, whose lives collided with mine on the course fate planned for us, may not like what I have written. Yet deep down in their hearts each one will know that the truth has been told.

My story, for now, is finished. My creed will ever be:

'This above all –
To thine own self be true,
And it must follow, as the night the day,
Thou canst not then be false to any man.'

All Futura Books are available at your bookshop or
newsagent, or can be ordered from the following
address:
Futura Books, Cash Sales Department,
P.O. Box 11, Falmouth, Cornwall.

Please send cheque or postal order (no currency), and
allow 40p for postage and packing for the first book
plus 18p for the second book and 13p for each additional
book ordered up to a maximum charge of £1.49 in U.K.

Customers in Eire and B.F.P.O. please allow 40p for
the first book, 18p for the second book plus 13p per
copy for the next 7 books, thereafter 7p per book.

Overseas customers please allow 60p for postage and
packing for the first book and 18p per copy for each
additional book.